African capitalism

Until recently the prevailing view of African capitalism has stressed its dependence on state and foreign capital and therefore its inability to make a significant contribution to African development. Drawing upon material from a number of countries and a range of academic disciplines, this book provides an analysis of African capitalism which offers a much more positive view of its role. A number of major constraints have combined to obstruct the emergence of dynamic African capitalist bourgeoisies: foreign competition, the cultural climate, the dependency factor in African economic life, the evolving class structure, the quality of indigenous enterprise and the nature of politics, ideology and state power. All these are assessed and found to be significant, but in the final analysis, in Africa as elsewhere, it has been in the arena of politics and ideology, centred on the struggle to exercise state power, that the fate of private indigenous capitalism has so often been determined.

AFRICAN SOCIETY TODAY

General editor: ROBIN COHEN

Advisory editors: O. Aribiah, Jean Copans,
Paul Lubeck, Philip M. Mbithi, M. S. Muntemba,
O. Nnoli, Richard Sandbrook

The series has been designed to provide scholarly, but lively and up-to-date, books, likely to appeal to a wide readership. The authors will be drawn from the field of development studies and all the social sciences, and will also have had experience of teaching and research in a number of African countries. .

The books will deal with the various social groups and classes that comprise contemporary African society and successive volumes will link with previous volumes to create an integrated and comprehensive picture of the African social structure.

Also in the series

Farm labour. KEN SWINDELL

Migrant laborers. SHARON STICHTER

The politics of Africa's economic stagnation. RICHARD SANDBROOK

Inequality in Africa: political elites, proletariat, peasants and the poor. E. WAYNE NAFZIGER

The African worker. BILL FREUND

Rural communities under stress: peasant farmers and the state in Africa. JONATHAN BARKER

AFRICAN CAPITALISM

The struggle for ascendency

PAUL KENNEDY

Senior Lecturer, Department of Social Science
Manchester Polytechnic

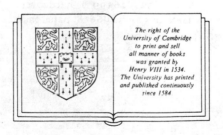

The right of the
University of Cambridge
to print and sell
all manner of books
was granted by
Henry VIII in 1534.
The University has printed
and published continuously
since 1584.

CAMBRIDGE UNIVERSITY PRESS

Cambridge

New York   Port Chester   Melbourne   Sydney

Published by the Press Syndicate of the University of Cambridge
The Pitt Building, Trumpington Street, Cambridge CB2 1RP
40 West 20th Street, New York, NY 10011, USA
10 Stamford Road, Oakleigh, Melbourne 3166, Australia

First published 1988
Reprinted 1990

Printed in Great Britain by
Redwood Burn Limited, Trowbridge, Wiltshire

British Library cataloguing in publication data

Kennedy, Paul T., 1941–
African capitalism: the struggle for
ascendency. (African society today)
1. Africa capitalism, to 1987
I. Title
330.12′2′096

Library of Congress cataloguing in publication data

Kennedy, Paul M., 1941–
African capitalism.
(African society today)
Bibliography.
Includes index.
1. Africa – Economic conditions – 1960–
2. Capitalism – Africa. I. Title. II. Series.
HC800.K46 1988 332′041′096 88–2563

ISBN 0 521 26599 1 hardcovers
ISBN 0 521 31966 8 paperback

RB

*To Sue, Anna, Daniel
and Rebecca*

CONTENTS

ACKNOWLEDGEMENTS

In addition to my wife, several people helped to keep me afloat and (hopefully) more or less on course during the writing of this book by providing valuable criticism, stimulating comments and by showing considerable interest. In particular, I would like to thank the following: Tony Berrett, for his wry but invariably pertinent observations and his strong enthusiasm for this project; two of my colleagues and friends at Manchester Polytechnic, Colin Barker and Phil Mole, who read earlier drafts of certain chapters and helped me to clarify and focus some important ideas; and Robin Cohen who guided and supported my endeavours at every stage. Naturally, however, I remain entirely responsible for all the views contained in this book and for any errors there may be.

I am also grateful to Manchester Polytechnic for enabling me to benefit from a one-term sabbatical during the early stages of formulating this project. Kate Baker's ability to convert my appalling handwriting into impeccably typed chapters in a very short space of time won my admiration as well as thanks.

ABBREVIATIONS

C.P.P.   Convention People's Party (Ghana)
I.C.D.C.   Industrial and Commercial Development
                Corporation (Kenya)
N.I.C.s   Newly Industrialising Countries
O.D.P.C.S.   overdeveloped post-colonial state

§ 1 §

THEMES AND PERSPECTIVES

This book explores two main themes. One concerns the role of local capitalism in the development of Black Sub-Saharan Africa up till the present time. Hopefully the discussion will succeed in demonstrating that indigenous entrepreneurs may well have a much greater contribution to make in the years ahead than hitherto. Moreover, until very recently this potential has not always been fully recognised by many African leaders and academics or by some interested Western observers and development experts.

This inevitably generates a set of questions which constitute the second theme: namely what, historically, have been the main constraints holding back the full emergence of African capitalists, what obstacles still impede them at the present time and to what extent have some of these constraints created more difficulties than others? Here it will be argued that the fate not just of local capitalism – in those countries where the market partly determines economic activity – but the prospects for African development in general ultimately rest more on the exercise of political will and choice than on any other single factor though, clearly, economic forces in particular are very crucial indeed.

Many newly independent governments viewed the prospect of capitalist development with suspicion. Private enterprise and profit were, after all, associated with Western domination. Moreover, as a vehicle for achieving balanced, self-reliant development and social justice, capitalism seemed to offer very little except continuing exposure to, and dependency on, metropolitan markets and capital, increasing inequality and a further erosion of Africa's unique cultural traditions. Both on practical and ideological grounds, therefore, many people regarded some kind of socialist development as infinitely preferable and, to a greater or lesser extent, a number of African regimes have experimented with various forms of collectivism and planned development. In the mid 1980s, while it is apparent that capitalist growth has so far bestowed few advantages on the majority of ordinary people, it has also become increasingly difficult to believe in the virtues of most self-styled African socialist regimes. The latter have not been particularly effective in raising living standards and reducing dependency nor are they noticeably less corrupt or repressive than capitalist ones.

If governments and some Western scholars were ambivalent concerning the prospect of capitalist development, their attitudes towards local capitalist classes were even more negative, if not actively hostile. On the face of it there were some grounds for this antipathy at that time. During the colonial period governments did not favour African entrepreneurs and foreign interests succeeded in establishing considerable control over leading economic sectors. The situation confronting local capitalists did improve considerably from the early 1940s but they were still confined mainly to agriculture and commerce by 1960. Moreover, the advanced technology and much of the capital required in the case of key development projects could only be obtained from abroad by encouraging foreign investment or by setting up public or joint enterprises financed by government borrowing, taxation, budget-deficit financing and other centralised policies. In any case, in the 1960s the development imagery shared by African governments, most Western advisers and international development agencies pointed to the importance of 'big' investments and the need to achieve large-scale shifts in economic practice and thinking. Individual, micro-level, private initiatives were identified as essentially peripheral to the main thrust of development strategy. They might also be tainted by traditional attitudes which involved elements of resistance to 'real' change. It seemed almost axiomatic, therefore, that state regulation and extensive public enterprise, alongside a greater or lesser contribution from foreign capital, would shoulder the main burdens of economic management. Private local capital, by contrast, could be expected to provide only a very marginal contribution.

By the 1960s, the theoretical basis for believing that the Western pattern of so-called bourgeois-led capitalist industrialisation still had some relevance in the Third World situation had also lost credibility – at least, given the usual terms in which that argument was couched. For example, Neo-Marxist underdevelopment theorists – who were becoming very influential by the late 1960s – were not alone in declaring that Marx had been quite wrong when, in the 1850s, he had contemplated the possibility that a resurgent Indian bourgeoisie might one day overthrow British imperialism and forge an independent capitalist path to national development. European political rule in India and nearly everywhere else in the Third World had indeed been terminated, but that did not mean that full-blooded, locally determined and self-reliant capitalist industrialisations were now a real possibility. Conventional economic thinking, too, with its emphasis on the benefits of international trade, capital flows, market-determination and private enterprise seemed naïve and misguided. The ideas put forward by the American sociology of development school also seemed increasingly unacceptable at that time since they appeared to offer little more than a thinly disguised apology for continuing Western domination. Moreover, in their writings some of these theorists had almost certainly exaggerated and misrepresented the leading role that Third World capitalist classes might play in spearheading socio-economic change. In any case, their ideas on this subject were rejected along with the rest of the theoretical package.

With the benefit of hindsight, however, there may now be a much stronger case for arguing that this analysis was partly mistaken and needs to be re-evaluated. For one thing, the belief that nineteenth-century Western industrialisation was led by powerful, rising commercial bourgeoisies who, having captured state power, were then able to remove the remaining 'feudal' obstacles to full capitalist development, is almost certainly oversimplified and may even be incorrect in the case of some countries. If so, then the argument that bourgeois-led transformations are impossible in twentieth-century Africa has little historical meaning and is probably irrelevant as a reason for insisting that local capitalist groups are therefore ineligible to make some kind of contribution to capitalist development or are incapable of doing so.

Secondly, while it is impossible to doubt the crucial role of the state in 'late' capitalist development it is important to make a very rough distinction between state-led (or induced) industrialisation (which is likely to include a certain amount of public ownership of key activities, at least in the early stages) – but where a vigorous private sector and market competition are also encouraged – and state-managed industrialisation. Here, a great many, perhaps most, economic activities are directly owned and managed by the state while private initiative is confined to certain limited areas. Although in practice most Third World countries operate at various intermediate points between these ideal-type situations the distinction is a useful one and is readily applicable to Africa where until very recently many countries have approximated more to the latter than the former. We will take up these important questions in Chapters 4 and 5.

Thirdly, it is probably inevitable – given the initial weaknesses of local capitalist groups – as well as desirable that foreign, public and cooperative ventures should be promoted on a considerable scale, as most Third World countries have done in recent decades. Yet there is no reason why any of this should preclude some attempt to foster a dynamic local private capitalism as well, unless countries are totally committed to some variant of bureaucratic socialism and perhaps not even then.

The emergence and consolidation of indigenous enterprise has been shaped and frequently held back by a number of major constraints operating over considerable periods of time. These can be briefly listed as follows.

1. *Africa's position in the international economy.* The terms on which most countries have participated in the global economy have often been highly unfavourable. This has been particularly evident during the last 10 years or so as a result of the rise in oil prices, mounting debts and high rates of interest, at least until recently, and a long period in which commodity export prices have tended to fall sharply (particularly during the world recession of the last few years) – more so, according to the World Bank, than for any other region of the Third World. Thus, between 1984 and 1986 the terms of trade for Sub-Saharan Africa declined by 15% and this represented only a further deterioration of an already worsening situation since the 1970s.[1] In market economies the ability of businesses to expand depends partly on the buoyancy of the home market. Since, under conditions of considerable dependency, this, in turn, is closely geared to export revenues, Africa's position in the world economy is obviously crucial. Nevertheless, the primary emphasis in this book has been placed elsewhere and this may mean that the realities of economic dependency have perhaps been given less causal weight than they actually deserve.

2. *State power, ideology and politics.* Both during the colonial period and since Independence governments have tended to act in ways that obstruct rather than encourage African capitalism, both because of the failure to provide direct assistance and to create a favourable national economic climate within the limitations set by the international situation. The position adopted here is that in the final analysis only independent states and their rulers can provide such a framework of institutions and incentives and most African regimes have so far failed to do so to the required extent. An individual government can do very little to alter the actual terms of exchange between the local economy and the international capitalist order. But it can affect the capacity of citizens and indigenous enterprises – public, private and cooperative – to take the appropriate measures required in order that their country can eventually acquire some kind of specialised niche in the world division of labour.

3. *Superior foreign competition.* Since the second half of the nineteenth century through to the European trading oligopolies and mining interests of the colonial period and the powerful transnational corporations of today, foreign capital has always enjoyed substantial competitive advantages. Not the least of these, in recent times, has been the power of international firms to demand special privileges from African governments as a condition of local investment.

4. *The cultural climate.* Traditional African value systems stressed the

moral virtues of (relative) economic equality and the obligation to redistribute surpluses. At the same time, the lineage basis of social organisation and kinship claims as well as the practices of polygamy and equal inheritance have all helped to create a cultural legacy which tends to threaten the legitimacy and the practicality of individual capital accumulation.

5. *The social relations of production.* Historically, capitalist development has presupposed the establishment of a thoroughly monetised economy, the formation of a pool of potential wage workers and the emergence of a group of individuals who were compelled to pursue continuous, productive investment and capital accumulation as the sole or primary means by which they could consolidate their class interests in an increasingly competitive market economy. In most of Black Sub-Saharan Africa this has involved the transformation of relatively equalitarian tribal societies into modern nation-states characterised by increasing degrees of inequality through a gradual process of socio-economic differentiation. Other conditions being favourable, it is likely that a 'critical' point has to be attained in the emergence of class relations before full capitalist development becomes possible. It is not clear whether such a threshold has yet been reached in all the countries under discussion.

6. *The national economic environment.* A supportive infrastructure, a well-developed home market and a secure investment climate are all essential for the successful pursuit of private enterprise. Again, certain elements of these have yet to be properly established in the case of many countries.

7. *The quality of entrepreneurship.* The resources, skills, and motivations displayed by the actors themselves, and their capacities for learning, will obviously be crucial in affecting business success. Several attributes will be important such as market persipience and responsiveness, sheer organisational ability, ingenuity and dedication. Many writers have been highly critical of African entrepreneurs, arguing that they often fail to evince these necessary qualities.

Clearly, these variables are interdependent. Each is contingent upon the operation of others although, as we have indicated, the second has been given the greatest explanatory weighting in the analysis that follows. It will become apparent that writers from different perspectives and subject disciplines attach varying degrees of emphasis to these variables. Indeed there is little or no common agreement not only on this but on most other questions relating to the causes and nature of economic development in Africa and other parts of the Third World.

One particularly important issue, in terms of the present study, concerns how best to conceptualise: (a) the key elements central to the exercise of business leadership within the individual firm and (b) the actual or potential impact of the entrepreneurial role upon the wider process of socio-economic change in developing countries. The way in which writers from different perspectives have approached these questions (and others relevant to the phenomenon of Third World entrepreneurship) will be spelled out in more detail later on. For the moment, however, it might be advantageous to offer some preliminary guidelines.

Anthropologists interested in entrepreneurship and socio-economic change have tended to focus their attention on those operating within small-scale semi-closed community situations. They point out that such entrepreneurs need to act first and foremost as social innovators whose ability to manipulate and evade established relationships and obligations enables them to neutralise or set aside the restrictions on economic enterprise that are often endemic in close-knit, traditional communities. By finding ways to circumvent such established loyalties and constraints whilst succeeding in setting up modern businesses, these entrepreneurs help to reshape pre-modern institutions and values in numerous micro-situations across rural and urban Africa.

For some of the writers associated with the sociology of development approach, Third World entrepreneurs were above all to be regarded as a major source of the cultural ethos of modernity. Driven, apparently, by powerful psychological orientations, certain special groups of entrepreneurs might bring a degree of energy, inventiveness and rational calculation to previously low-status economic activities sufficient to set in motion a dynamic process of national capitalist development. As the crucial originators of new values within economic enterprises these entrepreneurs would ultimately be seen to have played a dramatic, historical role in helping to spearhead the wider societal transformations associated with modernity and industrialisation. Both these approaches are explored in Chapter 7.

Economics is a complex discipline encompassing several different schools of thought whose proponents disagree on a number of important questions, including those relevant to the problem of Third World development and the nature of entrepreneurship. Nevertheless, despite differences of emphasis, it is probably true to say that most economists see the essential role of business leadership in terms of the ability to respond to market opportunities and then to build up business organisation so as to exploit those same opportunities effectively. Such activities almost certainly involve some degrees of risk. Some economists would also emphasise the importance of technical innovation in the sphere of business management as a key aspect of the entrepreneurial role. For the most part, the majority of entrepreneurs in a capitalist economy are regarded as having little choice but to follow the dictates of the market. But in doing so, whilst seeking to maximise profits in competition with others, entrepreneurs perform the essential task of consolidating and furthering the process of economic development and technological change. The research carried out by some economists on African business is discussed in Chapters 7 and 8.

As a complex body of ever-changing theory Marxism also includes a wide range of interpretations and important differences of emphasis. Basically, however, Marxist theorists regard business entrepreneurs primarily as agents whose essential function – and motivation – is to extract surplus value by paying their workers less than the value of what they produce during each production cycle and then to reinvest a portion of this surplus in order to expand business capacity, thereby accumulating capital (that is, assets capable of generating further wealth). By acting in this way during the early stages of industrialisation, and as members of a collectivity driven to compete against one another, this rising bourgeoisie gradually establishes the dominance of the capitalist system over all remaining vestiges of pre- and petty-capitalist production (for example, peasant family farms and previously independent, self-employed craftsmen). Simultaneously, these changes hasten the process of proletarianisation whereby a huge class of wage and salary earners is created whose members are unable to seek a livelihood except through selling their labour power. These and other ideas found in Marxist theory are discussed at several points in this book but especially in Chapters 2, 5 and 8.

Unlike the other perspectives we have just been discussing, Neo-Marxist underdevelopment theory views Third World entrepreneurs in an almost entirely negative light. Thus, entrepreneurs are regarded as 'compradors'; that is, as individuals or groups who willingly operate as the local representatives of, or agents for, foreign capitalists, perhaps mediating between the latter and other local groups. (The term 'comprador' was originally a Portuguese word used to describe the native representatives of Portuguese trading companies operating in various parts of Asia.) By earning their profits through the supply of auxiliary services for foreign interests, comprador entrepreneurs facilitate their country's continued subordination to outside influences thereby perpetuating national economic dependency and underdevelopment. The issues relating to African business groups and compradorship are discussed extensively in Chapter 6.

Each of these perspectives is intrinsically interesting in its own right though some are more useful than others. In order to pursue a comprehensive analysis we adopt a basically pragmatic approach towards these theories, drawing upon each as and when particular insights are relevant to a given question. Marxism, for example, offers a good deal of analytical purchase on questions relating to class formation and the preconditions and nature of capitalist production – issues that are highly germane to the discussion. Accordingly, a basically Marxist approach is used at various key points. Nevertheless, in stressing the exploitative nature of the social relations of ownership and control upon which the capitalist labour process is built, Marxists tend to take for granted, and show little interest in, the more mundane matters of day-to-day business practice and organisation; the 'technical' framework for profit-making and capital accumulation. Yet, if African entrepreneurs experience difficulties in this area and need assistance it would seem important to clarify the precise problems which arise. Thus, the research findings presented by various social scientists who have made a point of investigating the nuts and bolts of entrepreneurial decision-making also receive a good deal of attention.

For a discussion of these themes a number of decisions had to be made concerning the scope of the enquiry. Firstly, the material which has been used is drawn mainly, though not entirely, from studies that were concerned with 'modern' business activity associated with Western influence and the commercialisation of African economic life, particularly manufacturing, contracting, retail and wholesale trade and services. Secondly, the emphasis is on enterprises which possess a 'firm-type' organisation; business is pursued in permanent premises (however simple), the owner is self-employed on a full-time, long-term basis, at least a few people are employed and there is a minimum investment in plant and equipment. Consequently, a coherent system of rules, pertaining to internal relationships and the external environment, can be clearly discerned. Thirdly, we are interested in business proprietors who are both willing and able to display a capitalist orientation, that is, their business activities are oriented towards profit with a view to achieving expansion and capital accumulation. They do not see entrepreneurship primarily or only as a source of steady income – a 'living'. By contrast, whether by choice or necessity, the vast majority of people who are engaged in commercial activity are petty producers rather than capitalists. Their earnings only suffice to help reproduce the household to which they belong and to refurbish business stocks.

Fourthly, since the discussion is concerned with capitalist enterprises employing a firm-type structure and operating in the modern sector, certain kinds of business activities which are both extremely significant to African economic life and which attract vast numbers of participants receive relatively little attention: for example, small-scale commercial farmers, those who trade in traditional African goods and services, urban artisans and petty traders. Women, in particular, are casualties of these decisions because even in West Africa – where they have played a very considerable role in market and other kinds of trade, food processing and a host of other activities for a long time – the majority is still confined to petty production. Fifthly, some countries inevitably figure much more prominently than others. Being more developed, having governments favourably inclined towards indigenous enterprise or both, they have offered better opportunities for research. Finally, throughout the chapters the terms 'capitalist', 'entrepreneur', 'business proprietor' and so on, are used synonymously and interchangeably even though they have sometimes been given specific meanings by particular researchers.

❦ 2 ❧

ECONOMIC DEVELOPMENT
DURING THE COLONIAL PERIOD

Many scholars have been highly critical of the colonial record, arguing that governments often failed to establish the institutions, class relationships and economic processes capable of generating a sound basis for future self-sustaining industrialisation and national economic autonomy. To the extent that this was true it obviously has important implications for the development of African capitalism. However, some writers have been much more critical than others and the intellectual bases for their concerns have varied a good deal.

As far as the emergence of a significant entrepreneurial class is concerned it will become apparent, both in this chapter and the next, that it is useful and justifiable to regard the Second World War as a political and economic watershed. Before this time the development of African capitalism was retarded not only by the general economic climate but also by a number of specific constraints which did not affect other groups to anything like the same extent, if at all. Indigenous enterprise was largely confined either to traditional activities in which European firms had no commercial interest, such as the internal trade in foodstuffs and cash-crop production, or to the least profitable small-scale commercial ventures at the bottom of the European-dominated trading hierarchy. From the early 1940s, however, the economic climate improved for all types of business while many of the constraints formally experienced by local entrepreneurs began to ease and new opportunities appeared.

Neo-Marxist underdevelopment theorists, and others, argue that until approximately the middle decades of the nineteenth century European interests in most parts of the Third World, and certainly in Sub-Saharan Africa, could be served without the necessity for very much direct political control or intervention.[1] However, by the mid and late nineteenth century the rapidly industrialising Western economies required growing and regular supplies of cheap raw materials (primary goods or commodities) for factory production and secure access to expanding, and preferably captive, markets. Thus, it was necessary to find ways of 'encouraging' Third World native populations to seek involvement in the new, required forms of production. At the same time they would gain access to the cash needed to purchase Western goods. Only a much more direct and extensive usurpation of formal control by the European powers could guarantee these conditions.

Once in control, the metropolitan powers were primarily concerned to structure the territories they had acquired so as to meet the needs of various European interest groups. One such group consisted of the trading companies who wished to extend and deepen their long-established commercial links with various West African economies. Amin refers to this huge area as 'Africa of the Trade Economy'.[2] Here, the main aim of colonial governments was to encourage peasant cash-crop production on a much wider scale than had previously been possible, thereby fostering new kinds of export production. In those regions, usually adjacent to the coast, where the local people were already accustomed to a money economy and had accumulated financial resources from earlier production – the oil-palm producing areas of the Niger Delta, Dahomey and the Southern Gold Coast and the groundnut economy of Senegambia – peasants did not normally need much encouragement to extend their cultivation or to experiment with new crops. Further inland, or in areas where cash-crop production was much less established, various measures were used to ensure increased participation in the colonial economy: for example, the imposition of hut or poll taxes, the extension of the European commercial frontier through improved communications and investment in an enlarged trading network and enlisting the support of those chiefs who were willing to place their authority behind European demands for forced and other kinds of labour.

In much of East and Southern Africa, the regions Amin designates as 'Africa of the Labour Reserves', previous contact with European trade and culture had been much less in evidence.[3] In addition, two other kinds of metropolitan interests were able to stamp their demands upon colonial governments: the mining companies whose proprietors wished to exploit valuable mineral deposits, especially those found in the Rhodesias and South Africa, and prospective white settlers. Unlike West Africa, therefore, the main priority of colonial governments was not to encourage peasant cash-crop production but to promote a large-scale male migrant labour force whose members would seek employment in the European-owned mines, plantations and factories.[4] Accordingly, draconian measures were usually needed in order to incorporate African societies into the colonial and world economy, including land alienation, discriminatory taxation and the imposition of legal constraints on the scope and kind of economic activity Africans were permitted to pursue. Nevertheless, in some areas, for example parts of Kenya, Tanganyika and Uganda, commercial peasant farming did eventually emerge.

There is little doubt that in many parts of Africa colonisation did create the conditions whereby new sources of wealth were generated. The cultivation of cash crops for export increased in an especially dramatic way. Starting in the 1880s, cocoa exports from the Gold Coast, for example, were 50,000 tons in 1914 but rose to 200,000 tons by the mid 1920s and reached the level of 300,000 tons in the mid 1930s.[5] According to Amin, groundnut production in Senegal – already established before the onset of colonial rule – began on a large scale in the 1880s.[6] The harvest reached 600,000 tons in the 1936/7 season. So striking was this expansion that some observers described these changes as nothing less than an 'economic revolution'.[7] It has been estimated that the real value of West African exports rose by approximately 15 times between 1906–10 and the late 1950s.[8] This expansion was much faster than that which occurred in the preceding 50 years. Moreover, the production and expansion of many traditional craft goods also grew as incomes rose during these years.[9] Thus, by no means all indigenous products were ousted through competition from Western consumer imports.

These remarkable increases in agricultural output and the ability of many African societies to relinquish large numbers of male labourers for European employment were made possible by a number of underlying changes. On the European side there was the increased investment in infrastructure, the establishment of a relatively stable political–legal order, the dissemination of new ideas, skills and information and the introduction of fiscal and other inducements. But African social structures also proved extremely responsive and adaptable. Particularly crucial were the following: the ability of many societies to 'release' men from former warrior and hunting activities now that these were rendered either illegal or redundant by colonial rule;[10] increased male participation in agriculture, especially the tendency for men to take over cash-crop cultivation; the increasing workload borne by women everywhere but particularly in those regions where men were now absent for long periods of time;[11] and the ability of farmers to fit new crops into their existing systems of food production, their willingness to adapt traditional social institutions to the requirements of commercial activity and to experiment with new types of farming practice.[12]

However, in the view of many Neo-Marxist writers, these economic changes fell far short of promoting the possibility of long-term, viable and autonomous economic development in the continent as a whole. There were several reasons for this.

Firstly, not only were the African colonies structured to meet the needs of Western interests but these needs were normally rather narrow in scope. Underdevelopment theorists are not alone in making this kind of assessment. Writing about the West African experience, Hopkins, an economic historian, has observed that at least in the early period of colonial rule 'the expatriate role did not extend much beyond the general function of connecting West Africa to international markets. It was Africans who grasped the new opportunities . . .'[13] Consequently, a very uneven, distorted and incomplete pattern of development emerged in most areas. Typically, certain enclaves of intensive peasant cash-crop production, plantation agriculture or mining activity coexisted uneasily with vast regions and sectors that were starved of capital and whose inhabitants were only marginally exposed to the forces of modernisation.

Another manifestation of the limited nature of colonial policy was the financial stringency and conservatism in budgetary matters demanded by metropolitan governments. Any expenditure on roads, education or agricultural improvements had to be financed out of local revenues, especially customs duties on imported goods and head or hut taxes, depending on the colony.[14] Arguably, this was a very short-sighted policy which stunted the pace and depth of economic development. Then there was the failure, in most colonies, to seriously undertake the development of manufacturing, at least until the Second World War, and only then in certain processing industries. Moreover, this conservatism on the part of colonial officials was reinforced by a similar indifference displayed by the big trading companies and banking interests. During the 1930s expatriate firms in Africa responded to the economic crisis by contracting the scale of their retail operations, establishing agreements designed to reduce competition by engaging in market sharing and demanding government preference in such things as the allocation of import licences as against African, Asian and Lebanese businesses.[15]

Secondly, the incorporation of Africa much more firmly into the international capitalist order and the colonial policy of encouraging the emergence of specialised economies based on the export of raw materials subordinated economic progress to the uncertainties of the world market. Already-weak economies were made even more dependent and vulnerable to forces outside their control. There is certainly no lack of evidence to support this argument. Thus, during the period from the late nineteenth century until the First World War and from 1945 through to the Korean war boom and then during the late 1950s, world prices for most African exports increased quite considerably.[16] As the terms of trade became more favourable so imports and expenditure rose and the living standards of many Africans who responded to these incentives showed marked improvements. In the 1950s, rising export earnings, and therefore market expansion, were key factors which led to investment in manufacturing, especially in import substitution and agricultural processing industries. (Import substitution involves the attempt to replace imports, especially of consumer goods, by fostering a local manufacturing capacity for the domestic market.) But these periods of economic growth and rising government expenditure were largely determined by military, political and economic changes taking place in countries far removed from Africa.

Moreover, at other times, African economies fared much less well. For example, the short-lived post-war boom of 1920–1 was followed by a severe slump. This had a particularly devastating impact on small indigenous enterprises, especially in the more developed economies of the Gold Coast, Senegal, Sierra Leone and Nigeria. During the 1920s there was a partial recovery in world prices for African products but these were insufficient to promote much economic growth although other improvements, such as cheaper transport and an expanding road network, did bring some benefits. The great depression of the 1930s and the disruption to world trade caused by the Second World War also imposed a long period of falling prices and severe economic stagnation. In many areas African development was virtually halted.

Thirdly, underdevelopment theorists have maintained that the outward drain of capital to the metropolitan countries is the key element perpetuating poverty and backwardness in the Third World. Partly this export of capital occurs because foreign companies never display more than a short-term or immediate interest in the progress of the poorer countries. Their real focus of concern lies in the lucrative markets at the centre of the world capitalist system. High profits normally stem, it is said, from the ability of large oligopolistic companies to use their coordinated control of Third World markets in order to manipulate prices. Through their networks of mostly small intermediaries they can buy cheaply from the mass of dispersed, largely unorganised and relatively poor producers and then sell imports dear, thereby benefiting from unequal exchange in both sets of transactions.

To what extent European companies did engage in unfair trading practices by exploiting their monopoly position in order to make super-profits is not altogether clear but there are some fairly strong indications that this was indeed the case. Certainly, on a number of occasions during the 1920s and 1930s farmers in several West African colonies attempted to withhold sales of cash crops. Also, some traders tried to establish African companies with the intention of securing alternative and direct outlets for the sale of African produce in America and Europe.[17] Such moves were largely motivated by the belief that Africans were being cheated by the big companies. Thus, in many colonies a series of company mergers did take place during the inter-war years so that a few large European firms virtually controlled most produce buying by the late 1930s. Also, many governments imposed quotas on cheaper Japanese goods during the 1930s in order to help home manufacturers at a time of severe world depression but this can hardly have benefited African consumers.[18] Then there is the case of the statutory marketing boards (for the purchase of export crops) which were introduced in a number of British colonies during the Second World War. These government boards awarded most of their patronage to European firms. They also fixed the prices paid to African farmers at relatively low levels. The funds accumulated by the boards were mostly invested in British government securities, thereby helping to finance the metropolitan war effort and post-war reconstruction. Several writers have argued that these official outflows of capital during the 1940s and 1950s constituted a serious cumulative constraint on colonial development.

Several recent Marxist writers have offered a rather different critical interpretation of Western intervention in Africa. They claim that colonial domination singularly failed to set in motion the full conditions for 'primitive accumulation' or to bring that process anywhere near to completion. Marx argued that before the capitalist mode of production can perform its historic task of developing the productive forces in any given society, the class relations dominant in the old order and the unproductive labour processes encapsulated within them must be broken down and largely destroyed. He regarded two forces for change as central to the process of 'primitive accumulation': the gradual spread of commerce and money-based relations which eat away at the tissues of the old society, whilst increasing the availability of mercantile wealth in the hands of a primarily commercial bourgeoisie, but also – at some point in time – the often forcible exercise of political power through the offices of the state.[19] The ascendant classes who seek to bring about these political interventions do so in order to speed up the process whereby they can consolidate and extend their direct control over the means of production. Only then can they 'reconstitute' the various labour processes still operating at the heart of the old economy in more productive and profitable ways. Under capitalism this control is based on private ownership. Accordingly, primitive accumulation mainly involves political interventions which have the effect of exposing economic activity and possession to the full impact of competitive pressures (leading eventually to the centralisation of both ownership and production into larger and more efficient units). Such changes, in turn, separate the mass of direct producers from their means of production, especially land, or accelerate the process by which this occurs. This simultaneously drives the direct producers out of self-sufficiency and compels them to sell their labour power as the only remaining source of livelihood.

It has been argued that, in Africa, instead of destroying the lineage-based societies they encountered, Western capitalist interests and colonial rulers sought to preserve them wherever possible. Consequently, the capitalist mode of production was unable to penetrate fully to the core of the old order and establish its hegemony except in certain white settler enclaves and a few modern 'growth poles'. One explanation for this failure is that the traditional institutions found in many pre-colonial African societies proved to be extremely resistant to external influence.[20] African people were able to adapt to commercial pressures and respond to European demands and yet retained their basic institutions of chieftaincy, communal land ownership and lineage organisation. Anthropologists, sociologists and historians, too, have commented on the resilient and accommodating nature of African culture and society. Iliffe, for example, talks about the synthesis that emerged between commerce and tradition.[21] The new influences put down roots that were nourished by the old society.

Other Marxist writers like Kay and Taylor, however, insist that this provides only a small part of the explanation.[22] Kay's analysis of this question is particularly relevant and comprehensive. He argues that by the end of the nineteenth century industrial capital had established its supremacy in the West. But in doing so it left much of the Third World, including Africa, as a final preserve for merchant capital and did not seriously attempt to penetrate and restructure most of the non-Western world. Partly, this was because the needs of Western industry could be served perfectly well without the necessity for difficult, risky investments in productive enterprise on a vast scale all over the Third World.[23]

By its very nature merchant capital operates in the sphere of circulation, earning a return by buying and selling commodities. It also strives, wherever possible, to secure a monopoly so that it can impose its own terms and prices on consumers and producers. To attain a monopoly position trading companies may try to secure the assistance of the state, they may strive to outwit and undercut rivals, engage in mergers and amalgamations with competing firms in the attempt to fix prices and market shares, or a mixture of all of these. The really important point is that historically wherever it operates, and because of its concern with purely exchange transactions, merchant capital lacks the means or the incentive to fully break down the pre-capitalist societies on which it preys and establish the basis for more advanced forms of development. It partially destroys the old order but does not replace it with a more productive one and in this way it obstructs and delays the transition to industrial capitalism.

This pattern of limited, mainly commercial, capitalist penetration is said to have benefited Western interests in various ways. It also had a number of important long-term implications for African development. Firstly, the political changes made possible by colonial government enabled merchant capital to transform the majority of Africa's tribal cultivators into peasants.[24] Like peasants everywhere else, African cultivators were now obliged to yield a regular surplus in the form of various tax payments to governments and through contributions to the profitability of commercial companies. Also, in those areas where migrant labour was encouraged, most workers retained customary land rights in their home areas. Accordingly, they were not a 'true' proletariat in the Western sense.[25]

Secondly, in their different ways, the European trading companies, mining interests and white settlers, all pursued certain overriding objectives with respect to the African peasantry. When migrant workers employed by mines or plantations were ill, too old to work or no longer required, during a period of recession, their employers did not want the burden of supporting them. European companies were also reluctant to pay proper wages and provide suitable living quarters in urban areas (or permit a level of taxation sufficient to enable governments to supply these services). The advantages of cheap labour and a minimum investment outweighed the disadvantages incurred by employing a largely unskilled, inexperienced and temporary labour force. Where peasant cash-crop production predominated, trading companies had neither the intention nor, perhaps, the resources to compensate farmers during periods when world prices were falling or contribute to the development of alternative economic activities in the rural areas. What all these interests required was low-cost production involving a minimum of risk and yet high profitability. The economic and political logic was inescapable: devise policies designed to ensure that traditional African society rather than the capitalist sectors would bear a large part of the true cost of reproducing the latter's labour power.[26]

Thus, thirdly, all over Africa colonial governments took steps to preserve many aspects of African socio-economic life as a continuing refuge for the urban and rural casualties of the Western money economy. For example, wherever possible, chiefs were incorporated into the colonial administrative system and sometimes their traditional powers were strengthened so that they actually became less accountable to ordinary people. They continued to administer some tribal laws and customs. In most areas, communal land rights were safeguarded and kinship/community-based systems of welfare and protection continued to operate for some time. Also the control that male kinsmen and husbands had previously exercised over the reproductive and economic activities of women, in many societies, were upheld by some colonial authorities.[27]

The uneasy coexistence, across economic sectors and geographical regions, of pre-capitalist and capitalist modes of production – the one an essential precondition for the success of the other – was particularly evident in the case of Southern Africa. In Southern Rhodesia, for example, Arrighi has observed that the designation of certain lands exclusively for African settlement was fundamental to the evolution of white mining and agricultural-settler interests.[28] Only by taking steps to preserve a reasonably viable socio-economic base for potential African workers and their families could Europeans guarantee the availability of supplies of labour as and when these were required. A similar argument has also been put forward to explain the evolution of the highly repressive system of racial segregation, and eventually Apartheid, in South Africa, with its policy of maintaining the tribal 'homelands' as a means of regulating the supply and flow of African labour, in accordance with changing market needs and in conjunction with the detested Pass Law system.[29]

There is a further revealing twist to this general argument that European commercial interests held back African development, especially in the case of the trading companies. Because it operated primarily in the sphere of exchange, merchant capital's scope for counteracting a squeeze on its profit margin was very limited indeed given that it had little or no direct control over peasant producers.[30] Attempts to manipulate prices and markets by establishing monopoly conditions provided a temporary solution but had no effect on the wider problem, namely, finding ways to reduce costs, to improve the productivity of labour and diversify the economy. The general policy of preserving the rural areas as reservoirs of cheap labour meant that even mining and plantation interests did not necessarily possess strong incentives to respond to falling profit margins by investing in better methods of production or broadening their economic activities; even less so when they also enjoyed various forms of subsidy and protection from colonial governments.

By contrast, industrial capitalism in the metropolitan countries operates according to a very different logic. Partly this is because individual capitalists are normally permanent residents in their own country of origin and so wish to live in an expanding economy with a prosperous future. Up to a point, they are also likely to be accountable to the demands of powerful, organised political groupings and to the state, whose officials will normally seek to foster the conditions for a successful national capitalism. But some writers argue that Marx's model of the dynamics of industrial capitalism as a mode of production provides rather more compelling reasons why individual companies operating in the metropolitan countries are much more likely to act in ways that generate a productive expanding economy than their colonial counterparts.[31] Faced either with increasing competition and falling prices or with the demands of an organised work-force, or both, in theory industrial capitalists cope with the problem of declining rates of profit by seeking to enhance their ability to exploit labour. This is achieved by raising the productivity of the work-force through constantly striving to improve the production process. In this way capitalists can reduce the labour-time required to produce a given quantity of commodities. Depending on the power of organised labour, at a given point in time, this may lead to higher wage levels. Moreover, this same activity generates improvements and expansion elsewhere in the system since capitalists have to buy in new machinery in order to improve productivity. At the same time, by reducing the costs of production it stimulates effective demand in the wider economy (providing these advantages are passed on to consumers in lower prices). As Brenner observes, it is this process whereby class conflict and competition compel capitalists to generate relative rather than absolute surplus value from their employees that is at the heart of the capitalist mode of production.[32] In principle, these changes and conflicts, proceeding continuously within and between different economic sectors, endow industrial capitalism with its enormous capacity to develop the productive forces and improve the real living standards of the majority of people even while it continues to exploit those same people. According to the Marxist writers whose arguments we have considered, the possibility that this benevolent spiral of capitalist development could become a reality in most sectors and regions of Africa was still a very long way from being capable of fulfilment by the end of the colonial period. Primarily this was because foreign capital had failed to bring the process of primitive capital accumulation anywhere near to completion.

So far we have drawn upon viewpoints which paint a very unfavourable picture of colonial rule and Western capitalism. Other writers, however, though still critical in their analyses, offer a rather different and perhaps more positive view of the colonial era. Some of these writers operate mainly within the framework of conventional economic theory while others are Marxists who have recently tried to re-evaluate the impact of European imperialism on Africa and elsewhere.

For most economists, the establishment of free markets is the absolute and essential precondition for economic development. This requires that all previous customary, legal, religious and political constraints on the movement of people, resources and money, as well as the expression of wants, are removed. Once trade is liberalised and competition is firmly established as the principle determinant of what gets produced and by what means, then market demand will grow. This, in turn, will stimulate enterprise and therefore innovation, investment, employment, the division of labour and economic growth. Thus, it is not so much the spontaneous supply of entrepreneurs that determines whether and when economic development will accelerate, as some sociologists and anthropologists have suggested. Rather, new forms of business leadership are called into being by market forces.

Another very influential argument is that free trade between countries is generally beneficial to all those who participate and so it should be encouraged.[33] This is linked to the theory of 'comparative costs' and goes back to Adam Smith and David Ricardo. At its simplest the theory states that countries are not equally endowed with the same climatic, physical, social and other resourses. Thus, the costs involved in producing different commodities vary from place to place. Accordingly, it makes good economic sense for each country to specialise in the production and export of those goods wherein it possesses natural advantages and to import from abroad all those commodities which it could produce at home only at much higher cost. In this way, growing national specialisation fed by international exchange will operate as a vehicle for economic growth.

Some contemporary economists believe the potential advantages of unrestricted international trade to be so considerable that they have continued to urge independent African governments to resist the temptation to provide tariff protection for infant home industries beyond a certain minimum point and to permit the more or less free import and export of capital and goods.[34] They remain suspicious of calls for protection against superior foreign competition, arguing that this may enable inefficient local producers to remain in business and raise the prices that local consumers are forced to pay, thereby reducing the overall level of market demand and distorting the allocation of resources. The majority of economists, however, including those with a Marxian orientation, believes that there is a strong case to be made for a degree of protectionism. These economists point out that this has been one of the keystones of industrialisation for all late-developing countries whose capitalists would otherwise have been compelled to compete on very unequal terms with more established producers.

The theory of comparative costs is linked to a further idea, which involves the assumption that the subsistence producers of Africa and other parts of the Third World were unable to make full use of the labour, land and other resources available to them in the pre-colonial era because the absence of market outlets meant there was no incentive to do so.[35] Instead, people spent much of their time engaged in ceremonial, military and other non-economic activities. The relatively low and highly dispersed population existing in most parts of pre-colonial Africa has also been seen as a major factor holding back the growth of market demand. Spread out over vast areas, and living in a hostile environment that made transport and trade highly expensive, African cultivators inevitably strove to be as self-sufficient as possible. But in such societies, made up of innumerable, small and largely self-contained communities, the extent of economic exchange, and therefore the possibilities of technical specialisation, innovation and large-scale production, were severely limited.[36] Only when European trade and, eventually, colonial rule provided a 'vent' or channel through which goods and services could pass in and out to the external world did it become worthwhile and possible for people in traditional societies to divert previously under-utilised labour and other resources into cash-crop production or employment in order to purchase goods unattainable in the indigenous economy.

Some economists have also stressed the 'dualistic' nature of economic development once colonial rule was established.[37] The inflow of Western capital then gave rise to a modern, highly productive economic sector. This became the focus for rapid development partly by attracting and absorbing surplus labour from the quite separate traditional sector. The latter was supposedly characterised by a basic subsistence orientation, stagnation, low productivity and the under-utilisation of resources. Gradually, the flow of labour from the traditional into the capitalist sector, the resulting increase in productivity and wealth and the dissemination of modern technology and new attitudes leads to an eventual breakdown of the original dual economy and prepares the way for a genuine and rapid process of economic development.

It is not difficult to see how theories such as these could be interpreted in such a way as to lend a degree of apparent credibility to the attempts by colonial governments and European interests to justify their activities in Africa. It is partly for this very reason that many writers, influenced by other disciplines and perspectives, have often been critical of such thinking and have labelled it as 'bourgeois'.[38] Dependency theorists have been particularly scathing in their attacks on conventional economic thinking because it appears to legitimise imperialism by suggesting that so-called backward economies positively need large doses of Western capital, exposure to world market forces, and so on. But for Neo Marxist thinkers these provide a recipe for underdevelopment not for Third World economic progress.

It is not easy to resolve such huge differences in interpretation nor do we need to attempt such a task here. What can be said, however, is that colonial rule did bring certain advantages. Modern forms of transport, administration and education were established where none had existed before. Most regions were connected to the expanding world economy and the inhabitants experienced new opportunities and incentives to produce for and sell to a much wider market than had hitherto been possible. Many Africans experienced a rise in living standards and a wider range of occupational experience became available (primarily for men). The foundations – if only that – of modern technology, science, professionalism, capitalist agriculture and industry were laid down. At the same time, the processes of rural and urban class differentiation and proletarianisation were at least set in motion, albeit very unevenly, whilst stateless societies were incorporated into larger national entities under the apparatus of state control.

The critics of colonial rule are clearly quite right to point out that as a vehicle for achieving balanced, self-reliant economic development, capable of bestowing tangible benefits on the majority of a country's population, colonialism was inevitably flawed in all sorts of ways, although arguably it did prepare some of the groundwork for such a transformation. External interests and alien rulers can never have the same interest in bringing about long-term national economic development as indigenous classes and elites, nor is there the same prospect for making them accountable for their actions. However, by the same token, colonialism did eventually come to an end and, as Warren and other writers have begun to argue in recent years, the potential value of political independence as a crucial step towards the attainment of some degree of economic autonomy should not be underestimated.[39] Although the legacies of colonial rule and the ability of external forces to shape the local economy and society do not miraculously disappear once government is handed over to local people, there is greater scope for harnessing state power in the pursuit of national development. If this were not important then the phenomenon of late development – the ability of countries to catch up with and even overtake the industrial pioneers – would not be explicable. It may be very much more difficult to engage in this 'catching up' exercise in the late twentieth century than it was a hundred years ago, particularly when countries have experienced a long period of colonial domination. But the examples provided, for example, by Mexico, Brazil and some of the South-East Asian countries (nations which have remained firmly within the Western capitalist orbit) suggest that opportunities to obtain a certain kind of national development still remain.

Another possible counter-argument to the criticisms of colonial rule offered by Marxist and Neo-Marxist writers concerns the desirability of raw material production for export as the leading sector for African development. Again, Warren, for example, has questioned whether a realistic alternative strategy for bringing pre-capitalist societies into the world economy was readily available during the early period of colonial rule.[40] A start had to be made somewhere. Certainly, in some parts of West Africa, cash-crop export production was already established and entirely under indigenous control. At the time, particularly in view of the paucity of resources available to colonial governments, it seemed sensible to build on what had already begun and to encourage activities which fitted easily into the existing pattern of socio-economic life with a minimum of disruption. No doubt, African leaders would have given much greater emphasis to manufacturing had they been free to do so. But it is difficult to see how they would have financed the necessary changes without also placing considerable emphasis on primary production as a key source of funds for further expansion.

There is also the question of what kinds of resources were available to the metropolitan powers when they elected to assume control of the African continent in the late nineteenth century. Thus, in order to finance extensive and deep industrial transformations in a number of African colonies metropolitan governments would have needed to transfer massive quantities of capital away from the home economies, abandoning the basic premise that colonial development had to be basically self-financing.[41] Even if this had been politically possible – and it almost certainly was not – it is very doubtful whether the wealth-producing capacities of the colonial powers at that time were sufficiently advanced to make such a colossal and rapid funding exercise at all feasible.

Some idea of the relatively meagre dimensions of the entire world's industrial base at the time when Africa was being actively colonised, compared to today's levels, can be gauged from the following quotation taken from Harris's book, *Of Bread and Guns*. Taking steel production as a valid and useful index of industrial capacity he develops the following argument.

Modern raw steel production began in the 1870's. It took some fifty-seven years for the world to produce its first 100 million tonnes of output (1927), and another twenty-four years to reach its second (1951). But it was only eight years more before the third, in 1959. By 1973, more than 700 million tonnes poured from the world's steel mills and by now – despite world contraction – the total is something over 800 million tonnes. Since 1951, the world has increased its output of steel four times over. And production has spread. Now the orange glow in the night sky can be seen by peasants in India, Korea, Mexico, Brazil, Indonesia; from the rooftops of Cairo; from the fishing boats off the coast of Anshain in China.[42]

Turning to the question of world production as a whole, Harris points out that between 1950 and the mid 1970s world gross product increased approximately two-and-a-quarter times.[43] Yet, despite these impressive records of international industrialisation in the twentieth century there is still a very long way to go before output is able to match the as yet unmet needs of most people living on our planet. According to Harris, the 'world's industrial revolution has only just begun'.[44]

It was not only the African colonies that were adversely affected by the two world wars and the intervening recession of the 1930s. The pace of economic expansion slowed down in much of Africa because the colonies were so dependent on overseas markets. But by the same token this was part of a world-wide process and there were also many problems in the metropolitan countries: unemployment, economic stagnation, if not contraction, the destruction of capital stock, and so on. Moreover, even without the appalling consequences of the great depression, large numbers of people in the Western countries in the early decades of this century were still very poor indeed, and not only among the rural farm population.[45] Some regions and economic sectors were still relatively unaffected by mechanisation and modern forms of transport, power and communications until the First World War and beyond. In fact, the enormous advantages of motor transport, which played such an important role in opening up the African hinterlands to commerce and economic opportunity from the 1920s onwards, were established more or less simultaneously in both Europe and the colonies.

If these observations contain any validity at all it would seem unrealistic as well as unhelpful to push the criticisms of colonial policy and European capitalism too far. When Africa was colonised at the end of the nineteenth century the European economies were very much less developed than they are now. Yet the two leading colonial powers, Britain and France, particularly the former, had already undergone a longer period of industrial development than the span of years – approximately three-quarters of a century – through which the African experience of colonial rule would ultimately pass.

It is obviously difficult and perhaps misleading to single out one particular aspect of the colonial experience and its consequences and to argue that this was more damaging than any other. Nevertheless, arguably it was not only the economic legacy of colonial rule that continued to blight African progress after Independence – the failure to create the conditions whereby a much higher level of development could be speedily attained – but also the institutional legacy of colonial government itself and the politics of this period: the discrimination in the allocation of public resources, the tendency to foster monopoly and an excessive reliance on bureaucratic regulation used in the service of particular interests. These and other problems were highly damaging for African capitalism (especially in East and Central Africa), as we shall see in Chapter 3. The precedents established during this period continued to shape government policies and practices after Independence in various ways.

Whatever the verdict historians and others eventually reach concerning the record of European involvement in Africa during the colonial period, it is important to note the significant and often quite positive developments that took place in the period from the Second World War until the early 1960s. By the late 1940s, it was clear that the tide of African nationalism, already well under way as a result of the retrenchments caused by the depression years of the 1930s, especially in West Africa, and gathering momentum during the Second World War, was running high. Sooner rather than later the era of European rule in Africa would come to an end. Furthermore, the American government placed a good deal of pressure on the colonial powers at this time, urging them to plan for eventual decolonisation. There were many reasons for this but primarily American leaders were anxious to open up the world to their own powerful commercial interests and wished to pre-empt the possibility that more and more frustrated anti-colonial movements might move in a leftward political direction if steps were not eventually taken to meet some or all of their demands for national autonomy. These different pressures almost certainly worked to sharpen the minds of Europeans in Africa quite significantly and go a long way towards explaining why many colonial governments became much less conservative and more development oriented in their policy formulations during these years.

At the same time, world economic expansion meant that both the volume of raw material exports and the prices earned by African commodities, relative to imports, rose substantially. In the West African case, for example, it has been estimated that there was a sixfold increase in that region's total importing capacity between 1945 and 1955.[46] According to Kilby, Nigeria's total import market grew by 14 times in the period between 1946 and 1964. In fact, he points out that the greater part of Nigeria's twentieth-century economic expansion up to the mid 1960s took place after the Second World War.[47]

The establishment of modern methods of transportation in the early decades of the century had already exercised an enormous impact on market development. However, again, in Nigeria, Kilby shows how the existing transport network expanded rapidly in the post-war period and this reflected the underlying tendency for the economy to expand and was also a major factor contributing to that growth. Thus, between 1945 and 1963 the number of commercial vehicles travelling on Nigeria's growing road network grew from 1,500 to 24,000.[48] In addition, technical advances at this time, in particular the use of lighter vehicles of stronger construction and important savings in fuel consumption, reduced transport costs considerably thereby stimulating further market growth.

Together, political pressure and improving economic prospects helped to generate a number of further important changes both in colonial policy and in the climate for enterprise. Among the most significant of these were the following. Attracted by a growing market and, no doubt, by the need to establish a commercial bridgehead in the African economies before they became politically independent, a number of Western companies increased their investments at this time so that the inflow of private foreign capital rose quite considerably. In Kenya, for example, Swainson has shown how during the 1950s and 1960s a number of transnational corporations invested in modern plantation agriculture, raw-material-processing plants and consumer-goods industries.[49] The flow of capital into manufacturing was particularly rapid. In 1951, manufacturing industry already made up 12% of Gross National Product (G.N.P.) and by 1956 there were more than a hundred manufacturing and industrial establishments in Kenya employing over 50 persons.[50]

Secondly, overseas aid in the form of grants and loans also increased quite considerably after 1945.[51] Much of this aid was spent on the expansion of health and educational facilities as well as water conservation and public utilities. The main aim here was to raise the level of technical proficiency among sectors of the African population through various training programmes in addition to improving public welfare. Thirdly, these various capital inflows and the wealth they helped to generate increased government tax and revenue. Meanwhile, government income was also rising because of the customs duties levied on the increasing volume of imports and the funds accumulated by the marketing boards. Rising revenue enabled governments to expand public-sector investment generally, in line with the more relaxed attitude towards local market expansion. The much more central role of government in the colonial economies in turn helped to generate and sustain several further and largely beneficial changes. For example, there were more job openings in the public sector. In some countries agricultural extension services were expanded so that African farm productivity rose. Central and local government contracts for buildings, roads and various services provided expanding business opportunities for foreign and indigenous entrepreneurs.

Fourthly, in the 1950s, the old-established trading companies began to switch their local capital into manufacturing activity just at the same time that the transnationals were also seeking new investment outlets in certain African countries. Sections of the Indian and Levantine commercial communities, in East and West Africa respectively, also transferred capital into manufacturing during this period.[52] Underdevelopment theorists tend to argue that this decision to develop the productive forces outside agriculture using modern technology was both too little and too late and so could only deepen Africa's economic dependency on metropolitan capitalism. Many economists and some economic historians, on the other hand, have pointed out that for the most part manufacturing did not become economically viable in most African colonies until the 1950s or so. There were several aspects to this.

Commodity production and the development of a money economy had to reach a critical level over mainly subsistence production as a proportion of Gross National Product (G.N.P.). Swainson estimates that in Kenya the subsistence sector contributed approximately 60% to Kenya's G.N.P. in 1929 but this had fallen to one-third in 1948.[53] The growing importance of the monetised sector, in turn, was related partly to a second factor: the rapid post-war expansion in cash-crop production, in many colonies, mainly for export, which massively increased the level of effective demand for all kinds of goods and services. Increased government expenditure also helped to stimulate economic growth and local consumption. Eventually, at some point during the 1950s, a commercial threshold was reached at which it became both profitable and practical to begin manufacturing mainly consumer goods for the growing local market without the need for too much tariff protection from imports and without forgoing the economies of large-scale production.[54] Several writers have argued that these structural changes could have begun a few years earlier if the marketing boards had not continued to cream off a substantial portion of the rising post-war export earnings so that spending power increased more slowly than might otherwise have been the case.[55] Nevertheless, living standards did eventually improve, as did the commercial opportunities available to capitalist entrepreneurs both large and small.

The switch into industrial investment by the European companies was also, in part, a response to increasing competitive pressures since it became much easier at this time for smaller companies to enter trade on a profitable basis. But this brings us to the subject of the next chapter, namely, the specific effects of colonial policy and Western capital on the various forms of African enterprise.

§ 3 §

COLONIAL RULE AND AFRICAN ENTERPRISE

Most writers would probably agree with the proposition that colonial governments and foreign interests failed to realise all the potential for African economic development during the years of European hegemony although they would disagree as to the reasons for this and the extent to which it was true. But the inability or unwillingness of Europeans to establish the basis for full and proper capitalist development might not have mattered quite so much had local classes been able to emerge instead whose members were more disposed to undertake the task of genuine national economic transformation at some later date. This is the subject of the present chapter: the effects of colonialism on African enterprise. We will see that the more general difficulties in the economy as a whole resulting from economic dependency and the incomplete establishment of capitalist relations were compounded by two additional problems specific to indigenous entrepreneurship. One stemmed from the attitudes of colonial officials. This varied from indifference or a marked reluctance to provide assistance to downright hostility and discrimination in dealings with indigenous interests. The second obstacle was the superior competition offered by foreign capital, a competition with which Africans were normally ill equipped to cope and against which they received little or no protection.

GOVERNMENT RESTRICTIONS: MAINLY EAST AND CENTRAL AFRICA

A number of scholars have pointed to the way in which colonial governments often showed a marked tendency to rely on a wide range of bureaucratic measures in their efforts to manage the territories under their control. By contrast, free market forces and small-scale economic activities were often regarded with suspicion. Thus, in addition to wielding all the usual instruments of modern economic control – fiscal, monetary, public spending policy, foreign exchange controls and so on – colonial rulers also tended to assume additional regulatory powers and exercised these primarily in order to consolidate and protect the needs of favoured Western groups. In effect, government power was often used in order to create or enhance monopolistic tendencies and interests. On the whole these strategies were rather more pronounced in East and Central Africa than in 'Africa of the Trade Economy'.[1] That the exercise of discriminatory state power was highly advantageous to certain European interests did not pass unnoticed by many Africans, including some who later became involved in the various Independence movements. These perceptions may well have influenced the way future African leaders viewed the relationship between economic development and state power. In what ways did colonial policy impede African enterprise?

In the early colonial period, not only did African farmers and traders receive little, if any, help, but they were also exposed in many colonies to deliberate legal and administrative restraints. These were applied much more systematically and comprehensively in 'Africa of the Labour Reserves'. The most widely used restriction involved the need for traders to purchase a government licence. Sometimes cost alone was sufficient to prevent Africans from entering trade, given the low value of their likely sales turnover in relation to the licence fee. In addition, the issue of these licences was frequently hedged around with various rules concerning eligibility, the particular activities for which they were valid and the areas where licensees were entitled to operate.

In Northern Rhodesia, for example, local people were prohibited from operating stores in towns except in African locations.[2] Restrictions were also imposed on the kind of goods Africans were allowed to sell so that their trade would not impinge on European storekeepers. Moreover, in most urban areas the government supervised beer halls and did not permit legal indigenous bar ownership until 1961. Local people were also forbidden to register companies on their own land. In effect, all this meant that for a large part of the colonial period most kinds of business and commercial farming were rendered more or less illegal for Africans.

Discrimination in the issue of licences was also common in Kenya and Uganda. In these colonies, Asians were not allowed to own land or invest in commercial agriculture but they were encouraged to develop trading interests. By contrast, in Uganda, the 1901 Trade Licensing Act tried to eliminate Africans both from hand ginning and small-scale buying and selling of raw cotton despite the fact that such activities were eminently suitable avenues for indigenous commercial advancement.[3] The 'Cotton Rules' of 1918 tightened up the criteria of 'eligibility' for dealing in cotton and established particular locations for its purchase.[4] In the 1930s even the trade in native produce was brought under government control. The Native Produce Marketing Ordinance restricted the issue of purchasing licences to a few 'reputable' firms, thereby excluding most small itinerant African produce buyers, and stipulated particular buying centres in each area.[5] Statutory marketing monopolies of this kind, created largely for the purpose of restricting trading opportunities to certain designated interests, were also established in Northern Rhodesia and Kenya.

Whilst trading licences served as a general control on indigenous business activity some governments also devised additional and more specific constraints. In both Kenya and Northern Rhodesia limits were placed on the amount of credit that non-Africans were allowed to extend to local businesses.[6] Ostensibly, this was designed to protect Africans from the possibility of chronic indebtedness but since few businesses can survive or expand without receiving credit at some point, this rule acted as a brake on commercial endeavour. In Uganda the Coffee Ordinance of 1930 effectively prevented small entrepreneurs from entering the coffee-curing business or from exporting this commodity by confining these activities to large companies.[7] In Kenya, the government responded to the clamour from white settlers against competition by banning coffee cultivation among African farmers in the 1920s on the pretext that it was necessary to prevent the spread of disease from supposedly poorly managed to well-managed farms. Later on, in the 1930s, this prohibition was partly lifted but African cultivation was still confined to certain, mainly remote, areas and was only permitted on a small scale.[8]

For reasons that will become clear later on, colonial authorities in West Africa were much less prone to use administrative and legislative measures against indigenous enterprise. However, some instances did arise. In the Gold Coast, Africans whose land contained diamonds were forbidden to engage in mining operations unless these were confined to 'native' methods.[9] Moreover, licences had to be purchased before diamond mining was legal and these were only issued at the discretion of District Commissioners. At the same time a levy was imposed on would-be entrepreneurs to ensure that they would be financially able to pay the export duties liable in the event of successful ventures. Howard argues that, in total, these measures substantially restrained African enterprise in this field. In the Ivory Coast, by the mid 1920s, both African and French planters were successfully cultivating coffee and cocoa but there was a serious labour shortage. Responding to the demands placed upon it the government instituted a system of forced labour. At the same time, it ensured that the French planters gained privileged access to the supply of unwilling labour. By the early 1940s, African farmers were virtually debarred from using recruited labour at all. Some were even forcibly removed from their plantations and their labour was placed at the disposal of Europeans. This continued until mounting political opposition compelled the government to remove this discriminatory labour code in 1946.[10]

In some countries, for example Southern and Northern Rhodesia, Uganda and Kenya – and, of course, in South Africa – not just one or two, but a whole package of measures were introduced in order to foster European business at the expense of African interests. In Kenya, up to the Second World War, the scope of such policies was particularly comprehensive, though after this time most were removed as the settlers lost some of the autonomy they had earlier exercised *vis-à-vis* the metropolitan government. Kenya is especially interesting because it is one of the few countries where, in the opinion of some writers, a strong and highly promising African capitalist bourgeoisie has emerged since the 1960s.

Some Europeans, for example the missionaries, were opposed to settler predominance.[11] But the white settlers eventually established a considerable influence over metropolitan officials and secured the kinds of measures against African enterprise that we have already discussed; trade licensing, credit restrictions, the introduction of statutory marketing monopolies granted only to non-Africans traders and the banning of African coffee cultivation. But these steps were accompanied by a whole series of further policies. By the late 1920s, approximately 20% of the usable arable land had been confiscated from the African population and allocated to the settlers. A law introduced in 1918 had already decreed that African 'squatters' residing in the areas granted to the Europeans must provide labour in return for 'tenancy' rights. Brett argues that this effectively reduced traditional African cultivators to the status of serfs. But land grants were insufficient to enable Europeans to survive and prosper in competition with African farmers. Thus, railways were financed from government funds, including many uneconomic lines, and these were disproportionately concentrated in the settler areas. (The same was largely true in the case of road building.) In addition, a graduated pricing policy was implemented on the various railway routes so that freight costs were lower in the European reserves. Veterinary and medical services were also provided for the European communities at considerable cost to the government. The Land Bank of 1931 provided low-interest loans for white farmers. This complemented other agricultural assistance, such as help with locust control and various extension services. Protective tariffs were introduced in 1922 on European farm produce. These operated in Tanganyika and Uganda, as well. Effectively, this meant that consumers in these territories were providing a direct subsidy to the European farmers in Kenya in the form of higher prices than would otherwise have been the case.

At the same time, government policy was formulated so that most revenue was raised from the poor African majority; native and poll taxes, high customs duties levied on the kinds of cheap articles, such as textiles, that were mainly purchased by African consumers. The Europeans, on the other hand, strongly resisted the imposition of income taxes which would have fallen mainly on them, given their higher incomes. This remained the case until the late 1930s. According to Brett's calculations, the African fiscal contribution to government funds was approximately 70% in the early 1920s and remained disproportionately high over a long period. Clearly, during these years African land, labour and money were being used to fund the emergence and growth of white settler capitalism. Kenya was therefore one of the very few countries in Africa where the process of 'primitive capital accumulation' was genuinely underway during the early colonial period. Unfortunately it was largely confined to central Kenya and was firmly under European rather than African control, at this time, though this was eventually to change.

Another colonial strategy that usually produced adverse consequences for local entrepreneurs in many countries was the policy of encouraging non-African immigrant minorities to settle and then take up an intermediate business role between Africa farmers and workers and big European commercial interests. In East and Central Africa this position was mainly taken by Asians, although in Northern Rhodesia East European Jews also became established in trade quite early on. The Asians became established in Kenya, Uganda, Tanganyika, Nyasaland and, to a lesser extent, in Northern Rhodesia.

In most East African colonies the Asians generally enjoyed certain advantages over their African rivals. Firstly, many began in trade at an earlier date, most already possessed some commercial experience and a network of business contacts, and some had benefited from the opportunity to accumulate a little cash for starting capital before they moved into trade.[12] Secondly, although they were subject to government regulations they were not usually restricted to anything like the same extent as their African counterparts.[13] Indeed, governments and European commercial interests were normally quite favourably disposed towards them. They were encouraged to develop their business role in the colonial economy as buyers of African produce and sellers of imported goods and usually had access to credit as well as employment in big trading enterprises.[14] Thirdly, as an ethnic minority group sharing certain cultural ties and bound together by the same experience of political and economic vulnerability that has always faced such marginal groups operating in alien environments, the Asians had every reason to maintain a degree of internal group solidarity, closing their ranks against outside interests. Whilst this provided the economic strength that comes from mutual support, it also tended to alienate them from the less advantaged African majority.[15]

The already poor competitive position experienced by most indigenous entrepreneurs was further weakened because, given the latters' slender resources and the credit and administrative restrictions they faced, most African traders were very small and could only obtain goods from traders who also operated at the lower end of the commercial system. In practice this meant obtaining their supplies of trade goods not from Asian whole-salers, who were reluctant to deal with Africans in the small quantities involved, but from Asian storekeepers. The mark-up on merchandise purchased at retail prices inevitably made African goods somewhat dearer, thus weakening their competitive position and confining them, for the most part, to operating in the least accessible and poorest locations and at very low profit margins.[16]

In parts of West Africa, too, immigrant minorities often flourished in business while African entrepreneurs languished, and for similar reasons. In Senegal, the authorities encouraged citizens of lower-middle-class origins to emigrate from France.[17] Both Amin and Cruise O'Brien point out that like the Levantine immigrants these *petits blancs* were often employed by French trading companies and some were given positions as intermediaries in the groundnut trade in the interior. In general they were encouraged to operate in commerce and many eventually became shopkeepers in Dakar or developed other business interests including the direct importation of European goods. We have already seen how, in the Ivory Coast, the colonial government helped French immigrants to evolve into a wealthy planter class. A similar situation arose in the Belgian and Portuguese colonies, too. In the British West African territories it was mainly the Levantines who, arriving quite early after the onset of colonial rule, quickly established themselves mainly as retailers and wholesalers of imported goods, though some Indians came as well. As in East Africa, the Levantines enjoyed certain advantages not available to Africans, such as access to credit, the opportunity to obtain government contracts and the receipt of import quotas.[18]

There is, however, another side to this story of relative Levantine and Asian success in business compared to African entrepreneurs. We will return to this later in the chapter.

FOREIGN COMPETITION AND LOCAL ENTERPRISE: MAINLY WEST AFRICA

In West Africa, the main problem confronting African entrepreneurs was the reality of superior foreign competition. Because European companies enjoyed certain clear business advantages, colonial governments were less inclined to intervene in the economy on their behalf compared to governments in East Africa. But there were other reasons why bureaucratic regulation with respect to indigenous economic activity was used more sparingly in much of West Africa: the absence of a white settler class; the need instead to generate peasant cash-crop agriculture rather than a large and steady supply of migrant workers; and the region's historical involvement in external trade, which had enabled European trading interests to establish deep roots in the local economy.

In order to understand the reasons for European commercial superiority it is necessary to introduce certain approximate distinctions between the different categories of local traders. (1) Merchants negotiated directly with shipping companies or overseas buyers and suppliers and then arranged to export African produce or import Western goods, or both, in their own right.

(2) Middlemen were traders who occupied an intermediate position between the merchant companies and those lower down the commercial chain. There were, perhaps, two main types of intermediary or middleman. (a) Many were produce buyers who dealt in the export of cash crops. They might have obtained this produce directly from the farmers or through a series of buying agents (brokers) and then sold the produce to merchant exporting firms. (b) Others were retailers and/or wholesalers whose livelihood depended mainly on selling imported goods directly to local consumers or through itinerant hawkers, or both. They obtained their trade goods through a network of suppliers which led sooner or later to a merchant. Both the produce buyers and the retail storekeepers were more or less financially self-reliant, though some kind of credit arrangement was normally endemic to most types of trading. These two activities could be, and often were, combined to a great or lesser extent. Some trading intermediaries might also be engaged in merchant activity.

(3) Brokers and sub-brokers operated at the bottom end of the commercial hierarchy. Using advances of cash or goods provided by merchant companies or independent produce buyers they sought out those who were willing to sell cash crops and arranged to purchase these crops on behalf of the company with whom they dealt. Invariably, brokers were financially dependent for funding their buying operations on bigger enterprises higher up the chain. In return for their services they received a commission and perhaps a salary according to the precise terms of their agreement.

If we ask what happened to these different kinds of local entrepreneurs as a money economy grew in importance from the late nineteenth century, and consider their relative influence at different points in time, the following picture emerges. African merchants had competed with European companies since at least the early years of the nineteenth century at several locations along the West African coast. One such case is shown by the mulatto descendants of European traders who operated from the ports and towns of the Southern Gold Coast. Some of these men were merchants of substance who competed successfully with Europeans. They exercised an increasing degree of political influence in the declining Fanti States, especially in the 1850s and 1860s.[19]

During the early years of the nineteenth century, when the British were trying to stamp out the slave trade, ships carrying the now 'illegal' human cargo were sometimes stopped and the captives deposited at certain points along the coast. Sierra Leone became especially important in this respect. Fyfe describes how some of these creoles eventually moved away from Sierra Leone and settled among the Yoruba of Western Nigeria.[20] Slaves were also repatriated from South America at this time. Most of these Brazilian creoles were settled in Dahomey and in the area around Lagos on the Nigerian coast.[21] Wherever they became established the creoles tended to become converted to Christianity and many received a Western education. In Sierra Leone some became professionals and held positions in the civil service. However, like the mulatto traders of the Fanti Gold Coast states, the creoles in Sierra Leone, Western Nigeria and Dahomey also became involved in the expanding trade in oil palm and other products during the period of legitimate commerce in the mid nineteenth century. Moreover, some of these traders were merchant exporters and importers who competed successfully with their European counterparts, especially in Dahomey and Sierra Leone where they founded leading families.[22]

The important nineteenth-century oil-palm trade of the Niger Delta area was also organised and controlled very successfully by Africans, in this case the rulers of the oil states.[23] Using slaves for transport and labour and an elaborate network of dependent middlemen chiefs, Nan Olomu of Warri, and Ja Ja of Opobo, the two most successful rulers engaged in this trade, held together a commercial enterprise stretching over a very large area. Nevertheless, the import–export trade connected to the oil-palm business was controlled by European firms not by African merchants. In fact, Gertzel points out that the expulsion of Ja Ja from his kingdom in 1887 occurred because he had previously tried to enter the export trade independently of the European companies by negotiating directly with a Birmingham hardware firm at a time of falling commodity prices.

It seems clear from this brief survey that even before the colonial era only a small proportion of the indigenous traders involved in the external trade along the West African coast were independent merchants in their own right. Moreover, those who had flourished in the middle decades of the nineteenth century, particularly in Sierra Leone, Dahomey and the

Gold Coast, were confronted with severe and increasing pressures two or three decades later as a result of falling commodity prices and the encroachment of European companies. Thus, most African traders ceased to operate as merchants in the years just before colonial rule was established. It is true that in the Gold Coast, for example, the rapid expansion of cocoa farming created a later generation of small, independent African merchants. However, most of these shipping companies were wiped out by the collapse in prices which occurred at the end of 1920.[24] The later insignificance of independent Gold Coast merchants is revealed dramatically by the following statistic. During the 1936/7 season less than 1% of the cocoa crop was shipped abroad by indigenous entrepreneurs. Elsewhere, the same process took place very rapidly and within a few years of the consolidation of colonial power.[25]

Turning now to the African middlemen or intermediaries, on the whole we find a similar story of decline in the face of European competition except that this took place a little later, in the years just before and after the First World War. Again, the case of cocoa trading in the Gold Coast is instructive. Southall has shown how up until 1913, Cadbury's the chocolate manufacturer, and the long-established European import–export firms, bought most of their cocoa from a small number of independent African produce buyers.[26] Smaller quantities were purchased from local farmers' cooperatives or farmer-traders. However, by the mid 1920s a few European firms not only controlled virtually all the cocoa export business but the great majority of once-independent African produce buyers had also disappeared. Henceforth, Cadbury and the other companies obtained their supplies from numerous small cocoa brokers widely dispersed in the rural areas. Indeed, all over West Africa the majority of indigenous produce buyers and retail storekeepers was forced out of business during these years. Many were offered positions as agents or brokers for the European buying firms or became company employees. In the retail business some Africans survived by obtaining goods on credit from wholesalers through the famous passbook system.

The relegation of most African middlemen to the role of brokers was partly a result of the enormous improvements that took place in transport and communications. The first railway construction work began in Senegal in 1881, in Sierra Leone in 1895 and in Western Nigeria in 1896. In the Gold Coast the railway line reached Kumasi in 1903, while the first lorries were being used in the cocoa towns close to Accra in 1907.[27] The spread of modern forms of transport quickly reduced freight costs, thereby accelerating the expansion of the money economy and cash-crop production while facilitating the increased mobility of people and information. These benefits continued to spread slowly into more and more areas over the next

30 years or so. But these developments also enabled the European trading firms to move inland away from the coast. As they pushed into the interior they established warehouses, collecting points and retail stores. In the Niger Delta, for example, even after Ja Ja had been deposed in 1887, the European firms based on the coast were obliged to accept the continued domination exercised by the middlemen chiefs over the oil-palm business until around 1900 when the Niger River was finally opened up for transport and the first roads into the interior began to be built.[28] Similarly, in the Gold Coast, once the railway and the associated road network had more or less linked most of the Eastern Region 'cocoa towns' to Accra by 1915, it was increasingly possible for Cadbury's and the European trading firms to establish their own agencies up country, displacing most of the African buying firms.[29]

The exceptionally volatile fluctuations in export prices during the 1920–1 period also exercised a powerful shaping influence on the fortunes of numerous local middlemen. Thus, world prices for several African exports rose sharply after the First World War. Cocoa, for example, increased from an average of 47 shillings per hundredweight in 1919 to 123 shillings at its highest point in 1920.[30] In the Gold Coast, this short-lived boom sucked in many new firms, both shippers and produce buyers. When prices collapsed at the end of 1920 numerous small entrepreneurs, European as well as African, rapidly went bankrupt, caught out with huge stocks of unsaleable cocoa.[31] Writers like Bauer and Southall point out that in the aftermath of these events, and in the absence of a strong local trading bourgeoisie, the European companies had little choice but to take over much of the existing produce-buying network and provide the finance required for future trade expansion.[32] However, severe price fluctuations did not discriminate between African and European commercial interests. Also, the growing market opportunities brought by the spread of rail and road transport ought to have helped local as well as foreign firms. What then were the additional factors at work which placed African traders at a disadvantage?

Most writers agree that European firms had access to resources that were not usually available to local entrepreneurs. Accordingly, without government assistance and a degree of protection African traders could not normally hope to compete successfully. But not only was competition unequal, in the opinion of some writers, it also became unfair as European companies resorted to various strategies designed to reduce free competition. It is also alleged that colonial governments did little, if anything, to counter these arrangements.

Access to a more plentiful supply of capital was by far the most important advantage available to some of the large European firms. This conferred crucial benefits. Firstly, according to Bauer, the extension of cash-crop production further and further afield meant that considerable working capital was required in order to hold large stocks of goods in transit for long periods of time.[33] There was also a time interval between buying farmers' crops and receiving payment for overseas sales. Furthermore, a growing network of collecting points, warehouses and retail/wholesale stores had to be financed. Once made, these investments generated a steady return over many years.[34] Secondly, produce buying was normally fairly competitive, but by the same token the advantage went to those who could afford to provide their brokers with the money to secure crop pledges from farmers. Thirdly, sometimes it was an advantage to buy produce at a time when prices were low and then hold these stocks back in the hope of future price rises, but again this required cash reserves. Fourthly, the larger firms could afford to offer slightly better or steadier prices to farmers thereby ensuring continuous supplies. Last, but certainly not least, the ability to ride out trade depressions or absorb losses in the hope of better times ahead was much more difficult for small firms.

Access to capital was also crucial in other fields of enterprise, too. In the Gold Coast Howard cites the case of gold mining.[35] Attempts by African proprietors to compete successfully were thwarted because the really profitable deep mining ventures were impossible without access to modern equipment, particularly machinery for pumping water. Both the capital and the technical knowledge required for such activity were simply beyond the means of local entrepreneurs. By contrast, Africans were able to dominate the timber business until the Second World War. Howard observes that, significantly, the main reason for this was European reluctance to enter the timber trade until the infrastructural amenities in the Gold Coast were much more developed.[36]

Local entrepreneurs also lacked the opportunity to establish direct and easy access to overseas companies: shippers, manufacturers, merchant suppliers or firms buying African produce.[37] European companies, on the other hand, could afford to operate offices in the metropolitan countries, they enjoyed informal contacts with firms in West Africa and overseas and they were sometimes formally linked through mergers, company agreements and interlocking directorates. Through these connections the expatriate firms enjoyed ease of access to information, markets and supplies. In addition, companies based in Europe normally preferred to deal with large orders and established customers with whom they shared certain common national and cultural bonds.

Finally, as in so many spheres of business activity, substantial economies of scale were available to large firms. According to Bauer, these economies could and did enhance further company growth and business concentration in the sphere of West African trade.[38] Among the most important of these were the possibility of obtaining discounts from overseas suppliers when goods were purchased in large quantities and reduced overheads per unit of output once investments had already been made in such things as bulk storage and financial management.

Several writers insist that competition between local and foreign traders was not only unequal but increasingly became unfair as well.[39] The three main agents presumed to be involved in this process were the expatriate import–export firms themselves, the banks and the government, while considerable collusion is supposed to have taken place between them. Those writers who have been critical of these Western interests on the grounds of unfair competition tend to make the following observations. They emphasise the trend towards oligopoly, the process whereby large overseas firms bought out small ones, especially during years of economic crisis, or where previously independent firms merged to form larger units.[40] One very famous example of this occurred during 1929 when two of the giant West African companies, the African and Eastern Company and the Niger Company (each established as a result of earlier amalgamations), merged to form the United African Company. It was certainly the case that ownership and market control became highly concentrated during the 1920s and 1930s. Thus, in 1932/3 the top four Gold Coast firms controlled 70% of cocoa exports whilst the top 13 firms exported over 90%.[41] By the late 1940s, six or seven firms operating in Nigeria handled somewhere between two-thirds and three-quarters of all the various forms of import–export trade.[42]

Oligopoly supposedly allowed the big firms to earn excessive profits, for example by market sharing. Once trade agreements were operational it was possible for firms to engage in price fixing, especially on imported goods. These activities tended to prevent new firms from entering trade and worked against existing small ones. Bauer cites several instances of known and reputedly unfair trading practice. He argues that several large European firms engaged in destructive price-cutting activities.[43] They held down the prices of imported goods in their stores to a level below that required to enable small newcomers to survive and prosper. Once the latter were driven out of business, prices returned to their original levels. In the British colonies, during the depression years of the 1930s, the big companies also placed pressure on governments to restrict the immigration of Lebanese families and Europeans of non-British origin so that competition would not increase, though this did not meet with very much response. Some European firms were able to secure sole distribution rights on certain imports of British brand-named goods that were especially popular among African consumers. Exclusivity of access, in turn, enabled them to charge higher prices than might otherwise have been possible at that time.[44]

The European banks, too, have been accused of acting unfairly in their dealings with Africans.[45] It is alleged that they often discriminated in favour of European clients, charged higher fees for the services they provided to indigenous people and operated secret preferential agreements with the large trading firms. More importantly, the banks normally refused to provide loans or overdraft facilities to African customers, most of whom were much more reliant on loan capital in order to achieve expansion than were foreign companies. By refusing such facilities the banks effectively reduced overall competition in the colonial economy as well as holding back African enterprise. The banks saw their main function as serving the interests of their brother capitalists with whom they also shared certain common perceptions of the African population. Another problem was that African entrepreneurs had great difficulty in obtaining the collateral needed in order to secure bank loans. Land was normally owned communally and in the early colonial period few Africans owned modern houses. Indeed, the widespread tendency for indigenous entrepreneurs to invest in real estate probably owed as much to the problems of providing security as it did to the desire for financial security and social status.[46]

Government policy in West Africa also appears to have contributed towards the reality of unfair competition. Central to this process was the fact that officials and the leading representatives of finance and merchant capital were obviously drawn together by common national and cultural ties. These were constantly reinforced by informal as well as formal contacts. Moreover, paternalistic and perhaps racialist attitudes towards African people were undoubtedly shared by many in the expatriate community, including government officials. These attitudes tended to generate the belief that even educated Africans who were involved in some kind of 'Western' activity, including business dealings, could not be expected to perform well or in a trustworthy manner. For these and other reasons governments offered little, if any, help to local entrepreneurs. Indeed, some officials are said to have exchanged information secretly with banks and investment houses in Europe concerning the financial prospects and reliability of certain African traders to the latters' detriment.[47]

During the 1920s and 1930s, for example, several schemes were floated by prominent Africans in the Gold Coast and Nigeria.[48] The leading men behind these moves also had strong connections with the National Congress of British West Africa. Founded in 1921, this organisation became the most important forum for opposition to colonial government by local businessmen during the 1920s, especially in the Gold Coast. One of the main figures in these projects was a man called Tete Ansah. The aim was to compete more effectively with European companies and regain some of the economic initiative for African farmers and traders. This was to be achieved by founding banks to finance African enterprises, setting up limited liability companies that would buy farmers' produce and ship it directly to America and Europe independently of the big companies and establishing cooperative buying facilities and stores. Wealthy farmers and others were invited to contribute funds. In the end these ventures failed and on several occasions it appears that financial chicanery on the part of some of the organisers was partly to blame. Many investors who, sometimes for reasons of nationalism, had been persuaded to provide cash and/or advances of cocoa in order to help these schemes get off the ground, lost their money. Certain financial discrepancies were never satisfactorily explained.

Nevertheless, both Hopkins and Holmes have argued that not all of the entrepreneurs involved in these schemes were men of dubious character. Many were legitimate as well as competent and deserved to be treated sympathetically by banks. Yet most failed to receive such commercial backing largely because of the collusion that took place between governments and bank officials, both of whom were unwilling to take the trouble to devise criteria for distinguishing properly between the different categories of African businessmen. Instead, these events simply reinforced European prejudices. For many years, the promising and the able were lumped together in the minds of Europeans with the swindlers and the incompetent.

At the same time, virtually no action was taken to restrain the moves towards oligopoly on the part of the big European trading firms. Nor did officials attempt to impose any kind of limit on restrictive trade practices such as market sharing and price fixing, difficult though this might have been.[49] Moreover, during the Second World War there was a general policy of increasing the degree of state regulation over the colonial economies in order to meet wartime metropolitan requirements for tropical raw materials while minimising the use of scarce shipping. The Produce Marketing Boards represented an important aspect of this change in orientation. In operating these statutory organisations, government officials tended to work in close liaison with the leading European firms. This intensified collaboration meant that the controls exercised by the government operated very much to the advantage of the leading companies, since it was they who received the allocations of import licences and shipping quotas.[50]

Finally, what local entrepreneurs needed in order to have some hope of competing effectively with foreign companies was a degree of government protection in the form of a guaranteed share of contracts in the case of public building works, a proportion of the import licence allocations or, preferably, both. In fact, however, the great majority of African traders and contractors received neither of these, whether before, during or in the years of economic growth immediately after the Second World War. Indeed, these allocations were invariably based on the criteria of 'past performance' and this automatically excluded newcomers, usually Africans, from serious consideration. No doubt it was unrealistic to hope for such policies at that time. However, it is unfortunate that colonial governments seem, if anything, to have moved in the opposite direction; what assistance they gave to private interests was received by those who did not need their protection.

Before leaving this section on foreign competition it is worthwhile remembering that in very many economic spheres local people flourished quite successfully during the colonial period and often benefited from the opportunities generated by the climate of general expansion and increased purchasing power. Thus, whenever local enterprise was actively encouraged by government (or the weight of bureaucratic restrictions were somewhat reduced compared to the 'normal' situation) and in those fields in which foreign capital had little if any immediate commercial interest (perhaps because an earlier, indigenous initiative made it unnecessary and unprofitable for Europeans to seriously dislodge Africans), or both, local enterprise tended to thrive, expand and adapt to the opportunities provided by improved transportation, urbanisation and regional specialisation.

Cash-crop production is one obvious and crucial example of this especially, though not exclusively, in West Africa. Not only was the emergence of successful commercial farming for export usually almost entirely African led and managed, but in some areas rural socio-economic differentiation (based either on existing inequalities associated with traditional roles or uneven access to earlier commercial activity) became quite pronounced as a result of such participation.[51] In the Gold Coast, for example, Hill demonstrated some years ago that the spread of cocoa farming in southern Ghana from the 1890s involved considerable variation in the ownership of cocoa lands and the extent to which labourers were hired.[52] On the basis of purchasing records by the Farmers' Council for the 1963/4 cocoa season, Beckman has calculated that approximately half the sales of cocoa at that time were made by 10% of the farmers most of whom employed a number of wage labourers (many of the latter being migrants from the North) in addition to kin.[53] At the other extreme, 12% of the cocoa crop was sold by about half the farmers whose land holdings were much smaller and who probably employed only one or two labourers, if any. The much higher incomes earned by the larger farmers were usually invested in education for children and house purchases or were used to fund additional rural enterprises such as money lending, transport and various kinds of trade including, sometimes, produce buying. An emergent stratum of 'kulak' farmers enjoying greater wealth than the majority (some of whom may have been in the process of acquiring private owner-ship rights over land as well) has been identified in a number of countries including Uganda, Tanzania and Kenya, to name but a few.[54]

Other important spheres of enterprise left as preserves for African skill and investment were the various trading activities involving indigenous foodstuffs. Long-distance trade, often in non-bulky luxury items, and managed by groups of full-time, professional merchants, had long been important in many parts of Africa and usually involved exchanges be-tween ecological zones.[55] But the economic expansion associated with colonialism and cheaper transport together gave a strong boost to certain kinds of trading in foodstuffs such as fish[56] (and to related activities like fish-smoking), yams and other staple crops while the long-distance trade in kola nuts and cattle, between the forest and savannah areas of West Africa, also increased dramatically. In Nigeria the exchanges of kola nuts and meat, primarily between the South-West and the North, were organised by the Hausa.[57] In Chapter 7 we will look more closely at the various ways in which the Hausa traders adapted to the developments associated with European rule. Although the trade in kola nuts and cattle did not involve 'modern' commodities – directly linked to Western influence and foreign capital – the ability to organise these activities profitably and to cope with changing economic circumstances did require sophisticated business re-sponses and skills. Moreover, the Hausa also initiated, financed and managed the extensive groundnut trade of Northern Nigeria during the years just before the First World War, and against the wishes and in-tentions of colonial officials who wanted to foster cotton production instead.[58] Thus, although they sold these crops to European exporting firms they continued to dominate the produce-buying business against all the trends we have discussed for other African agricultural exports.

Market trade in the growing urban centres also became an increasingly important focus for local enterprise, catering mainly for the rising popu-lation of relatively poor African consumers. In West Africa, women were able to play a leading role in many aspects of marketing and some invested their earnings in house purchase, lorry transport and other urban busi-nesses.[59] For a long time market trading was one of the very few legitimate fields of urban business endeavour open to indigenous people in many parts of East Africa, though men rather than women tended to occupy a dominant position. Also, despite the heavy weight of bureaucratic regulation and severe competition from Asian shopkeepers, a growing number of East African pedlars did manage to make a living by hawking imported goods in the rural areas.[60] Petty retailing of this kind was also commonplace and widespread all over West Africa. Like brokerage in the regions of export crop production it was often based on a system of credit advances from larger European or Levantine wholesalers or retailers.[61] Traditional craft activities of many kinds – handloom weaving, pottery, leather work, the production of simple household utensils, ornaments and tools, and so on – as well as 'new' skills, based on adaptations of Western goods, also provided an enormous and often expanding range of opportunities for petty producers.[62] At least up until the late colonial period it was by no means always the case that imported manufactured goods entirely displaced traditional activities. Indeed, rising incomes and population growth, among other factors, seem to have fostered an absolute expansion in many craft activities, even though in relative terms the demand for such products declined as a proportion of the expanding market.[63]

Although this wide range of indigenous business activities usually involved very small-scale enterprises and, as we have already indicated, they represented 'safe' areas in which European capital displayed little or no interest, some Africans did manage to establish themselves quite successfully in a few spheres of modern business. For the most part, and increasingly, this occurred in the prosperous years beginning in the early 1940s. However, in some colonies, important steps in this direction were achieved by local entrepreneurs in the years before the Second World War. One such activity was the timber business which, in the Gold Coast, was largely under local control at this time.[64] Transport was another. From the 1920s onwards – although much more so from the mid 1940s – indigenous owners ran small haulage firms, mammy lorries (minitrucks used primarily for cheap passenger transport), buses and taxis, even in the East African colonies.[65] Last, but not least, is the case of bread baking in Nigeria.[66] The industry was originally established by Brazilian creoles repatriated mainly during the middle years of the nineteenth century. These early pioneers transferred the relevant skills to Nigerians. In the twentieth century, as consumer purchasing power rose and tastes became more Westernised, so the number of small Nigerian-owned bakeries rapidly increased. Eventually, the introduction of the dough break (a machine for kneading dough) and the practice of retailing bread through commission sellers led to the emergence of somewhat larger enterprises, especially after the Second World War.

In one sense, this brief discussion showing both the extent and the particular fields of enterprise dominated by Africans during the colonial period only serves to highlight their vulnerability and intrinsic weaknesses compared to foreign business. Some of the examples discussed later in this chapter, concerning the often very limited successes achieved by chiefs and other privileged traditional groups who became involved in modern business activities, bears further testimony to this interpretation, at least for the period before 1940. Yet at the same time, this discussion also seems to point to a quite different conclusion: the extraordinary vitality, ingenuity and flexibility shown by numerous (and for the most part) illiterate petty producers of very limited means. If these indigenous entrepreneurs had received more encouragement and protection it is arguable that some might have spread their interests far beyond these largely traditional spheres and set down roots in certain areas of the modern economy even before the 1940s and with beneficial consequences for the future of African capitalism.

ALTERNATIVE EXPLANATIONS FOR POOR AFRICAN BUSINESS PERFORMANCE

So far we have considered those crucial factors impeding indigenous entrepreneurs during the colonial period which were almost entirely outside African control: government hostility or indifference, foreign exploitation and the unequal distribution of resources between European and local capital. In the present section, however, we examine some alternative ways of viewing the relatively poor performance of African entrepreneurs at this time.

Bauer's analysis of the import–export trade in West Africa provides a useful starting point.[67] He argues that most Africans did not appreciate how much capital and skill were needed in order to extend the commercial network into ever more remote regions. Storage, distribution, transportation and buying facilities had to be set up on a huge scale. Thousands of brokers at the bottom of the commercial chain needed finance so they could offer cash advances to farmers. In effect, by extending credit in this way the European companies were financing the African brokers whilst simultaneously, of course, ensuring a continuous supply of produce for their own export activities. For the most part, only Europeans possessed the resources required to establish such a comprehensive commercial system effectively and rapidly. Had the European companies not taken over this role during the early colonial period, then the spread of a money economy, the growth of export production and the rising living standards that followed might have taken much longer to become realities. This implication may be unpalatable and unproven but it is difficult to ignore.

Similarly, Bauer claims that the majority of farmers and local traders also misunderstood the necessary and important role that trade expansion played in opening up the economy generally. By reaching ever larger numbers of people and offering them money incentives to cultivate, traders made a crucial contribution to economic growth and so were just as entitled to earn profits as the farmers themselves.[68] But most Africans did not see the situation in this light. For them, trade was not productive so that even without oligopolistic price fixing and market sharing commercial profits were generally regarded as unjustified and exploitative. Price fluctuations, too, were normally interpreted in the same way. Like the majority of citizens in the West at that time, most Africans lacked the educational resources to comprehend that international price fluctuations were caused not only by the machinations of greedy expatriate companies, but were also due in part to world-wide changes in supply and demand outside the control of any single agent.

Moreover, to many people, produce buying appeared to be a relatively simple activity. Accordingly, it seemed both unjust and unnecessary that Europeans should dominate it. However, as well as ample capital, success in this field also presupposed considerable business experience, skill, access to contacts and the ability to cope with numerous uncertainties. Produce buying, therefore, was anything but straightforward. Several writers have shown how most of the entrepreneurs who did try to break into produce buying and exporting in the 1920s and 1930s found it very difficult indeed to do so.[69] Most could not afford to pay the same prices as their European rivals and rapidly discovered that patriotism alone was insufficient to induce shrewd farmers to part with their crops if it meant receiving less than a European firm would pay. In addition, honest and capable African traders had to contend with the reputation for unreliability and dishonesty earned by some of their predecessors and often found it difficult to overcome the distrust which many farmers felt towards them.

This reference to the problem not just of capital but also of unsound business practice leads on to a further topic, namely, to what extent was poor business performance due partly to entrepreneurial deficiencies. In order to examine this, it may be useful to look again at the fortunes of the Asian and Levantine traders of East and West Africa respectively.

In East Africa, some of the Asians who established successful wholesale and retail businesses in the early part of this century were descended from an earlier generation who had played an important part in the mid nineteenth-century trading system based mainly on Zanzibar.[70] At that time, some Asian traders exported ivory to India. Most, however, brought consumer goods from European import companies established in the area and supplied these to Arab and African traders on a credit basis. The latter organised caravans into the interior and sold imported goods to the inland tribes in exchange for ivory and slaves. With the building of the railway, which reached Nairobi in 1900 and Kampala in 1902, many Indians moved inland, established trading posts and began to import manufactured goods directly from Europe. Clearly, therefore, those traders descended from this class of coastal entrepreneurs and financiers enjoyed a head start over their less experienced and poorer African rivals at a time when the East African economy was beginning to expand at the end of the nineteenth century.

However, not every member of the Indian trading community was as fortunate as this. Many who later owned retail trading stores, originally came to East Africa as indentured labourers to build the railway and presumably relied mostly on savings from wages to get started in business.[71] Also, several writers have commented on the business skills and hard work shown by the Asians in building up their businesses. Brett points to their willingness to operate at low profit margins and the high propensity to save.[72] Many were prepared to live in rural outposts for long periods of time and operate at low levels of turnover. Marris and Somerset note that in Kenya the Asian habit of organising firms on a family basis made them very competitive in terms of running costs.[73] In addition some businesses were helped through kinship or caste connections.[74] In Uganda, Mamdani argues that the Asians tended to concentrate their efforts on business activity and this was the really important factor determining Asian success.[75] Because Asians lacked political power and occupied a position of social and cultural marginality, business offered the only real opportunity for them to succeed. They had everything to gain and nothing to lose by channelling all their energies, profits and skills into this activity.

The Levantines began to arrive in West Africa in the 1880s. Writing about the Gold Coast and Sierra Leone respectively, Garlick and Van de Laan claim that the majority came with little if any capital and many were illiterate.[76] To become established in business they had no choice but to work very hard indeed and eke out a thrifty existence for long periods of time. In fact, Garlick claims that many traders reduced their living expenses by living on their business premises, thereby earning the contempt of some Africans who commented disparagingly on the poverty of their life-style. Both authors praise other attributes of the Levantine business approach as well. Levantine businessmen were willing to operate in areas and in commodities where profit margins were often very low yet they stuck tenaciously to their business footholds until things improved. Most took the trouble to learn the vernacular wherever they became established. Their endurance and the fact that they remained in one place for long periods of time, and therefore the continuity of their business operations, enabled them to build up strong local ties. Since they knew the neighbourhood people well they could afford to offer credit to their mainly African clients. This not only aided business expansion, it also helped to push back the frontiers of the money economy more rapidly than might otherwise have been the case. In Sierra Leone especially many were also prepared to move up country and settle in remote towns and villages, where they filled the gap between the mass of African farmers and the larger European buying companies. In addition, Garlick's research, carried out in the Gold Coast during the 1950s, revealed that most Levantine enterprises, at that time, were efficiently run. Traders kept proper accounts, they recorded their sales, managed stock inventories in relation to sales, acquainted themselves with market changes and customer needs, supervised their finances carefully, usually gained reputations for reliability and had few bad debts.

Garlick and Van de Laan also point out that asceticism in combination with business skill and acumen explain the Levantines' success only in part. They possessed two further advantages. One was the importance of the family enterprise. This provided a low-cost, disciplined, trustworthy labour force, all of whose members could hope to benefit from their joint endeavours. At the same time, the perennial African problem, at the death of a business proprietor, of equal inheritance between the latter's children (perhaps involving competing claims from kinsmen as well) and therefore the tendency for business estates to be broken up, did not normally arise for the Levantine business community.

The reason for this brings us to the second advantage. Like their Asian counterparts in East Africa, the Levantines faced a precarious political and social situation. They lacked political rights and were widely resented by the local population who saw them as strangers usurping the business opportunities that rightfully belonged to indigenous people. European officials often treated the Levantines with suspicion and some called for strict immigration controls over the influx of non-Europeans. In these circumstances the Levantines had no alternative but to direct most of their resources into business accumulation as the only means available for establishing some sort of security. As Van de Laan argues, their business success owed more to political and economic necessity than to moral and technical superiority.[77] Indeed, for the most part, the latter were products of the former. Thus, given the lack of alternative openings as well as the absence of extended family pressures, it is hardly surprising that the second generation were normally willing to take over and consolidate the family business.

During the 1930s, when the economic climate forced the big European companies into a period of retrenchment, most of the Levantines appear to have held onto their earlier gains and survived to thrive in better days. Indeed, several writers have pointed out that a few relative newcomers to West African trade – A. G. Leventis in the Gold Coast was probably the most outstanding example – actually established leading positions in commerce during the 1930s and broke into the import–export business soon after.[78]

Van de Laan's analysis of the creoles and Levantines in Sierra Leone is also instructive.[79] In the late nineteenth century many creoles occupied important positions as produce buyers and a few were engaged in the import–export trade. However, soon after colonial rule was established they were displaced from these lucrative activities by the European firms. In the 1910s and 1920s trade spread further inland, but to take advantage of this it was necessary to settle in the railway towns or move into remote rural areas. Whereas the Levantines had very little to lose by exploiting these lowly opportunities, many creoles were simply unwilling to operate in such reduced circumstances. Those who did venture inland lacked the drive to pursue these trade possibilities with energy and determination or failed to establish the necessary connections with Freetown. Thus, it was the Levantines who mainly took over the role of brokerage for the European produce-buying firms. It was they, too, who came to dominate the internal trade in kola nuts and rice, who eventually took advantage of lorry transport and who gradually transferred their capital into retail trade, gold mining (from the 1930s) and diamond mining during the 1950s.

No doubt the creoles could have started in business all over again and, like the Levantines, slowly built from the bottom up until they had re-established new profitable enterprises. In contrast to the Levantines, however, they were not newcomers or strangers, lacking connections with African society. Also, their education and Westernised style of life meant that they enjoyed alternative opportunities outside business and could transfer their energies towards professional and bureaucratic occupations.

Clearly, the Levantine case demonstrates that where individuals or groups face a situation of multi-deprivation, strong personal motivations may generate an ascetic orientation towards economic activity of the kind Weber identified in the case of certain early protestant sects. This may provide a powerful substitute for the dearth of resources normally required for business success. In the present case, however, this asceticism and the energy, determination and rationality it sustained, did not stem from a set of shared cultural values existing in their own right, but originated as a response to the prevailing political, social and economic climate of inequality and power – a climate which confronted Levantine immigrants with a particular structure of constraints and opportunities.

The situation facing most Africans during the early colonial period was rather different. In parts of West Africa, privileged groups like the old coastal trading elite enjoyed alternative opportunities for personal success. If anything, these avenues became more rather than less promising as time went by because colonial rule provided conditions for the emergence of a much more diversified economy and occupational structure than had hitherto been possible. Although educated Africans were soon to be debarred from holding the highest positions in the system of colonial administration, compared to most indigenous people, they were in a relatively favourable position and were eligible for a growing number of opportunities in law, education, the churches, as junior clerks and storekeepers in public and private employment, and so on.

For the mainly illiterate, rural-based African majority, too, business enterprise did not offer a viable or realistic alternative at this time. Colonial governments and Western interest groups had very definite ideas concerning the role that most Africans should play in the new economies as cash-crop farmers or migrant workers. Once commerce and other modernising influences had penetrated into the interior sufficiently to expose increasing numbers of people to the demonstration effect (rising expectations of greater economic rewards generated by a growing awareness of the real material gains experienced by others) of modern business opportunity, European interests had already pre-empted the most profitable and accessible activities. No amount of business asceticism seemed likely to prevail against the might of European competition, government protection and periods of severe economic crisis. In any case, most people did not need to fall back on this stark alternative as a means of livelihood and long-term security. The majority of Africans possessed land rights and therefore access to the means of subsistence. They enjoyed the protection of customary relationships and could obtain cash through participating in the colonial economy by other means. Only when economic change, social and occupational differentiation and educational opportunity had reached higher levels and coincided with a period of sustained economic prosperity – starting from a much more developed base than had existed in the early period of colonial rule – would the conditions be favourable for a resurgence of viable indigenous enterprise.

TRADITIONAL AUTHORITY AND BUSINESS ENTERPRISE

Traditional rulers sometimes found ways to become involved in certain kinds of modern entrepreneurial activity as their societies underwent the transition to capitalist industrialisation even though other factions of the old ruling class may have been initially hostile or resistant to such changes. Something like this happened in Britain, Germany and Japan though with important variations. Similarly, during the last three or four decades the modernising governments in some Third World countries, for example Brazil and India, have offered certain inducements to traditional landowning groups in the attempt to accelerate agricultural change while incorporating these groups, and their resources, more firmly into the development process. Apart from the Ethiopian Highlands, in most of pre-colonial Sub-Saharan Africa a landowning gentry class, able to extract surpluses from a subject peasantry, did not exist. Nevertheless, like traditional rulers in other parts of the world, those chiefs, kings and religious leaders who survived the transfer of power to European rulers did enjoy certain advantages by virtue of their office and social status and these often provided resources denied to others. Such resources could be, and sometimes were, directed towards business enterprise. This involvement of chiefs and other privileged elements in some forms of modern enterprise, at the very same time that they were also helping to perpetuate certain aspects of traditional society on behalf of the colonial government, highlights one of the central contradictions of economic change during this period.

For these reasons it might be instructive to look briefly at the extent to which traditional authority figures played a leading role in the commercial developments that accompanied colonial rule. Moreover, it may be useful to consider the long-term consequences of this involvement for the process of indigenous capital accumulation. Numerous examples can be found in the literature for this period concerning traditional rulers and entrepreneurship, but the discussion will be mainly confined to the following countries: Sierra Leone, the Belgian Congo, the Sudan and Kenya.

Kilson describes the various ways in which chiefs in Sierra Leone used their position in order to further their business interests.[80] Chiefs had always enjoyed customary rights to tribute and labour. These rights were left more or less intact by the colonial authorities and so many chiefs were able to convert these into money. They did this both by marketing their share of agricultural produce secured as tribute and by selling the produce they obtained from diverting customary labour contributions into cash-crop production. In 1937 chiefs supposedly relinquished these rights in return for regular salaries but in practice they continued to exploit this source of wealth for some time longer. They also manipulated their crucial position as custodians of the system of communal land tenure. This involved at least two main processes. Some chiefs expanded their own holdings and turned such land over to cash-crop production. Later on, in the 1930s, when gold and diamond mining became one of the mainstays of the economy, along with export agriculture, the chiefs were able to claim rents or royalties from mining companies in return for land concessions.

As well as using such strategies for improving their financial position, chiefs were also entitled to receive money payments direct from the government. Until the 1930s, they were allowed to draw a small rebate from the revenue they collected in the form of hut taxes. They also received entertainment and other allowances by virtue of their official role as designated by the state. In addition, many abused their officially sanctioned fiscal duties by devising schemes to extract illegal taxes from the subject population and by embezzling some of the funds under their control. Kilson claims that chiefs engaged in these and similar malpractices in several other colonies, for example in Chad, Western Nigeria and Uganda.

During the early colonial period, chiefs in the Belgian Congo were also able to utilise their position as a stepping-stone to further wealth and status. Depelchin observes that there were two main ways in which this occurred.[81] Firstly, in some parts of the colony European officials tried to ensure that the early schools gave priority to the sons of chiefs, a practice not uncommon elsewhere in Africa, too. In any case, the expense involved in gaining access to secondary and higher education effectively debarred all but those whose parents were reasonably wealthy. Depelchin goes on to argue that the association between education and wealth almost certainly meant that a considerable proportion of those who belonged to the emergent class of *evolués* (highly educated and westernised Africans), who were destined to fill some of the highest professional and official positions later on, come originally from the chiefly stratum. Secondly, the colonial government instituted a system of financial remuneration whereby chiefs were rewarded according to the amount of cotton they could persuade the peasantry to cultivate.

That this, and possibly other sources of wealth, along with access to education for their sons, proved advantageous to chiefs and their families, as far as business activity is concerned, is borne out by Schatzberg's study of Lisalu, a medium-sized Zairian town.[82] In this research, carried out in the 1970s, Schatzberg found that a high proportion of the leading party and bureaucratic officials in the area came from similar social backgrounds. Their fathers and grandfathers had been mission educated, had participated in modern occupations and/or had enjoyed close contacts, at an early period, with European companies or officials. Moreover, behind this experience of privileged exposure to the main agencies of modernisation often lay the reality of traditional status: grandfathers enjoying chiefly office had been able to translate this advantage into education and modern-sector employment for themselves and their sons.

Duffield and Mahmoud have shown how in the Sudan, leaders of religious sects, such as the Mahdis, also benefited from the favours bestowed by colonial officers during the period before the Second World War, along with sheikhs, sultans and spokesmen for groups of Islamic migrants moving in from the West.[83] At this time, the British administrators were more favourably inclined towards traditional elites than the growing urban, commercial groups who sought Western education and positions in the modern economy. In certain areas, the British gave formal recognition to the rights acquired by those who had been loyal to previous governments during the eras of Turko-Egyptian and Mahdist rule. The colonial rulers also made land grants to some religious leaders and sultans. This made it somewhat easier for traditional rulers to adjust to the loss of revenue and labour caused by the abolition of slavery. It also enabled them to participate in the new wealth generated by the spread of cotton cultivation.

In other areas, some traditional rulers were granted licences to grow cotton on irrigated pump schemes during the 1920s, mainly on publicly owned lands. Again, this was done partly in order to foster loyalty to the colonial regime. During the 1930s and 1940s, native administrators – some of whom had formally been sheikhs and whose official role in the system was institutionalised during this time – and prominent local traders were also granted licences. Many of these licensees made considerable commercial gains from cotton production, especially during the Korean war boom. Some reinvested their profits in trading and other ventures such as mechanised agriculture, cotton ginning and oil mills. Thus, through the deliberate and discriminate exercise of state power the colonial government nurtured an emergent agrarian capitalist class drawn very largely from traditional office-holders. The nucleus of this class eventually went on to found one of the leading Sudanese political parties, the Umma Party. According to Mahmoud, the descendants of this class have remained both politically influential and commercially predominant up to the present time. They were strongly represented amongst the top one hundred Sudanese capitalists she investigated in 1976.[84]

In some parts of Kenya, as elsewhere in Africa, it was often members of chiefs' families who were amongst the first people to receive a mission education. This in turn often proved to be a useful channel for access to the most well-paid jobs as skilled artisans, white-collar workers, foremen and supervisors in the European sector. Kitching argues that those Africans who received the highest salaries from modern-sector employment during the 1930s and 1940s often invested part of their earnings in land purchase and improved farming practices, thereby establishing themselves as a minority capitalist landowning elite.[85] Cowen uses the term 'straddling' to describe this process of funnelling cash earnings from employment into capitalist enterprises.[86]

Another route to modern business, based partly on the benefits bestowed by traditional status, involved the manipulation and perhaps abuse of chiefly office whilst exercising executive power on behalf of the colonial administration.[87] In this way, chiefs might acquire land or livestock. Kitching also shows how despite the enormous obstacles imposed by the white-settler regime, a number of individuals and syndicates in the Central Region managed to establish modern enterprises such as diesel-powered maize mills, retail stores, haulage firms, lorry transport, and eventually, produce-buying companies. He observes that chiefs often played a prominent role in these business arrangements.

Finally, Kitching also discusses the role of the Local Native Councils, first established in the mid 1920s.[88] They were run by prominent locals who were nominated by the District Commissioners and then elected by a restricted franchise of mostly mission-educated young men, traditional office-holders and people with modern-sector experience. The Councils became an important avenue whereby progressive, increasingly nationalistic and ambitious men promoted development in their localities. For example, they encouraged agricultural improvements such as veterinary facilities and the establishment of demonstration centres where new crop varieties could be tried out. Council representatives also tried to set up loan schemes for local businessmen. Since chiefs and headmen as well as local entrepreneurs and the mission educated were strongly represented on the Councils, mainly because these were the kinds of people nominated by the District Commissioners, much of the economic activity fostered by them benefited those who participated in these same decision-making processes. To what extent the Councils actually channelled loan funds towards their own members and their kinsmen is not clear. However, it seems that some European officials certainly viewed the Local Native Councils as a vehicle for encouraging local notables to become established in business and so they may have turned a blind eye if and when such abuses took place.

It is possible to interpret this evidence concerning the links between traditional authority and entrepreneurship during the period mainly before 1945 both from a negative and a positive viewpoint. On the one hand, it would seem that in seeking to overcome the crucial obstacle to business enterprise, namely securing capital, chiefs were sometimes doubly advantaged compared to the majority of commoners. They could utilise and manipulate traditional resources – tribute or slave labour, custodianship of land, rights to agricultural surpluses, and so on – and they were often in a position to gain legitimate or illegal access to official government resources such as loan funds, salaries, tax revenue, public land, contracts and licences. Yet, despite these assets and with some notable exceptions, especially in the Sudan, central Kenya and perhaps in other areas, too, traditional office-holders were not normally able to transpose their advantages into concrete and lasting business achievements. If chiefs, with all the resources at their command, retained only a precarious hold on capitalist activity – outside cash-crop farming – then how much more difficult must it have been at this time for others.

At the same time, it seems very likely that the realities of an uncertain business climate prompted chiefs, their educated sons, kinsmen and the commoner population to reach certain conclusions. One was that education offered a much more realistic and promising avenue for future wealth and power than business endeavour. Certainly, the privileges enjoyed by individual European officials were based mainly on their previous educational attainments. Moreover, lucrative employment with promotion prospects in government administration, the professions and big companies all depended on educational attainment. Such job opportunities could be expected to increase as the economy grew. In any case, salaried employment seemed much more secure than business enterprise as a path to personal advancement. As Kilson remarks in the case of Sierra Leone, it is hardly surprising that many chiefs, as well as others who possessed the means to do so, increasingly invested their wealth not in business ventures but in education for their sons, nephews and other kinsmen.[89]

Perhaps, however, these experiences – or African perceptions of them – also contained certain possibilities for the future which were rather more promising. For one thing, the plight of traditional rulers and other less privileged Africans highlighted the various ways in which political power was absolutely crucial for economic advance. It was important in the obvious sense that only African control of the state and the end of colonial rule would ultimately open the way to full development on behalf of indigenous rather than foreign interests. But also, and more specifically, these experiences demonstrated that success in capitalist activity could be considerably enhanced as and when state resources were deliberately used in order to protect and nurture the needs of particular individuals or groups. Of course, in some countries future nationalist leaders reached a rather different conclusion as we shall see in the next chapter: that the state structures *per se* could and should provide the main avenues for private achievement and enrichment, but through public office in an economy organised through greatly enlarged bureaucratic and party structures. Thus, the state would not only lead the process of economic development, its officials would also directly manage it themselves. Nevertheless, it seems highly likely that in most countries many educated Africans did see the potential for a successful and significant African capitalism, providing state power was harnessed constructively and in appropriate ways.

Then there is the question of investment in schooling rather than business enterprise. Viewed in one way, the channelling of economic resources into education, in the hope that this would pave the way for kinsmen to eventually attain high bureaucratic, professional or political positions, represented a serious threat to long-term capital accumulation. On the other hand, it could be argued that by acting in this way traditional rulers were, in effect, constructing an alternative and potentially useful inter-generational route to future capitalist activity. Marxists and others have often regarded a long period of capital accumulation by an emergent, mainly commercial bourgeoisie as the primary route to productive capi-talism since at a certain point in time this class presumably finds it profitable to transfer mercantile wealth into industry. In fact, as we shall see in Chapter 8, this has provided only one path to modern African business activity in the era since the Second World War. Very often those entrepreneurs who did move into industry from trade gained more from the opportunity to accumulate experience and general skills during the time spent in commercial endeavour than they did from the chance to build up personal savings. After all, the ability to be successful in running modern large-scale enterprises, of the kind which became increasingly important during the years of rapid economic growth after 1945, required many assets in addition to capital: particularly the availability of overseas and local connections and technical organisational knowledge and experi-ence. If education offered a passport to employment and this in turn provided an arena for acquiring relevant experience and skills – at a time when very few people enjoyed such advantages – then investment in schooling and qualifications represented a potential boon rather than an obstacle to future African capitalism.

1940–60: AFRICAN CAPITALISM – RECOVERY AND ADVANCE

While it is important not to exaggerate the extent to which African capitalists made real advances during the two decades preceding Indepen-dence, at least in certain countries, neither should their gains be under-estimated. A number of factors were at work, helping to revive and improve African business prospects.

Many of the legal, financial and bureaucratic restrictions imposed on indigenous enterprises in earlier decades, especially in East Africa, were lifted in the post-war political climate. Thus, access to credit was made somewhat easier for would-be African borrowers and some of the prohib-itions concerning where Africans were allowed to trade, and in what goods or services, were removed or qualified.[90] But some governments went much further than this and actively tried to promote certain kinds of indigenous enterprise. We have already considered the case of the Local

Native Councils in Kenya. In Nigeria, too, certain policies were implemented that were deliberately designed to benefit local artisans and entrepreneurs. The restrictions imposed on the entry of foreign immigrants, for example, whose skills might enable them to compete directly with Nigerians, probably helped to extend the scope of local opportunity.[91] This was certainly so in the case of passenger transport, a sphere of enterprise which Nigerians soon came to dominate as the volume of traffic increased enormously in the post-war era. Local entrepreneurs became quite well represented in the more difficult market for freight shipment as well. The colonial government in Nigeria also made quite substantial attempts to encourage industrial entrepreneurship during the 1940s and 1950s. Kilby has examined these measures in some detail.[92]

One such policy, begun in 1946, involved trying to assist Nigerian textile producers to improve their technical proficiency, and therefore market prospects, through the provision of training schemes, research and advice. Eventually a few entrepreneurs were offered loans to buy power looms and other equipment. Then there were the industrial estates. These were set up to provide well-equipped sites for manufacturers and offered technical assistance, workshop facilities and other advantages at subsidised rents. The most famous of these was the Yaba Industrial Estate near Lagos which opened in 1959. Public lending agencies offering grants and loans to prospective Nigerian entrepreneurs were established, beginning in 1946. By 1949 there were four Regional Development Boards offering such assistance.

On the whole, Kilby is critical both of the way in which these schemes were run and the quality of the performance revealed by the Nigerian beneficiaries. In view of the constraints under which Africans had operated before the war – the relatively slow expansion of market opportunities until the 1940s and the poor provision of technical and commercial training – it is perhaps not surprising that many of those who responded to the improved economic climate at this time were initially ill equipped to move into some of the more demanding entrepreneurial roles, especially in modern industry. Many European companies were able to draw upon overseas as well as local managerial, financial and technical resources when the climate for industrial activity at last became favourable. Africans, by contrast, usually had to begin from scratch, largely unsupported by a local tradition of technical knowledge or customary social practices on which to base modern organisational techniques. In Chapter 8 we will consider the all-important question of the quality of entrepreneurship and the various weaknesses often displayed by African proprietors. For the moment, however, it is sufficient to note that in some countries aid was being proffered to local entrepreneurs in the years before Independence.

The attitudes of some Western companies also underwent a change at this time, both with regard to African enterprise and the long-term prospects for economic development. In Kenya, for example, Swainson has shown how, after the Second World War, the transnational corporations gradually became the predominant form of Western capitalist investment. One of the many consequences of this transformation was that the government and the big corporations interested in agricultural commodities took steps to improve the productivity of all the farming groups in Kenya. The Swynnerton Plan of 1954 represented one very important attempt to encourage African commercial agriculture by providing individual land titles, finance and technical advice.[93] This proved to be the forerunner of many schemes designed to transfer white-settler land back to African farmers, especially – as it turned out – to the more wealthy landowners. But what was also revealing was that several foreign companies also began to Africanise their distribution systems by extending wholesale facilities to local traders in the Reserves.[94] According to Swainson, their aim was to encourage the growth of an African trading class whilst simultaneously deepening the money economy and market demand. Thus, from the early 1950s firms like Shell Oil, Bata Shoes and British American Tobacco were operating schemes designed to guarantee bank credit to African traders.

Overseas companies were also instrumental in fostering a new kind of indigenous entrepreneur through the system of manufacturers' representatives. Industrialists with little or no previous involvement in Africa tried to establish a foothold in the expanding markets for consumer goods by encouraging suitable Africans to set themselves up as sole agents acting on their behalf.[95] While this obviously provided the companies with low-cost distribution outlets in the various local economies, the commercial experience, savings and business contacts which many of these representatives were able to accumulate enabled some to establish their own businesses at a later date.

During these years certain fundamental structural changes were working their way through African economic life and these altered the competitive balance between large and small firms. Kilby has examined this process in the context of Nigeria.[96] He argues that post-war prosperity led to rising incomes and therefore market expansion. Helped by falling transport costs this change increased the opportunities for small African and non-European entrepreneurs to enter trade, thereby increasing the competitive pressure felt by the old European trading companies. In the pre-war period, when markets were shallow and transport costs somewhat higher, traders had needed large amounts of capital in order to operate in the most profitable fields. Now, in the new climate small companies, enjoying a greater flexibility and lower overheads than the big companies, could function successfully in all kinds of trading niches throughout the economy, despite their rather limited access to capital. Faced by this growing tide of competition and falling profit margins and with an eye to the potential political credit they might earn in their relations with Nigerian leaders, the European trading firms wisely rationalised their operations and largely withdrew from trade into services and manufacturing. A similar process took place in other West African colonies.

Indigenous entrepreneurs also benefited from a number of more specific changes connected with the Second World War and its impact on colonial life. For example, many Africans were taught to drive while serving in the British army. Such skills were easily transferred to the transport business in the years of post-war prosperity.[97] Presumably a similar process took place with respect to other kinds of technical skills. Many soldiers were awarded gratuities on being demobbed and these could be, and often were, invested in improved farm practices, artisan workshops and small trading enterprises. In Ghana, and probably elsewhere, some of the earliest indigenous manufacturing, contracting and trading firms were established by people who had worked abroad for a time in the years just before, during and after the Second World War.[98]

Probably, however, it was rapid economic growth and rising market demand alongside the cumulative effects of gradually improving skill levels and wider occupational experience which provided the most important stimuli to African enterprise. Doubtless, the prospect of political Independence and the rising tide of nationalist feeling were also highly significant. Optimism for the future and a sense of increased personal and national confidence encouraged people to think in terms of long-term goals. It was true that even in the most developed African economies incipient African capitalist groups still had some way to go before their skills and experiences could be fully harnessed in the pursuit of viable strategies for national development. Nevertheless, at least in some countries, a basis for future economic growth had been laid down by 1960 and there were realistic prospects that local capitalism might play an increasingly important role in this process. How great this contribution might be and with what success and speed African entrepreneurs might respond to this challenge would depend on several factors, but above all, the nature of state power and politics after Independence.

§ 4 §

GOVERNMENT, POLITICS AND AFRICAN CAPITALISM SINCE INDEPENDENCE

States and the agents who control them have always played a crucial role in helping to create the conditions for a successful transition to industrialisation. This has been so irrespective of the commitment to either a capitalist free market or a socialist planned ethos, though the extent and nature of state influence over the economy has obviously been somewhat less evident, and rather different in form, in countries approximating to the former rather than the latter. Exactly how states intervened, what changes they introduced and which social groups played the leadership role has varied enormously from country to country. Today, the majority of the Third World countries remain within the Western capitalist orbit. They continue to rely on the operation of market forces and private incentives as one of the main mechanisms for mobilising effort and resources and for reaching decisions about production and investment, at least with respect to certain sectors and activities, and even though public ownership and government regulation are deemed necessary and beneficial for others.

One of the most important decisions modernising states with a basically market orientation have always had to confront concerns the question of what policies, if any, to pursue with regard to local capitalist interests. All of the nineteenth-century Western countries which followed Britain's path, with the possible exception of Tsarist Russia, regarded the emergence of a strong local capitalism not only as the main guarantee of economic development, but also as a precondition for the attainment of national economic autonomy. It was a matter of national pride as well as an economic necessity to encourage local enterprise at all levels.[1] In practice, fostering local capitalism and formulating policies designed to boost the prospects of industrialisation were indivisible and indistinguishable, one from the other. Third World countries in Latin America and Asia since the Second World War, and in some cases before, have also sought to protect and nurture indigenous enterprise to a greater or lesser extent,

although foreign and state capital have continued to play very considerable roles.

Even in those Third World countries where the emphasis given to public
activity and government regulation is very considerable, so long as some
private activity is also thought desirable, there would seem to be a number
of distinct advantages to be gained from actively promoting a vigorous
local capitalist class. For one thing, although it is probably no longer true
that metropolitan capital wishes to hold back Third World development,
and indeed may wish to promote it, nevertheless, individual foreign
companies can never have the same degree of long-term interest in the
attainment of higher levels of national development as local business
groups, since they and their families can anticipate fewer direct or permanent benefits from such advances in the future compared to nationals.[2] By
the same token, overseas firms cannot be expected to respond particularly
well or gladly to calls for sacrifice and change in the pursuit of national
rather than purely personal goals. Accordingly, foreign firms are likely to
pay their taxes even less willingly than indigenous capitalists and may
expect substantial inducements before they invest seriously in the local
economy. They may also be less willing to reinvest their profits and are
likely to seek numerous ways of legally or illegally exporting capital
abroad. Secondly, it is much more difficult to make foreign managers and
technicians directly accountable for the consequences of their actions in
relation to national need and interest.[3] Their families and friends probably
reside in the country of origin, to which they also will eventually return, so
that few need suffer the adverse consequences of mistakes or malpractices
for which they are responsible. Foreign managers do not usually share
strong cultural bonds with local citizens and company employees and they
are unlikely to participate in national politics or be forced to justify their
policies and practices to local voters and pressure groups on whom they
depend. Moreover, a strong national capitalist class, some of whose
members may invest abroad, can be expected to return at least part of their
foreign earnings to the country of origin, thereby offsetting the export of
capital by foreign companies.

Assuming that these advantages are indeed valid and worth pursuing we
will now consider what kinds of measures and practices have actually been
adopted by African states in the period since Independence with regard to
indigenous capitalism. Here it will become apparent that for the most part
governments have been markedly ambivalent in their attitudes towards
African enterprise and have often acted in ways that are harmful rather
than helpful. Later, we will argue that these 'policies' need to be viewed as
but one aspect of a much more deep-rooted syndrome of economic and

political processes characteristic of most African governments during the last 30 years.

GOVERNMENT POLICIES IN PRINCIPLE AND PRACTICE

In the nineteenth century tariff protection was widely used by late-developing countries in order to foster modern forms of local enterprise. Import restrictions against foreign goods are widely used by Third World countries today. However, the local presence of foreign firms already producing for the national market behind these same tariff walls, and whose activities are often integrated into the global operation of the transnationals, means that a genuine programme designed to assist local enterprise will also require some kind of indigenisation policy. Wherever public control and ownership have been thought desirable this has inevitably involved the partial or total nationalisation of foreign concerns.

By the mid 1970s the majority of African countries had engaged in various 'takeover' operations, usually in the fields of mineral extraction, petroleum, banking, insurance, public utilities like port installations and telecommunications, and to a much lesser extent, in some kinds of manufacturing.[4] Rood argues that one reason why it has been more difficult for governments to engage in full-scale nationalisation in the case of manufacturing is that in order to be competitive such enterprises normally require a continuous flow of up-to-date technical information and know-how from abroad and this is best achieved by retaining at least partial foreign ownership. Where private ownership is deemed appropriate, indigenisation policies have involved enacting laws banning foreign firms from operating in certain sectors altogether – normally in activities like retail and wholesale trade, brokerage, transport, food production and distribution and some consumer goods industries – or which prohibit them unless their annual sales turnover, capitalisation, or both, are above a certain minimum. Indigenisation laws often stipulate that henceforth local people must be permitted to hold a certain proportion of the equity share in those foreign enterprises that are allowed to continue.

In the Nigerian case, the 1972 Nigerian Enterprises Promotion Decree required foreign companies operating in the areas not exclusively reserved for Nigerians, or which were exempted on the grounds of size, to offer at least 40% of their equity shares to local people.[5] The 1977 Decree stiffened these requirements and insisted on 60% Nigerian participation in some areas and extended the 40% rule to even the largest and most capital-intensive industries previously exempt. Similar measures have been introduced in countries such as Malawi, Kenya, Senegal, Zaire, Uganda, Ghana and Zambia, among others, though they have not usually been as comprehensive as those adopted in Nigeria.[6]

Vulnerable local firms struggling to compete against much better endowed foreign companies may also benefit from various other kinds of direct government assistance. These might include the following: the provision of short- and long-term loans, possibly at preferential rates of interest; foreign exchange allocations; different kinds of technical, financial, marketing and management training schemes; and partial relief from the payment of taxes, rates and customs duties. Over the last 25 years many African governments have, indeed, attempted to provide some of these direct benefits in various guises and to different degrees.

Management and technical training centres, sometimes sponsored by the International Labour Office, have been established in Uganda, Kenya, Ghana and Malawi.[7] Industrial estates and craft centres providing subsidised workshops, equipment, basic amenities and access to management and technical skills have also been provided, for example in Swaziland and Kenya.

Then there are the many types of loan schemes. A number of countries, including Senegal, Ghana, Nigeria, Kenya, Zambia, Malawi, Lesotho and Swaziland, have operated such schemes. We will see in Chapter 7 that some commentators believe a shortage of capital to be much less of a problem than is commonly supposed. Nevertheless, during the colonial period foreign-controlled banks in most African countries were never very interested in providing overdraft or loan facilities to Africans and this often continued for a while after Independence. Moreover, businesses in every country require access to loanable funds at certain times. Certainly, indigenisation programmes can only be viable if individuals either possess savings already or can borrow money in order to buy out departing foreigners.

In some countries governments have placed pressure on Western banks to set aside a proportion of their loanable funds for local firms, sometimes supported by government-backed credit guarantee schemes, as in the case of Ghana in the early 1970s.[8] Alternatively, or in addition, state banks were given the task of providing loans for small businesses. Some governments set up special banks funded wholly or partly by the state, possibly designed for specific purposes such as agricultural development, craft industries or funding the take-over of overseas trading companies. Government-financed National Development Corporations were also established in some countries, for example in Lesotho, Swaziland and Kenya.[9] These institutions normally enjoy wide-ranging powers, including the ability to take up equity shares in foreign or local companies as well as loan provision. Between 1965 and 1976 the highly successful Kenyan Industrial and Commercial Development Corporation (I.C.D.C.) lent more than Kenyan £5 million, mostly in the form of three-year loans to traders and industrialists.[10] A large proportion of this capital was advanced specifically to enable Kenyans to acquire the businesses of non-citizen Asians.

This brief description does not, of course, exhaust the possible extent of state help. Other measures might include the following: the provision of credit-guarantee schemes to enable local entrepreneurs to import much-needed machinery for local manufacturing from overseas suppliers; export subsidies; reduced custom and excise duties or lower rates of interest if these are used primarily in order to develop export industries; restrictions on the availability of local bank overdraft or loan facilities to foreign companies, and so on.[11] Measures like these have been widely used in the Newly Industrialising Countries (the N.I.C.s) of South-East Asia. So far, however, they have been much less in evidence in most African countries with the partial exception of Kenya and Nigeria.[12]

There is a third and very important form of government assistance to local business that requires separate consideration. This concerns the possibility that in seeking to supply its numerous agencies and departments at central and local level with the enormous range of inputs they require – the army and police, social services, educational institutions, the various branches of the civil service, and the different parastatals (government boards exercising regulatory powers over the economy, public utilities like water and electricity and corporations run more or less like conventional firms, but publicly owned) – the state might channel a certain proportion of these contracts towards local firms. In most advanced countries, governments tend to direct the largest volume of their business towards local firms as a matter of course. Municipal, regional and national-level building projects are the most outstanding examples of this. Moreover, at times of national crisis the government of some (now) advanced countries guaranteed to purchase virtually all the goods produced by particular firms at favourable prices in order to create an even more secure climate for growth and economic diversification.

The Japanese government adopted this approach towards certain local firms in the early stages of industrialisation and the American government operated similar policies during the Second World War. In most African countries, however, deliberate government discrimination in favour of local firms when awarding contracts has been much more problematic. In part, this is because foreign companies may still exercise a considerable hold over certain economic sectors despite indigenisation programmes, so that governments do not always have much choice, but there are also other factors at work, as we shall see shortly.

It has been pointed out that public expenditure in most African economies is probably no higher as a proportion of Gross Domestic Product than elsewhere in the Third World and typically it is much lower than in the Western developed countries.[13] Nevertheless, at the present time a very considerable proportion of national production and distribution remains 'uncaptured' either by foreign or local modern-séctor enterprises, though this may change rapidly in the future. Instead, this activity is largely under the control of numerous petty producers of all kinds and part-time marketeers or falls within the sphere of subsistence where transactions are still dominated mainly by ascriptive rather than commercial criteria. Accordingly, the share of national emplóyment, production and market demand dominated by government patronage and concentrated in those modern sectors of the economy that are crucial to private firms is inevitably of great importance to them, in relative terms. In a harsh, fiercely competitive economic environment, where local firms operate at a disadvantage alongside foreign companies, the ability to gain access to regular government business may make the difference between survival or failure, growth or stagnation. In dependent economies the ability to cope with government contracts as well as other kinds of business will also hinge on the ability to import spare parts, materials and equipment. Thus, the allocation of foreign exchange quotas between different firms provides the state with yet another lever of potential control – one that may operate in tandem with the distribution of contracts – and constitutes yet another resource for which local capitalists must compete.

One way in which African governments have used their economic clout, ostensibly and in part with the intention of directing business away from foreign firms and towards local enterprise in the field of distribution, has involved setting up national trading corporations. These parastatals were then granted a very large share of the available import licence allocation. In effect, this meant they could dominate the import–export business while simultaneously controlling the retail–wholesale distribution system, by making certain specified trade goods available to indigenous firms in preference to the big foreign companies. During the 1960s, the governments of Ghana, Uganda, Malawi, Kenya and Swaziland all established institutions of this kind. Of course, state monopolies have also been widely used to regulate many other areas of African economic life, such as building construction, shipping and fishing. Probably the most important and ubiquitous examples of this are the produce-marketing boards which operate in many countries. In British West Africa, for example, they were originally introduced during the Second World War. Again, one of the principal reasons for continuing to operate marketing boards is that they provide a vehicle for deliberately reducing the profitable business opportunities available to overseas companies in favour of local enterprise, whether state or private. The boards have the power to grant trade licences so that only particular individuals or organisations are entitled to buy peasant cash crops and then sell them at fixed prices to the state.

On the face of it, the kinds of measures we have outlined, and which were in fact introduced to a greater or lesser extent by many African governments, seem to add up to a considerable programme of support designed to foster local capital. Sadly, however, in the majority of countries the reality has proved to be very different from the appearance. In his analysis of the political climate for African capitalism since Independence, Iliffe has identified three types of regime and associated business experience.[14] 'Nurture capitalism' exists where governments operate with a clear ideological commitment to a basically capitalist ethos and deliberately try to foster a vigorous local business class in certain economic sectors. By so doing, they anticipate that one day indigenous capitalism will come to dominate most areas of the economy. Here there is a marked coincidence of interest between politicians and business groups rather than a perceived conflict or rivalry. Iliffe claims that so far only in Nigeria and Kenya have governments seriously tried to create the conditions for nurture capitalism. Elsewhere, some states have tried to actively suppress the local business class – as in Nkrumah's Ghana after 1961 and Tanzania. Alternatively, office-holders and politicians have sought private property and business interests through exploiting their privileged access to state resources, creating thereby a kind of 'parasitic capitalism'.[15] Among the examples he gives for the latter are Zaire, Liberia and the Ivory Coast.

These basic distinctions provide a useful starting point for our analysis of government policies with respect to local business. The question we want to consider is as follows: how, and to what extent, were the policies and practices we have already outlined – measures that were capable, in principle, of being used to benefit local enterprise and which were often designed, ostensibly and partly with this in mind – actually aborted in practice?[16]

To begin with, there are a number of countries where little or nothing has been done to assist African entrepreneurs. If anything, many governments seem to have been antipathetic, if not downright hostile, towards most forms of private, local capital and have striven to impose legal and other restrictions, confining the latter to narrowly circumscribed activities. Clearly, this has been most evident where regimes have been committed to an avowedly socialist development strategy and seek planned, equitable development free from the insecurities, inequalities and external dependency regarded as inevitable in market economies. Guinea, Mali, Ethiopia, Somalia, Mozambique and Benin, among others, all belong to this category. The Marxist regime in Ethiopia, for example, has confined private business to a few areas such as weaving, grain milling and hotels, whilst it has limited such enterprises to individual ownership, prohibiting capital pooling and preventing any one individual from owning more than one enterprise.[17] Tanzania after the 1967 Arusha Declaration is another case in point. Here, economic priorities were henceforth firmly directed towards cooperative rather than capitalist agriculture with the emphasis on rural rather than urban development. Emphasis was also given to improving majority living standards in the key areas of health, water supply, education and communications (what later came to be regarded by the World Bank as the 'Basic Needs' approach). At the same time, political and other inequalities were to be contained by imposing the 'Leadership Code' on political and bureaucratic cadres as well as professionals. This forbade such people from running private businesses.[18]

However, a supposedly socialist ideology and practice is not the only factor at work here. Thus, Zambia's ideological pronouncements on socialism and humanism did not preclude decisive government action to sponsor the previously weak local business class. This was done by providing protection from foreign competition initially, by banning non-Zambians from nearly all retail and wholesale trade and from certain other economic activities such as transport in 1970 and by providing loans through the Industrial Development Corporation, among other things.[19] According to one writer, by intervening in this way, the Zambian government has ensured that as the class of indigenous owners becomes stronger so the future actions of the state are likely to become progressively subject to its demands.[20] At the same time, some governments whose leaders have openly pursued a staunchly pro-capitalist course have nevertheless tended to be markedly reluctant to encourage certain forms of local enterprise and have preferred to rely instead on a mixture of state and foreign ownership.

The Ivory Coast government under Houphouët Boigny is probably the most outstanding example of this, although Sierra Leone and Malawi probably represent quite similar cases. (The Malawi government did attempt to indigenise rural distribution in the late 1960s and provided credit facilities, but these measures were later rescinded.)[21] Most writers regard Houphouët Boigny's government as flagrantly 'neo-colonial' in its approach to economic development, but also reluctantly concede that its record of sustained economic growth is second to none in Black Sub-Saharan Africa.[22] French and other foreign capitalist interests have been offered considerable inducements to invest in the Ivory Coast economy, and expatriate technicians and managers still play a key role in the various parastatals as well as private enterprises.[23] Moreover, an unashamedly export-oriented growth strategy has been pursued. By contrast, apart from the African planter class who control a large share of the prosperous agricultural export sector, and whose members often enjoy close family connections with the educated elite, there has been virtually no attempt to foster an Ivorian industrial and commercial class or to indigenise foreign firms.[24]

Then there is a second group of countries where some steps were taken with the declared intention of aiding local capital, but the actual implementation of these policies has often left a good deal to be desired, at least for certain periods of time while particular regimes were in power. Senegal, Liberia, Ghana, Uganda and Zaire are among this group of countries, although some of the practices or malpractices adopted with respect to indigenous capital have been widespread among other regimes, too. Close examination of these countries reveals that the steps taken to help local capital tended to end up in one or more of the following ways: measures were half-hearted and limited in their scope and therefore largely inefficacious; policies were not fully enforced so that foreign interests simply regrouped and directed their resources to other areas of the economy or remained more or less entrenched in the sectors they had previously dominated; or, having made certain concessions, governments then withdrew these at a later date and diverted them towards political insiders who then became the main beneficiaries. We will now consider some cases.

Even before his apparent conversion to a more state-oriented quasi-socialist strategy in 1960, the small loan schemes introduced by Nkrumah's government in order to assist Ghanaian entrepreneurs were very limited in scope.[25] Later on, the regime's policy of overcoming external dependency and seeking economic diversification through industrialisation was implemented by attempting to channel resources towards the rapidly expanding state sector rather than assisting local private capital. Thus, the National Trading Corporation received most of the important licence allocation but used this to build up its own distribution network mostly at the expense of small traders, many of whom found their quotas reduced or abolished. In building construction, a large proportion of government tenders were directed towards the newly created National Construction Corporation, while many small contractors found themselves excluded from government lists, especially if they were politically out of favour.[26]

In Senegal a certain amount of help was offered to local enterprise in the 1960s and early 1970s.[27] The French were ousted from the groundnut trade after Independence and their activities were taken over by a state marketing board which was later encouraged to operate in conjunction with village cooperatives. Some restrictions were placed on the Lebanese in 1964. In 1968 the banks were persuaded to provide credit for local firms while a special organisation was created in 1969 to offer investment capital to Senegalese entrepreneurs and to carry out research into their needs.[28] The 1972 Investment Code offered special help for local firms, such as tax exemptions and technical assistance, in addition to providing inducements designed to attract foreign capital. In practice, however, these policies remained largely unenforced or proved difficult to implement. Amin claims that in 1972 African entrepreneurs still received only 6% of the available short-term loans and by 1974 less than 10% of commercial business was in African hands.[29] One problem with the 1972 Investment Code was that the minimum investment required before applicants were eligible to receive benefits was set too high and was therefore inaccessible to the majority of Senegalese entrepreneurs. Similarly, the loans on offer through the auspices of the government body created in 1969 imposed restrictions that rendered most applicants ineligible to receive them.[30]

The Uganda government under Obote in the late 1960s also appeared to offer some assistance to African traders.[31] This took the form of loan facilities and a promise that the National Trading Corporation and the state marketing boards would issue licences to local entrepreneurs. In this way a substantial proportion of the market share in the import–export business and the internal retail–wholesale trade would, supposedly, accrue to Ugandans. As in Nkrumah's Ghana, however, these measures were never given the chance to really take effect and were soon replaced by policies involving a quite different aim. Between 1966 and 1969 the members of what Mamdani calls the 'bureaucratic bourgeois' – leading officials in the ruling party and the state apparatus – began to divert the business opportunities available through the licensing powers granted to the various monopoly state organisations towards their own private firms, largely excluding the true African commercial class.[32] Further attacks were made on African entrepreneurs in 1970. Licence fees were increased to the point where most small traders were no longer able to afford them and the state monopolies began to assign licensing rights – for example in corn milling, transport and produce buying – mostly to the larger, privileged firms, again squeezing out many smaller entrepreneurs.[33]

Indigenisation measures were also introduced in Liberia but these were used by members of the ruling group in order to implant themselves as sleeping partners in Lebanese companies.[34] In Zaire, too, the measures introduced between 1973 and 1975 designed to strengthen the local business class and promote economic development actually produced a very different result, largely because of the manner in which they were implemented. In 1973, European-owned small- and medium-sized businesses in trade, agriculture and light industry were confiscated. But instead of being sold to experienced African entrepreneurs they were mostly given to about 2,000 'acquirers': powerful members of the governing political elite and bureaucracy closely linked to, and dependent on, Mobutu's system of authoritarian personal rule.[35] A year later 'radicalisation' was introduced whereby much bigger foreign enterprises were taken over by the most powerful political insiders. There followed a period of severe economic disruption caused partly by the incompetent and avaricious way in which this commercially inexperienced class of acquirers managed their enterprises. Faced with massive tax evasion, rising unemployment, shortages and price increases, the government handed the radicalised businesses back to their original owners in 1976, though Zairians retained 40% equity participation.

So far our analysis of the different ways in which African governments have apparently tried to foster local capital has been concerned mainly with the actual content of the declared policies and their inadequacies. However, in the case of many countries these measures and their shortcomings represent only a small part of the underlying political realities that have been at work and have generated only a fraction of the political problems with which African entrepreneurs have had to contend. The failure in most countries to genuinely assist local capital can only be properly understood in relation to this wider context.

One very important clue to the true political situation is provided by the case of the business 'minorities' – the Levantines, Asians and other foreign groups – and what happened to these junior partners in 'neo-colonialism' once indigenisation policies were placed firmly on the political agenda. However unjust it may have been, given their long-standing contribution to African economic life, the foreign minority groups were the obvious candidates for any really serious policy designed to evict foreign capital in order to make room for local firms. Although in several countries, like Senegal and Uganda, the minorities were no longer confined solely to the role of commercial intermediaries and had moved into manufacturing and other key economic sectors, on the whole, and compared to metropolitan capital, their bargaining positions were not very strong. They were the prime targets for bitter African resentment both from indigenous traders and the general population, since their pronounced involvement in commerce had always exposed them to the full force of local consumer discontent concerning price rises and shortages. Unlike Europeans they enjoyed few cultural, administrative or political ties to the rising educated African elites and their countries of origin had little to offer independent Africa in exchange for concessions to their nationals. The great majority of Asian or Levantine firms were relatively unsophisticated in organisation and employed mainly family labour. Those involved in manufacturing tended to employ labour-intensive production systems and were run on an owner-manager basis. In these respects, most were not dissimilar to the new African enterprises struggling to become established in the decades just before and after Independence. Why then, despite their relative lack of political leverage and the introduction of indigenisation measures, did a large proportion of the Asians and Levantines manage to retain a significant business presence in so many countries; 'retreating' to sectors exempt from legislation, regrouping to form bigger enterprises or simply continuing their old activities?

The answer given by several writers is quite clear. Whatever they may have said in public, African bureaucratic elites wished to exploit both the political vulnerability and commercial resources provided by the foreign minorities for their own private purposes. In return for legal immunity or access to state-sponsored business opportunities and public resources, African politicians and officials knew they could exact personal bribes and sinecures (directorships or partnerships), as well as funds for political purposes and other rewards. In addition to being wealthier, in many cases, than local entrepreneurs, it was much easier to squeeze benefits out of groups whose very existence as legal citizens was open to government manipulation and whose members possessed little or no political or cultural influence over the general population. Moreover, unlike an expansionist African capitalist class, legally free to spread its commercial tentacles ever wider, the foreign minorities need never become future political rivals to government and bureaucratic elites. In countries like Ghana, Uganda, Sierra Leone, Senegal and Liberia, among others, therefore (and during the crucial early post-Independence period when arguably it was most important for a strong African capitalism to take root and flourish), the minority groups tended to survive and some of their members even grew in economic importance.[36]

The case of Uganda under Obote in the late 1960s is particularly instructive. Like Nkrumah's regime earlier in the decade, Obote's government indulged in a good deal of socialist as well as anti-imperialist rhetoric. A severe political and economic crisis took place in 1969. This was caused partly by a collapse in the currency but also by the measures adopted by Asian and African traders in their attempt to resist the extention of state control over the economy.[37] At the same time, the African commercial class was demanding the expulsion of the Asians and a final resolution to the vexed question of foreign domination of the key economic sectors. Despite the underlying causes of the 1969 crisis, the government reacted by increasing the state's role in the economy even further, partly through nationalising certain foreign concerns but also by using the state monopolies to allocate trade licences to the more powerful and established members of the Asian commercial bourgeoisie. Simultaneously, individual government officials and politicians sought nominal positions as directors both in the subsidiaries of the transnationals based in Uganda and in prominent Asian businesses.

Thus, in common with some other regimes the Ugandan bureaucratic bourgeoisie was quite prepared not only to tolerate, but to openly forge an alliance with certain factions of those very foreign interests against whom some of its ideological pronouncements had previously been directed and at the same time that it was proclaiming the necessity for socialist planning and national economic autarky. It appears that it was not really opposed to capitalism and private profit so long as this remained under foreign ownership and therefore partly subject to private and public manipulation.

This was revealed even more clearly by the way the government proposed to deal with the question of Asian citizenship. The 1969 Trade Licensing Act decreed that non-citizens could only continue to trade if they obtained valid permits. These, in turn, were only available to Asians whose businesses enjoyed a very large turnover so that, in effect, approximately two-thirds of the non-citizens (those who lacked passports and therefore eligibility for citizen status) were henceforth legally excluded from trading. Mamdani argues that, fearing the possible consequences of this move, especially an increased economic role for African businessmen, the Obote regime contemplated granting citizen rights to about 30,000 Asians who would then be able to continue in trade. This proposal was announced in December 1970. By doing so, the Ugandan bureaucratic bourgeoisie was declaring its preference for an Asian rather than an African capitalist class. The military coup that brought Amin to power took place soon after this and one of its most important consequences was the mass expulsion of the Asians.

Clearly, contradictions and paradoxes abound here, as elsewhere in the politics of African economic life. Thus the contrast between preserving a strong foreign capitalist presence, including sections of the minority interests, in an apparently socialist economy, while deliberately repressing or discouraging a local capitalist class is hard to ignore. So, too, is the irony that though underdevelopment theorists point tirelessly to the realities of dependency and foreign control over African economic life, and many political leaders have vigorously accepted these arguments, in practice the latter also appear to have believed that they could control foreign firms more easily than a future powerful African capitalist class and they have viewed the spectre of this with greater trepidation.

In some countries where an attempt has been made to exclude certain foreign interests from particular economic sectors in order to encourage local firms, it has been the politicians, military officers and bureaucrats who have tended to benefit most from these opportunities rather than genuine, experienced African entrepreneurs. State loans set aside to fund takeover operations have been used disproportionately by top people, their families, friends and clients. Alternatively, it has been relatively easy for government officials to acquire illegitimate resources through embezzling public funds, accepting bribes or by utilising personal and political connections with banks and other agencies.[38] Moreover, as we have seen, a very large proportion of available business opportunities depend directly on public-sector contracts, put out to tender, or indirectly on the ability of officials to wield the various levers of bureaucratic and monopolistic control over economic life, particularly the issue of foreign exchange quotas and licences to operate trading and other businesses. It was not difficult for officials or politicians to arrange that as and when these opportunities became available, with the exclusion of foreign interests, or as new areas for state franchise operations were opened up, that they and their relatives were among the main beneficiaries. To some extent these practices have been apparent in most, perhaps all, African countries over the last 25 years, including, for example, Liberia, Zaire, Malawi and Sierra Leone, but they have also been commonplace in Nigeria, one of the countries supposedly characterised by nurture capitalism.[39]

Of course, the various strategies we have outlined, including indigenisation policies, do not exhaust the ways in which state power has been used for private enrichment. Corruption, theft and nepotism have occurred at all levels in African bureaucracies, as many commentators have observed, and have been possible wherever the growing regulatory powers of the state have impinged on the formal economy. In addition, various forms of graft, employment and career opportunities have been created with the establishment of more and more parastatals. In Ghana between 1960 and 1966, in Uganda at the end of the 1960s and in other countries pursuing a supposedly socialist programme, employment – particularly for the politically privileged – in the rapidly expanding socialised sectors of the economy provided the main avenue for private wealth creation rather than the diversion of state resources into business activity as such. This is, perhaps, an important variation on the main patterns of personal enrichment, though all are based on the ability to manipulate political power and bureaucratic office.

THE POLITICS AND ECONOMICS OF STATISM

It can be argued that the attitude and policies displayed by many governments with regard to local capitalism represents only one aspect of a much more general and widespread phenomenon in post-Independence Africa. This is the tendency towards 'statism' in the pursuit of economic goals. Hyden is one of several recent writers who have discussed this phenomenon. He has observed that:

African governments throughout the continent have given preference to bureaucracy over market as the principal mechanism of assigning resources and income in society. African governments inherited a sizeable bureaucracy from the colonial powers ... government leaders also inherited a functioning market but they essentially abandoned it in favour of political intervention through an expanding state bureaucracy.[40]

We have already encountered some of the main manifestations of statist economic direction: marketing boards, national trading companies, public corporations, foreign exchange controls, and the licensing of different kinds of business activity. But, in addition, many governments have also attempted to control the distribution and price of essential commodities, domestic food supplies, petrol and so on. These operate in addition to the 'normal' range of administrative, fiscal, monetary and protectionist measures that all modern capitalist states exercise to some degree. Dislike for the operation of market forces as the main way of regulating economic life and a deep distrust or even fear of individual private enterprise are obviously two sides of the same coin.

But it is not only indigenous capitalists with small- or medium-sized firms whose activities have been constrained by the various forms of state regulation. To a greater or lesser extent so, too, have market traders, fishermen, self-employed artisans as well as many other urban petty producers and, most important of all, the mass of cash-crop farmers in the rural areas.

Statist policies with regard to the peasantry typically involve at least two main dimensions. Firstly, several researchers have pointed critically to the long history of misguided government attempts to interfere in peasant farming through various forms of administrative, legal and political coercion, particularly since 1945.[41] These policies were usually built on a mixture of ignorance – concerning the complexivity of village life and traditional farm practices – and misplaced faith in the superiority of Western agricultural technology and its suitability in the African situation. Secondly, governments have sought to extract increasing amounts of wealth from peasant agriculture in order to fund various development projects, finance bureaucratic expansion and subsidise urban living standards. This has mainly been achieved through the simple expedient of continuing to operate the monopsonist system of state purchasing first introduced during the Second World War. This enables governments to extract a kind of export tax through the operation of a two-tier pricing system.

Ghana's case is not untypical. Between 1947 and 1965 the cocoa economy yielded over 40% of its earnings to the government and the Cocoa Marketing Board in one form or another.[42] The public share of cocoa income was actually larger than this because this figure does not include the indirect tax income derived from imports financed, in turn, by cocoa earnings overseas and the government borrowing made viable partly by the prospect of future cocoa exports. Falling world prices in the 1960s led the government to impose a series of cuts in the producer price. By 1964, therefore, the real purchasing power of a load of cocoa had fallen to about half its pre-Independence value.[43] Not surprisingly, farmers eventually responded by cutting back production and investment. In the 1970s they resorted to smuggling cocoa over the borders into neighbouring Francophone countries in massive quantities in order to obtain a better price paid in hard currency.[44]

In Ghana and many other countries, therefore, what emerged during the 1950s and 1960s, to a greater or lesser extent, was a particular kind of development strategy involving the following tendencies: a policy of diverting rural wealth towards the state, an unwillingness to tolerate, assist or give free rein to most forms of indigenous private enterprise while retaining an important foreign business sector; and an increased reliance on various forms of public-sector enterprise and bureaucratic economic regulation. Recently, a number of writers have argued that statist development policies of this kind are both a consequence of certain underlying political tendencies and at the same time they have helped to generate and reinforce a characteristic syndrome of social and economic structures and processes. It will be useful to explore some of these associated patterns of political and economic life.

At the political level two closely related phenomena are apparent to any observer of the contemporary African scene: the central importance of the state as the focal point of emergent economic conflict and a marked tendency, in some countries, towards coercive personal rule. Since Independence the state has been perceived by the various contenders for power and wealth as by far the most important source of personal and group improvement. Thus, the state, rather than the market or the sphere of production has been the main area in which struggles for the control of scarce resources have been fought out. Individuals, parties, factions, ethnic or regional groups and classes-in-formation have competed to gain a degree of control over the means of coercion and regulation operated by the state so that some of the national wealth can be channelled in their direction. In this process, political elites, bureaucrats and the military have inevitably enjoyed an enormous advantage over other groups. At the same time, a number of underlying tendencies – the continuing strength of ethnic and regional loyalties, the colonial legacy of bureaucratic coercion and African political inexperience, the absence of a tradition of impartiality in the exercise of state power and the existence of a relatively undifferentiated economy still orientated partly towards subsistence – have meant that in many countries government possess little if any real legitimacy. By the same token, governments can often exercise power in an unrestrained fashion. Social organisations and pressure groups are weak and under-developed and politicians and bureaucrats cannot easily be made account-able to and through an established ethos that stresses the importance of public duty and national responsibility. Indeed, a coherent and organised 'public' barely exists. In this situation African leaders have increasingly resorted to a blend of personal rule and the exercise of force in the attempt to retain power and manage the state economy and society.[45]

Sandbrook refers to this form of government as 'neo-patrimonialism'.[46] Weber originally used the term 'patrimonialism' to refer to a widespread form of pre-modern traditional authority.[47] Here, the ruler's ability to exercise power in a stable and legitimate way derived typically from his long-standing personal relationship with dependants to whom he allo-cated rewards, usually some kind of salary. In return, these dependants were obliged to exercise the ruler's delegated authority in a proper manner sanctified by the force of custom to which the ruler, too, was ultimately responsible. Neither the ruler nor his lieutenants were supposed to exceed the bounds of authority established by custom or practice. But Sandbrook goes further than this. He suggests that in some countries a variant of patrimonialism, referred to by Weber as 'Sultanism', has become estab-lished where the ruler lacks any kind of legitimacy.[48] He secures the loyalty of his dependants by handing out special rewards and opportunities which only they are eligible to receive and perhaps, also, by advancing those with whom he shares a special ethnic or kinship relationship. Coercion may be employed against outsider groups and interests. In Africa, the attempt by certain rulers to wield power through a combination of force and the personal loyalty owed by favoured clients has been strengthened by the instability created as a result of intense competition between sub-elites to gain access to state resources. Virtually all forms of economic enterprise have been adversely affected by the arbitrary, unpredictable and insecure political climate generated by this situation.

In some countries, for example, Ghana, Uganda and Zaire, the cumu-lative effect of the tendencies we have outlined were so devastating that large sectors of the economy either disintegrated altogether or the people involved in them were driven by necessity to develop an alternative or 'second' economy.[49] Faced with falling returns for their cash crops – due both to declining world prices and excessive government taxation – many peasants have retreated from export production, partially or totally. Al-ternatively, they have tried to obtain hard currency by selling direct to neighbouring, more prosperous countries. Both responses reduce or re-move one of the state's major sources of income. In Zaire, for example, the illegal sale of coffee took place on a vast scale in the late 1970s.[50] It involved smuggling (using private planes, trucks, bicycles or simply headloading crops along forest paths) and various kinds of fraudulent exporting in-cluding under-invoicing or deceiving officials as to the product's quality. It has been calculated that whereas the official volume of coffee exports in 1978 was 90,000 tons another 60,000 tons were sold abroad illegally. A similar story is told of ivory, gold and other exports.

There were many other ways, too, in which the people of Zaire and other countries sought to cope with adversity, partly caused by excessive state control over the economy and manifested in such things as severe food shortages, inflation and the collapse in the provision of essential services. MacGaffey discusses the following strategies, among others, adopted by Zairians: hoarding food in case of shortages and then using it for speculative purposes; distributing goods through barter and kinship networks; black-market sales of scarce goods such as beer and petrol at many times the official price; bribery; and theft from large state and private organisations.

In extreme cases of national economic decline people may withdraw from the formal or official economy altogether. In Ghana during the 1970s and early 1980s escape represented one of the most important aspects of the emergence and consolidation of *Kalabule*, the second economy. Urban dwellers left for their rural farms.[51] Peasants grew foodstuffs instead of cocoa, Ghana's main export, or smuggled it across the borders. In addition, technicians and professionals of all kinds sought employment in Nigeria or the neighbouring Francophone countries. Paradoxically, there-fore, in extreme cases, one of the major consequences of statism – in addition to economic stagnation and even decline – is that the state loses much of its control over the formal economy anyway, and therefore its ability to obtain revenue and direct resources whether for productive or essentially parasitical purposes.

In many countries a statist development orientation has also been associated with a whole syndrome of interlocking economic policies and practices. Thus, a number of governments have given priority in their development strategies to the pursuit of rapid industrialisation, mainly by setting up import-substitution industries, and by concentrating on big national prestige projects. They have pursued these aims mainly – and perhaps unavoidably given their nature and scope – by relying on state corporations and foreign enterprise. But inevitably these policies have given rise to a new and crucial dependency on expensive imported capital-intensive technology and on the need to invest in complementary edu-cational and other kinds of infrastructure. The need to finance such a programme has often compelled governments to undertake a number of further policies. Among others, these include the following: borrowing from the world banking system whenever a country's international credit-rating made this feasible; offering inducements to foreign capital; engaging in budget deficit financing, monetary expansionism and imposing higher taxation; encouraging or permitting exchange rates to be overvalued thereby, in theory, cheapening the cost of imported capital and technology; and encouraging a further intensification of cash-crop production so that an even greater volume of resources could be transferred from the peasantry to mainly urban-based public-sector institutions and activities.

These measures in turn have created a number of problems. African economies have become further exposed to Western financial pressures, including the conservative policies imposed by the International Monetary Fund and other world institutions, as well as subject to the increased risk of capital outflows in the form of debt servicing and repatriated profits. Overvalued currencies have made exporting very difficult, further heightening the tendency towards balance of payments crises. Higher taxes have fallen disproportionately on the poor, through their purchase of consumer goods and services, while the better off have often been able to use their social connections in order to evade income tax.[52] In any case, an increased tax burden and the inflation brought about by a combination of monetary expansion, food shortages and high-priced imports have further eroded the incentives that ordinary people might otherwise have had to work harder, invest and pursue enterprising endeavours.[53]

The massive diversion of resources from the cash-crop peasant economy to the public sector – where officials have often deployed this wealth wastefully on ill-conceived projects and bureaucratic expansion – have aggravated these problems. For, as Williams observes, this flow of wealth has reduced the demand for the kinds of goods that rural people might purchase 'in favour of goods consumed by governments and their beneficiaries. This may well have held back local industrialisation, by shifting demand to goods which cannot be produced locally or which can only be produced at a high cost, and away from goods which are manufactured locally.'[54]

Thus, statism – as described, a dislike of the market and vigorous local enterprise, a preference for extensive bureaucratic regulation and an expanding public sector alongside a still-important foreign capitalism that is more accessible, perhaps, to manipulation – has often gone hand in hand with the decision to rely heavily on advanced technology and both have been associated with rural stagnation, growing inequality and political repression. Of course, there is nothing intrinsically wrong with placing a central emphasis on advanced technology. Indeed, as we shall see in Chapter 6, it is probably impossible for African countries to achieve economic development and social progress unless their governments, technocrats, professionals and entrepreneurs can find ways to gain ready access to the immense competitive and other advantages that such technology can provide, just as their counterparts in other Third World countries are currently trying to do. However, advanced technology needs to be absorbed and used in such a way that instead of contributing to the destruction of the underlying local economy it provides a leading edge which can assist in its transformation: liberating energies, harnessing skills and resources and accelerating productive change over a broad front. In other words, to be effective imported high technology has to be supported by competent government and used so as to complement indigenous resources as part of an active strategy designed to foster all forms of enterprise.

Unhappily, in too many African countries statism and the policies which have tended to accompany it have given rise to, and in turn been sustained by, a quite different set of circumstances. What has often prevailed, to a greater or lesser extent, depending on the country, is a 'zero-sum' situation. Individuals, elites and groups have been locked into a perpetual conflict where narrow interests are pursued at the expense of others and the wider community. Success in the attainment of wealth, power and status is perceived in terms of a struggle where each contender strives to monopolise the finite and eventually dwindling volume of national resources; it is not seen as something which normally results from productive investment or the sustained management of resources through continuous enterprise nor can it be so assessed or measured in the current circumstances. Bona fide capitalist entrepreneurs, too, may be compelled by the logic of the political–economic situation to act in much the same way as everyone else: namely to seek narrow short-term gains by plundering the national cake rather than contributing to its enlargement. Indeed, it may very well be foolish and counter-productive to do otherwise.

Even if some of the rivals for state power seriously resolved to engage in more productive activity, the consequences of their own former actions, and the actions of others, make this very difficult indeed. Economic stagnation or even decline, arbitrary, inept government and administration and chronic uncertainty do not provide the conditions whereby either the would-be accumulators themselves, or the majority of citizens, possess the means or the opportunity to actively expand the productive base. Rather, officials, political leaders and others tend to squander their wealth on luxury consumption, they invest it in real estate and foreign banks or engage in speculative activity. They act in this way not only because such ventures are considerably easier and offer greater security but also because there are no compelling political or economic forces at work capable of inducing them to do otherwise.

Alternatively, as we have seen, in some countries, individuals have taken advantage of their privileged insider position as members of the bureaucracy and political establishment in order to acquire the resources needed to set up in business and have then relied, perhaps, on guaranteed government contracts to provide market opportunities. Here, the question arises whether the misuse of state power on a massive scale in the pursuit of personal wealth may yet generate the possibility of some kind of future capitalist expansion by concentrating scarce social wealth in the hands of a relatively educated minority who might be in a better position to use it productively than the mass of ordinary citizens. Several writers have speculated on the likelihood of this occurrence.[55] They have referred to this 'redirection' of wealth as a form of 'primitive capital accumulation'. Strictly speaking, Marx used this term to denote a much wider process whereby some kind of political intervention, often involving the use of force, in a still largely pre-capitalist society, has the effect of separating some of the direct producers from their means of production, rendering them available to the capitalist labour process as workers while simultaneously transforming them into consumers.

Be this as it may, the argument is an interesting one which may well point to certain promising possibilities. Nevertheless, at least two very considerable obstacles lie in the path of such an optimistic prognosis. So long as statist policies, arbitrary government and economic stagnation, which represent the other side of the coin to this pattern of accumulation, persist unabated and are, indeed, sustained by it, then the wider political and economic environment will remain largely hostile to all kinds of sustained local capitalism, including the one in question. But, in addition, his privileged insider position and access to unearned resources and opportunities means that this kind of capitalist is not really accountable, in the full sense, to market forces and so he has little incentive or need to innovate or seek efficiency. Yet by his very existence, along with others, he may effectively block or retard the emergence and progress of more productive and less protected capitalist entrepreneurs.

Two conclusions seem to emerge from this discussion. Firstly, where countries retain a degree of commitment to private incentives and market forces as one major plank in a strategy for economic development, the considerable advantages obtained by relying on foreign capital (and a healthy public sector) do not and should not preclude a parallel and complementary emphasis on local private initiatives of every kind. Ultimately, there is no substitute for a vigorous local capitalist class. Secondly, what all countries seeking to undergo industrial transformation require, in addition to a strong indigenous capitalist bourgeoisie, is a disciplined, highly competent and patriotic class of bureaucrats and professionals who supervise the offices of the state. This has always been the case. In fact, the latter may be more crucial to successful economic development than the former. In Chapters 6 and 9 we will return to this question and consider what are the prospects for the emergence of competent, constructive bureaucratic and political classes – some of whose members may also be engaged in private business activities alongside career employment – in some African countries in the years ahead. For the moment, however, we turn to another more immediate issue: namely the question of why statism, and in particular the tendency to discourage local capitalism, has been so prevalent in Africa until now.

⸹ 5 ⸻

CLASS FORMATION AND STATE POWER

As its title suggests this chapter explores two closely related phenomena: the problem of class formation and the stage this had reached by the time of Independence, especially the position of the African capitalist bourgeoisie, and the fascinating but difficult question of the post-colonial state and its role in economic development. We begin with a brief summary of some of the relevant debates.

1. Most writers agree that at the time of Independence indigenous classes in Africa remained largely incipient or embryonic in form.[1] What existed in most areas was a form of mercantile capitalism. To a greater or lesser extent the cash nexus shaped most people's lives at the level of household relations and domestic consumption as well as the inter-personal rivalries and tensions to which these sometimes gave rise. But money relations had not yet penetrated to the more fundamental level of the means of production and subsistence. In most areas, because the African peasantry remained effectively in control of land, continued to produce some subsistence crops and still received a degree of protection from customary practices based on ascriptive relationships, they were cushioned from the full impact of market forces and so were 'uncaptured' by the state or by merchant capitalism despite their involvement in cash-crop production, or migrant wage labour, and monetary exchange.[2]

2. The embryonic character of classes at the time of Independence applied to indigenous business groups as well. As we saw in Chapter 3, local entrepreneurs had begun to flourish in many colonies especially after 1945, but they occupied a rather marginal position. Most were confined to trade, contracting and transport and normally operated at the lower end of the commercial hierarchy. Even in some parts of West Africa, with its long history of involvement in international trade, there were very few African retailers, produce-buying firms or import–export traders. In some areas – for example parts of Tanzania, Uganda, Kenya and the Ivory Coast and Ghana – a small class of rich peasant-farmers or farmer-traders were in the

process of emerging, but they were usually confined to a few prosperous areas and most possessed usufruct (the right to enjoy certain benefits derived from farming land formally owned by other individuals or some corporate entity) rather than private ownership rights over land. Also, they normally employed family members or migrant wage workers (who retained land rights in their home area and were paid partly in kind) rather than fully proletarianised wage labourers.[3] Central highland Kenya and parts of Zimbabwe may well have been exceptions to this general pattern.

3. A number of Western writers and a good many African politicians drew certain conclusions from all this. (a) Because the capitalist relations of production were incompletely established in most countries and given their weak position, even within the mainly mercantile economy then in existence, local capitalists lacked the economic base needed in order to repeat the supposed achievements of their nineteenth-century Western counterparts. Thus, African capitalists were unable to exercise a degree of political clout sufficient to win them a solid and leading hold over state power; they were unable to establish bourgeois hegemony. (b) By the same token, local business interests could not play a leading role in national development, especially in view of the very advanced technology characteristic of late twentieth-century economic life. (c) Furthermore, some leaders argued that since African businesses would require considerable help from the state, if they were to compete successfully with foreign firms and contribute significantly to the development process, the state might just as well retain control of these resources and invest them directly in public enterprise. There was often more than a hint of moral disapproval in such assessments concerning the helpless, state-dependent and basically comprador nature of local capital.[4]

More than this, in some countries, political leaders and certain Western academics also voiced strongly held ideological preferences to the effect that as a development strategy capitalism was inappropriate, given Africa's culture and history, and was discredited by its obvious association with Western imperialism. For example, Sekou Touré of Guinea denied the existence of social classes in the African context except in so far as these were a hangover from the invidious inequalities introduced by colonialism.[5] For Julius Nyerere of Tanzania, after the Arusha Declaration of 1967, economic individualism, class differentiation and private ownership were irrelevant to Tanzania's development prospects and potentially destructive of the valuable African tradition of communal production and distribution.[6]

These assertions with respect to class formation and the position of the African bourgeoisie seemed to point inescapably towards the need for a strong state-led development strategy relying heavily on some kind of mix between public and foreign investment. But further support for this view-point came from at least two other very influential sets of ideas, both primarily academic in origin: the question of 'late development' and its peculiarities, especially in the Third World context, and the debate concerning the special nature of state power in post-colonial Africa.

4. In a series of essays written during the 1950s and 1960s, Gerschenkron argued that the role of the state in establishing the wider conditions for economic development tends to increase in proportion to a country's backwardness compared to those that are more advanced.[7] Gerschenkron was mainly interested in countries like Germany and Tsarist Russia, whose development was 'late' compared to that of Britain or perhaps France, but his ideas generated a far wider interest. The kinds of state-imposed changes that Gerschenkron had in mind – changes not dissimilar to those Marx subsumed under the concept of 'primitive capital accumulation' – included the following: completing the 'liberation' of the productive forces by abolishing what remained of feudal institutions and privileges, particularly serfdom and guild organisation, thereby creating private property in land and removing the obstacles to labour mobility; moving some way towards the establishment of equal citizenship rights; channelling government resources into all kinds of modern infrastructure or encouraging private interests to do so; and assisting local enterprise by giving preferential government orders to domestic producers, providing tariff protection, encouraging credit-creation by private banks, offering government guarantees against imports of capital or expertise, and so on. Direct government investment in certain kinds of enterprises, at least for a time, had also been important in some countries.[8]

Gerschenkron also pointed out that relative backwardness usually had other consequences such as the need to rely on borrowed technology in the early stages of development, the importance of a very positive ideological climate usually linked to some form of nationalism and the rapid emergence of large-scale enterprises in the leading economic sectors due to the application of advanced techniques. Also, because changes occurred very quickly there was a much sharper discontinuity between the old and the new society than had been the case with early industrialisation. Moreover, definite advantages were available to late developers because of their ability to imitate, borrow and build upon the highest achievements of the countries that preceded them.[9]

Some writers interested in Third World development have remained deeply sceptical concerning the advantages of the interventionist state in overcoming relative backwardness, particularly neo-classical economists. However, most scholars from a variety of disciplines and perspectives have taken it for granted that the role of government is probably even more critical in the late twentieth century. Indeed, the very notion of 'development' testifies to this, since it involves the idea that purposive action can be taken in the pursuit of economic goals. There is, of course, an important difference between the nineteenth-century Western experience and the so-called developing countries today. For the former, with the possible exception of Tsarist Russia, the state's role mainly involved what White calls 'parametric' measures.[10] Here, governments established a broad framework for economic change but private economic actors retained a certain degree of independence, collaborating with the state rather than being completely dominated by it. More recently, states have resorted to 'pervasive' measures, as well; they intervene directly in some aspects of economic decision-making and ownership, reducing or even eliminating the independence of the private sector altogether. White distinguishes between 'state capitalist' countries, where private and public entrepreneurship coexist and the state both collaborates with and exercises control over private interests, and 'state socialist' regimes involving the virtual abandonment of private capital. A number of regimes occupy an intermediate position.[11]

5. The theory of the overdeveloped post-colonial state (O.D.P.C.S.) and the debates associated with it have occupied the attention of many scholars including some interested in the African situation. Initially the theory stated that, in order to serve the needs of metropolitan capital whilst simultaneously mediating between the various local and foreign interests, colonial governments tended to establish a heavily bureaucratic state structure.[12] Accordingly, the state's influence was 'overdeveloped' in relation to the underlying, and still only partially transformed, socio-economic system. At Independence its enormous potential for wielding power meant that the O.D.P.C.S. was a valuable prize and class factions and elites naturally competed for its control. Yet, in most African countries indigenous classes were relatively unformed; neither a unified national bourgeoisie nor any other dominant class was able to exercise hegemony by virtue of its control over the means of production. Instead, various *petit bourgeois* factions – rich peasants, small traders, civil servants, political and military elites – struggled to capture the O.D.P.C.S.

Most writers who have thought about this question operate within a Marxist perspective. Here, considerable rethinking has taken place during the last 20 years or so on the general question of state power. Yet it is still maintained that ultimately the state apparatus is always in some real sense under the control of a dominant class. State officials may exercise relative autonomy, sometimes acting in ways that hurt the interests of particular dominant class factions, but over the long term they serve the latters' generalised needs and interests.[13] Since in the African context and by common consent there was no obvious contender for the position of dominant class, the question obviously arose as to exactly whose interests were being served by the O.D.P.C.S.

The situation in Tanzania during the 1960s and 1970s offered a favourable arena for the complicated debates generated by this problem and various 'solutions' were offered. Some writers argued that, by exercising the institutional levers of power installed during the colonial period and enlarged since Independence, political elites in Tanzania (and perhaps elsewhere) might transform themselves into a ruling class enjoying a greater or lesser degree of autonomy *vis-à-vis* metropolitan capital.[14] Others claimed that the various *petit bourgeois* factions who competed for state control could only function as a 'governing class', compelled to manage the economy primarily on behalf of the 'true' bourgeoisie whose members lived in the West.[15] A few writers have pursued these arguments in a different direction. Saul, for example, argued that the very inchoate nature of African politics and society might provide favourable conditions, in certain circumstances, whereby a radical *petite bourgeoisie* might wield state power in the pursuit of a genuinely equalitarian socialist path to economic development, relatively free from external control and without passing first through a capitalist stage.[16] Tanzania and Guinea Bissau, among other countries, were cited as possible candidates for such a solution and indeed both regimes have engaged in serious experimentations along these lines.

Apart from Gerschenkron's theory of late development all of these debates and arguments tend to depict approximately the same general scenario, one that highlights the peculiarities if not the uniqueness of the African situation. Thus what stood out at Independence was the centrality of the state. It seemed inevitable that the state would become the site where future struggles would be fought out between emergent classes and the primary source of those very resources without which no future class would be able to attain dominance. But the state's centrality was clearly of key importance to the question of economic development as well. At the very least, governments would be called upon to take the initiative in shaping economic change whilst under the jurisdiction of various classes-in-formation. In certain cases some form of socialist planning and ownership might be possible, perhaps even the only realistic alternative.

Without doubt these theories and arguments have been extremely useful in helping to identify some of the crucial dilemmas present in post-colonial Africa. Yet, it is also possible to claim that these analyses actually conceal certain very difficult notions and the full implications of these have not always been sufficiently spelled out. Moreover, some of the underlying assumptions are either incorrect or misleading. Consequently it has some-

times been all too easy for certain politicians and others to draw inappropriate conclusions or to cloak their own ideological and personal interests
with a mantle of academic justification. Space does not permit the full and
comparative analysis which these questions properly deserve but a few
observations may be useful.

Firstly, it is important not to exaggerate the extent to which indigenous
business activity was inhibited during the colonial period. As we saw in
Chapter 3, despite the very considerable obstacles confronting local entrepreneurs, especially the restrictions imposed by government, the superior resources and competitive superiority enjoyed by foreign firms and
the dependent, uneven nature of development, in many colonies Africans
did manage to establish a significant economic bridgehead in trade, transport and contracting – albeit at the lower levels – in addition to commercial agriculture. But more important, in some countries Africans made
very considerable advances in the years between the outbreak of the
Second World War and the time of Independence. A substantial improvement in the conditions of world trade boosted African economies as a
whole, colonial policies became less restrictive towards indigenous enterprise, governments adopted more expansionist economic strategies and
some foreign companies began to cultivate local business interests. In any
case, in most colonies it was not until the 1950s that foreign capital itself
began to regard serious investment in manufacturing as feasible and
desirable. Thus, the 'lateness' of industrialisation can hardly be regarded
as a symptom solely of local capitalist weakness, particularly since most of
Africa was still under European control at this time. In fact, the gains made
by indigenous capital in the space of only 20 years or so, starting from a
very narrow and relatively small base, could perhaps be viewed as a
considerable achievement rather than as cause for concern, at least in some
countries – an achievement offering considerable future promise.

Secondly, much of the argument concerning the inherent weakness of
African capitalism, and therefore its irrelevance as a major vehicle for
development, is based, implicitly or explicitly, on a comparison with
Western countries. Here, supposedly, the rising commercial bourgeoisies
captured sufficient control over their respective states to force declining
feudal classes to accommodate their demands. This resulted in the removal
of most remaining obstacles to full capitalist industrialisation and the
implementation of policies highly favourable to the bourgeoisies' eventual
economic dominance. As a major theoretical component in Marx's ideal-
type model of the rise of capitalism, which can be usefully applied to
concrete historical cases, this construction is valid. However, it is only an
abstract guide to analysis and a very generalised one at that. The realities,
of course, have always been much more complex. In the early stages of

capitalist transition an incipient commercial bourgeoisie may constitute an important, even a major, political force. It may, for instance, demand state intervention to hasten development. But in an economy where the capitalist mode of production is nascent rather than dominant, by definition, bourgeois strength still rests primarily on mercantile activity. It is not yet based on the ability to directly command and mobilise the productive forces through extensive private ownership, since the majority of direct producers (mainly peasant family farms) have not been completely separated from their most important means of production, land.[17] Therefore at the very least the bourgeoisie must share power with other classes and its hold over the state can only be partial at best. Similarly, if commercial groups seek to impose political change through the exercise of state power in order to bring about the final removal of those same obstacles to full capitalist production which (according to Marx) money, wealth, commodity production and trade cannot achieve by themselves, then, since bourgeois control over the state at this stage is only partial, it follows that the intrusion of such political forces will necessarily require the support, the acquiescence, perhaps even the leadership, of other classes. Thus, a capitalist bourgeoisie proper can only attain its full political and economic potential, and therefore a dominant hold over the state, during and as a direct consequence of the actual process of industrialisation, not before this process is fully underway.

Even in Britain, the country on which Marx's theorising about the pre-history of capitalism was largely based, and where very special historical changes going back centuries preceded the rise of the factory system in the 1760s or thereabouts, the bourgeoisie was not the only source of economic change. As Moore makes clear in his analysis of Britain – one example of the path to modernisation he typifies as 'bourgeois revolution leading to democracy' – sections of the nobility became involved in commercial agriculture (based increasingly on free wage labour rather than serfdom) at a relatively early date and certainly from the sixteenth century.[18] Consequently, and unlike their European counterparts, they were never seriously opposed to commercialism or to the bourgeoisie. Both classes shared common interests, for example the desire to impose restraints on the absolutist ambitions of the monarchy, especially with regard to the Crown's attempt to prevent land enclosures in the first half of the seventeenth century and to interfere with colonial trading monopolies, but also the desire to see British commercial influences expand overseas. By the mid eighteenth century the conditions for industrial capitalism were largely in place, particularly the near-destruction of the peasantry. But the point is that the imperatives of the market were not confined to traders and urban manufacturers, but were present throughout all Britain's social strata, including the landed nobility, and despite the latter's ultimate dependence on state power to guarantee legal rights over land. Moreover, although the commercial bourgeoisie helped to determine the key political interventions that prepared the way for full capitalist industrialisation – including the restrictions imposed on the monarchy in the seventeenth century and government support for overseas trade and colonial acquisitions through the policy of mercantilism, and so on – it did so in partnership with the nobility rather than as the dominant force. Indeed, the landed nobility continued to exercise considerable control over the state right through until the last decades of the nineteenth century, when its economic base in agriculture began to be seriously undermined. Even then aristocratic power was not completely eclipsed by the bourgeoisie.[19]

In countries like Germany and Japan the state's role in fostering the changes required to support industrialisation was much more intrusive. However, as Moore suggests when discussing his second route to modernisation – 'revolution from above leading to fascism' – the bourgeoisie was much weaker still in these countries and certainly did not control the state prior to, and as a precondition for, capitalist development.[20] In both cases the groundwork for industrialisation was laid down by state officials and political rulers who had strong ties to the landed classes and with support from the monarchy and sections of the army and imperial bureaucracy, albeit reluctant support. Without the actions taken by these reforming elites (including the establishment of national unity in the case of Germany) in pushing through essential reforms and key economic changes, the industrial bourgeoisies in these countries probably could not have risen to a position of ultimate economic pre-eminence, though they were compelled to share power with the remnants of the nobility and reactionary elements until well into the twentieth century.

This brings us to a third argument. In certain circumstances, for example during the drive for industrialisation, state officials may be able to exercise a considerable degree of autonomy *vis-à-vis* the emergent or declining classes. In some countries successful modernisation has probably been based, in part, precisely on this eventuality. According to Skocpol one reason why this may occur is because modernising state officials share particular interests.[21] They rely for income and status partly on their long-term career prospects as professional bureaucrats in a government hierarchy that must remain free from external domination if their position is to be assured. Also, their training, occupational position, the expectations of citizens and their own sense of official responsibility endow state rulers with an interest in the maintenance of law and order and national security. In order to successfully safeguard state and nation from possible internal revolutionary turmoil or external aggression they may be prepared to force through drastic changes related to modernisation. The effectiveness of such measures also depends on the fact that as government officials they, and they alone, are in actual possession of the coercive powers available to the state and enjoy the experience and technical mastery needed to wield them with competence. Changes may be imposed even against those groups with whom they share – or once shared – a common class background, perhaps in land ownership or the privileges and prestige of superior rank in the social hierarchy.

The classic example of this process, of course, was the Meiji Restoration in Japan during the 1860s and the events surrounding it. Here, a section of the Tokugawa nobility – often upwardly mobile, usually higher samurai, mostly Westernised and innovative and originating primarily from the Satsuma and Choshu regions – whose members had earlier come to play a central role in the national bureaucracy imposed a series of radical reforms on Japanese society.[22] These included the abolition of aristocratic status and the secure economic claims over peasant surpluses previously enjoyed by the daimyo and samurai, Japan's greater and lesser nobles.

Both Skocpol's and Trimberger's analyses deserve respect because both avoid the simplistic class reductionism sometimes found in Marxist writings, where power invariably reflects economic interests. Yet equally, their work does not exaggerate or mystify the causal significance of political variables, an intellectual tendency concerning which Marxists have been justifiably sceptical. Thus, ruling elites and state officials do sometimes act independently, but they also have interests of their own and these may coincide with long-term national interests.

Fourthly, although the political changes imposed by modernising state rulers were crucial to the industrialisation process in most Western countries, officials did not attempt to swamp private economic initiatives or subordinate these entirely to their own official perceptions and interests. At the same time, although late development may involve ever increasing doses of state intervention, this does not mean that governments need to crowd out the sphere of private initiative to the point where it ceases to be viable altogether. Instead, and however reluctantly in some cases, nineteenth-century elites took steps to strengthen local capitalism in the likely knowledge that by doing so and by encouraging industrialisation this would eventually expose them, and the old ruling classes, to the increasing demands of the rising bourgeoisie, the urban working classes and new technocratic/professional groups as well.[23]

Turning now to the African situation, it is clearly undesirable to push the historical comparisons too far. In any case, as we will see, African societies and their leaders today face a number of daunting problems which nineteenth-century rulers mostly did not need to confront. Nevertheless, it may be that the foregoing discussion does contain some points of relevance to contemporary Africa. For one thing, the challenges of late development and the enormous importance of state power in 'managing' this process are not new. Also, as the experiences of the newly industrialising countries of Asia and Latin America clearly demonstrate there *is* a real potential for economic change in the late twentieth century; meaningful development opportunities and choices are available to governments. Establishing a momentum for successful industrialisation has always been a traumatic and threatening process. Moreover, modernisation inevitably imposes awesome responsibilities on state rulers, especially the need to reach a number of difficult decisions the consequences of which are uncertain. At times these decisions have required a degree of competence, wisdom and an element of personal and class sacrifice from those who wield state power. Nor, historically, has it been the case that modernising rulers were only able or willing to impose changes because they were puppets governed by powerful class interests. In all these ways, therefore, the situation facing African governments since Independence cannot be regarded as wholly unique or unusual.

Furthermore, the requirement that an indigenous capitalist class must always possess a strong and possibly leading command over state power – based on an underlying economic strength – before it is eligible to receive government assistance, or as a pre-condition for being allowed to play an important role in economic modernisation, seems an extremely 'hard' test to apply in most African countries. The severity of this test is revealed partly by comparisons with earlier industrial transitions in the West where indigenous capitalists did not always wield a particularly strong influence over the state in the early stages. Yet this did not deter governments from rendering them assistance. Nor did their initial weaknesses prevent these bourgeoisies from learning how to shoulder some of the economic tasks associated with modernisation. The capacity to wield political power and the ability to play an increasingly important economic role are separate not identical processes, though clearly one may lead to the other. ‾ here is another difficulty. The political situation confronting incipient business and other privileged groups in Africa around the time of Independence was quite different from that experienced by their Western counterparts at a comparable period of development. In most European countries and Japan during the period leading up to the first phase of industrialisation the lower orders did not enjoy the same degree of electoral franchise as in Africa during the 1950s and 1960s so that their immediate hopes and political preferences did not have to be taken very seriously. Political victories did not depend on the ability of elites or rising classes to organise mass electoral machines almost from scratch. Eventually, modern party politics could no longer be ignored, but by then the die was cast firmly in favour of capitalist values and interests.

The circumstances which brought African nationalist movements to power did not favour emergent capitalist interests. Independence movements normally consisted of loose alliances of ethnic, regional, educational and other sectional interests, each clamouring for their special demands to be met. Given the reality of mass party politics, a widespread franchise and the need to hold unwieldly confederations of interests together, the opportunities inherent in the political process usually rested with political leaders who enjoyed popular appeal and possessed the skill required to manipulate party machines. In most African countries local business groups had little to offer ordinary people, not much chance of gaining widespread sympathy for their specific needs – privileged as they were, relative to their compatriots – and little hope of competing for power effectively with politicians. It is difficult to see how things could have been otherwise.

Nevertheless, some writers claim that in Kenya the two conditions required for bourgeois hegemony in the post-Independence era did apparently coincide: the emergence of a fairly strong indigenous capitalism during the colonial period and its ability to gain a strong hold on the newly emerging state. Something rather similar also took place in countries like Nigeria, the Sudan and perhaps the Ivory Coast but not to the same extent. Other countries like Ghana and Uganda experienced the first condition but not the second. Before we examine the Kenyan case it is important to make several points.

The Kenyan situation is indeed rather exceptional and it is not surprising that it has attracted a good deal of attention. In part, its exceptionality stems from the relative success of the Kenyan economy since Independence, at least compared to other countries, and this in turn is almost certainly related in some way to the emergence of a strong capitalist bourgeoisie enjoying state support.[24] Secondly, in considering the rise of the Kenyan bourgeoisie, writers like Leys and Swainson adopt a basically classical Marxian interpretation. Leys, in particular, makes his position quite clear when he argues as follows:

In noting the important role of the state in facilitating this movement of African capital out of circulation and into production, we must avoid the mistake of attributing to it an independent role. Its initiatives reflected the existing class power of the indigenous bourgeoisie, based on the accumulation of capital they had already achieved . . . Unless the exercise of state power after 1963 is grasped as a manifestation of the class power already achieved by the indigenous bourgeoise, it can lead to serious mystification. The most common form of this is to see the state's economic role as expressing the 'modernising' vision of the state bureaucracy (the 'elite').[25]

Thirdly, although the highly competent and far-ranging analyses offered by Leys and Swainson deserve respect, exemplifying as they do some of the best research on contemporary Africa in recent years, it may be important not to read too much into their interpretation. Partly this is because they may have exaggerated the significance of the link between the attainment of bourgeois wealth and state power. In addition, it is possible that others will apply their view of the Kenyan situation as a theoretical yardstick to other African countries thereby perpetuating misunderstanding, since on this basis it might be argued that a leading role for African capitalism is only 'possible' − or can only be tolerated − where such interests are sufficiently strong in economic terms to secure a commanding influence over state power. As we have tried to argue, such a view may be both unwise and inappropriate when measured against an alternative historical perspective. Briefly, then, how did the Kenyan capitalist bourgeoisie emerge?

According to some observers a class of mainly Kikuyan accumulators first appeared in central Kenya even before the onset of colonial rule. Leys cites the extensive research carried out by Cowen as providing valuable confirmation of this view.[26] Thus, through a combination of long-distance trade, migration in search of new land and cattle raiding a group emerged whose members increasingly owned or controlled both land and livestock. Writing from an anthropological perspective, Marris and Somerset offer a rather similar picture of early Kikuyu enterprise.[27] Hard work and individual effort in the pursuit of social achievement, they argue, enabled some exceptional individuals to amass wealth. This involved a step-by-step graduation from extensive land clearance and farming to participation in risky expeditions involving trade with the pastoral Masai and eventually to the emergence of a few talented organisers capable of leading such large-scale caravans.

Leys claims that for a time colonialism blocked this process of accumulation, since land alienation, the establishment of government-enforced European monopolies over the most valuable cash crops and exporting, in addition to competition from Asian traders in the reserves, combined to prevent most Africans from engaging in modern forms of capitalist enterprise until the 1950s.[28] However, a few of the more privileged elements, especially government-appointed chiefs and their kin, did enjoy new opportunities: the ability to buy land and invest in small businesses using funds acquired illegally through the misuse of office and early access to mission education. Kitching also attaches considerable significance to early, privileged access to schooling.[29] Those who benefited from this often assumed leadership positions in certain Kikuyu organisations which eventually played a key role in the Independence movement. Others were able to secure better-paid supervisory or skilled jobs in the European sector, investing their earnings in land acquisition, capitalist farms and small businesses. Swainson dates the early emergence of an embryonic capitalist class from the 1920s and 1930s but sees events after 1945 as especially crucial.[30] Like Kitching, she argues that colonial assistance programmes, often channelled through the Local Native Councils, were important because they provided small loans and contracts to a favoured few. After the Second World War some European companies also played a part by extending distribution facilities to African traders in the reserves.[31] Since help was mainly directed towards chiefs, people connected to them and to existing entrepreneurs, it tended to accelerate the process of class differentiation.

According to Leys, the crucial stage in the rise of the mainly Kikuyu capitalist bourgeoisie was, of course, the Independence period and its aftermath. The Kikuyu played a dominant role in the nationalist movement.[32] In addition, because of their earlier investment in education, the emergent capitalist minority and their kin were especially well represented in the state apparatus. Thus, after 1963 state power was used to enable the Kikuyu bourgeoisie to assume ownership of the former white farms and then move into urban real estate, road transport, the higher levels of trade and eventually into some branches of manufacturing.[33] For example, in the mid 1960s, Western advisers and government officials argued that African settlement schemes were expensive and often unproductive in national economic terms. Henceforth, public funds for land acquisition and farm improvements would be mainly available to those who could offer collateral security against loans and demonstrate their ability to engage in successful farming.[34] Normally this meant that funds went to the wealthy, existing large landowners or people who enjoyed political and bureaucratic connections. Other forms of state help included the rapid expansion of the 'small loan schemes' for commerce and industry through the I.C.D.C. and the Trade Licensing Act of 1967. The latter excluded non-citizens from certain kinds of trade. Leys also points out that the Kikuyu bourgeoisie increasingly acted so as to outmanoeuvre rival classes by banning the Kenyan People's Union Party in 1969, establishing a state-controlled trade-union organisation and prohibiting strike action, among other things.[35]

Arguably, however, there are certain difficulties involved in accepting Leys' and Swainson's interpretations of these developments, especially that offered by Leys. Although it may be perfectly true that a class of African owners and commercial entrepreneurs had established an important presence in the late colonial period, this is not the same thing as saying that an African bourgeoisie had attained a pre-eminent economic position. Asian and white settler capital and the transnationals remained firmly in control of the most important economic sectors, though the former two groups were politically in retreat due to changes in colonial policy after the Mau Mau revolt. Also, Leys' theory mainly applies to the Kikuyu in central Kenya who only made up about 20% of the population. In any case, until Independence African capital was mainly concentrated in trade, distribution and commercial agriculture so its achievements differed little from those gained by local entrepreneurs in several other countries, such as Ghana and Nigeria.

What may be much more significant is the fact that the Kikuyu minority managed to dominate the leading nationalist party, the Kenya National African Union. Their political activism was partly due to the peculiar circumstances of land alienation and the relatively intense exposure to capitalist penetration which occurred in Central Province where most Kikuyu lived. These experiences helped to make the latter especially responsive to nationalist demands. At the same time, the ethnic fragmentation of Kenyan society meant that as the largest group the Kikuyu were able to dominate the political situation and it has proved difficult for other groups to mount a sustained counter-alliance. By contrast, in some other African countries, such as Nigeria and Uganda, politics have tended to be dominated by strong ethnic or regional discontents. These have often swamped other considerations and generated bitter conflicts that undermined stable government or prevented the formation of clear class alliances capable of operating above ethnic differences. The partly fortuitous nature of the political circumstances prevailing in Kenya may have greater explanatory significance in accounting for Kikuyu political dominance than their pre-established economic base in agriculture and trade.

Thirdly, it has been the willingness of party and state officials to foster indigenous capitalism that is the really important and possibly unique feature of the Kenyan situation. Superior Kikuyu educational attainment and therefore their strong presence in the state bureaucracy and politics was no doubt partly responsible, but many other African countries also experienced the uneven impact of colonial change leading to severe imbalances in the ethnic composition of educated officials at Independence. Anyway, educated leaders and bureaucrats in many African countries have remained largely unresponsive if not hostile to the needs of local capital. But government officials and politicians in Kenya have not only used state power to benefit local enterprise, despite its initial weakness compared to foreign capital, they have also tended to engage in private business activities in their own right, placing their own personal funds at risk as well as loans obtained from the public purse. They have often pursued productive business ventures in addition or in preference to luxury consumption, overseas savings or essentially speculative activities.[36] Again this contrasts strongly with the situation in other countries where state power has been used to amass private wealth but mainly of a non-productive kind. Thus, the special feature of the Kenyan situation lies less in the ability of an economically predominant class to capture direct state power or buy off the bureaucracy, but has more to do with the willingness of educated officials and politicians to view private business endeavour and public office-seeking not as mutually opposed activities – one of which could only be pursued at the expense of the other, given the realities of underdevelopment and resource scarcity – but as overlapping and complementary endeavours, both of which could be followed simultaneously at the individual and the national level.

Part of the explanation for this crucial difference in perception compared to other African countries, as Leys and Swainson both suggest, may be found in the special nature of colonial intervention especially in Central Province. Land alienation, the struggles of white settlers to establish capitalist farms, their demands for long-term state support and eventually the investment by foreign companies pursuing productive and not merely trading activities, all combined to deepen and extend the pre-colonial tendency towards individual land ownership noted by Cowen, Leys and Kitching. Thus, in some areas the means of production became commoditised and subject to individual rather than communal control. Of course, this process underwent a marked acceleration after Independence with the various land settlement schemes which were based on the assignment of individual property rights to land.[37] This in turn probably exposed a minority of African farmers more fully to the uncertainties of the market and therefore the imperatives of accumulation: the opportunity and the necessity to invest profits in new endeavours and to improve productivity instead of simply extending the area under cultivation.

However, the emergence of private property in rural land is unlikely to be the only factor at work. In the Ivory Coast, for example, the emergence of a class of African planters after 1945 and their strong political links with the ruling group did not generate a government deeply committed to fostering indigenous capitalism or whose members have been conspicuously involved in directly productive enterprise as private citizens.[38] In addition, there are other countries like Zambia (and perhaps Swaziland and Lesotho) where local business groups occupied a weak economic position, mainly in commerce, at Independence and were not especially well represented in politics and government.[39] Nevertheless, writing about the Zambian situation, one writer has argued that in the late 1960s the Kaunda government did take substantial steps designed to foster a strong African business class despite the latter's lack of political clout.[40]

These cases suggest that the ideological preferences shared by politicians and officials, their development images and perceptions concerning their own best opportunities for personal advancement in the context of wider national interests may also influence policy-making in certain potentially significant ways. These, in turn, have obviously been shaped partly by history and culture. While it is important not to endow cultural and ideological factors with a greater explanatory significance than they actually possess, or to deny the extent to which they are given meaning by the social relationships of production, nor is it necessary to ignore their potential autonomy as agents of change. Perhaps, therefore, the much firmer hold which the lure of continuous business endeavour seems to have had for many educated and powerful Kenyans, seen as a realistic and preferred goal for personal endeavour, compared to other Africans, owes something to the earlier experience of white-settler farming and other European investments. Here, migrant workers saw productive enterprises in operation over a long time period and they knew that discriminatory state power was a crucial ingredient in their success. But they were also exposed to the role-model of the practical business organiser, involved directly in day-to-day technical, financial and managerial problem-solving activities as embodied in the white farmer and his supervisory personnel.

This experience of the origins of European wealth in productive, commercial enterprise surely contrasts strongly with the more typical African image of the European: the mainly sedentary, office-bound person shuffling bits of paper around, whose eligibility for status, power and relatively high earnings normally hinged on the possession of non-vocational educational qualifications; someone who was typically unconcerned with practical and commercial matters, and, above all, a person who was secure in his position as a company or government employee. This more usual African perception of the European reinforced the traditional view of success and prestige typical in pre-colonial African society; namely the belief that wealth and status tended to originate in power and office rather than the other way round.[41]

The contrast between Ghana during the Nkrumah period and Kenya also throws some doubt on the argument that a strong business class able to influence political debate is an essential precondition for receiving firm government assistance. By the early 1950s Ghanaians were well established in commerce, transport, contracting and, of course, cash-crop farming.[42] Moreover, some were already setting up small-scale manufacturing firms alongside the move into industry taken by European trading firms at this time.[43] Several writers have shown how Ghanaian entrepreneurs were quite heavily involved in the various political movements that emerged during the late 1940s and 1950s, voicing their discontents and demands, seeking representation in the political parties and trying to influence government policy at local and national levels.[44] Business leaders were often in the forefront of demands that much sterner measures be taken against British banks. Anger was expressed at the continued outflow of cocoa revenue to support British currency reserves. Also, the general tardiness of the Nkrumah administration in failing to tackle the problem of economic dependency and foreign domination was attacked.[45] Yet despite their position of relative economic strength, the incipient bourgeoisie failed to consolidate its political hold on the government during the years before and after 1957. In 1960 the regime became committed to a statist development strategy that made basically no provision for a private indigenous contribution of any significance and very little material assistance was offered to local entrepreneurs even before this date.[46]

The reasons for this are complex and open to numerous interpretations, but the following explanation may have some validity. Ghana's capitalists were fairly evenly distributed across most of the prosperous southern ethnic groupings. Regional issues did intrude into the political scene in the mid 1950s, particularly with the formation of the Ashanti-based National Liberation Movement, whose members were angry because the Convention People's Party (C.P.P.) government insisted on holding cocoa prices down at a time of high world prices.[47] However, on the whole, no one ethnic group was able to dominate the Independence movement and, in the crucial period leading up to the 1951 election which brought Nkrumah and the C.P.P. to power, ethnic issues were subordinate to the more important question of the strength of national fervour concerning the timing of decolonisation. By the same token, the commercial changes that had taken place, especially in the south during the preceding decades, had generated a considerable degree of class differentiation. The clash of interests between the urban and rural masses, some of whose younger members had gained literacy, on the one hand, and the farmer-trader-chiefs and remnants of the old professional coastal elite groups on the other, not only cut across ethnic divisions but provided one of the main themes of nationalist politics – a theme that Nkrumah and his party were able to project as their own.[48] To many ordinary people, Ghana's bourgeois groups appeared as elitist, privileged and linked to imperialist interests through their contacts with European trading firms. They were also not very adept at engaging in mass electoral politics, though had they been so, they would still have faced the problem of persuading the less privileged to give their policies and needs political priority.

However, the social origins of the C.P.P. activists, their shared perceptions concerning how best to promote their own long-term interests and their ideological inclinations may have also shaped the political and therefore economic realities confronting local capital. Beckman, for example, argues that the activists in the C.P.P. tended to be young, elementary school leavers and members of the urban and rural *petit-bourgeois* stratum whose families had experienced some benefit from change but not at a very high level.[49] Rural members tended not to come from backgrounds in cocoa farming and related trading activities. In common with some of the right wing C.P.P. leadership and party founders, many of those who were involved in the lower echelons of party organisation did have some kind of small private business interests. But for the majority, bureaucratic employment and the prospects of common advancement in one or other of the expanding party and government organisations offered a much more secure and promising avenue for personal advancement than sustained business activity. Eligibility for these positions depended on a certain level of educational attainment but also on political loyalty and ability. In any case, the growth of the public sector and the extensions of government control also offered numerous opportunities for engaging in private activity through the misdirection of public resources.

One example of this process of self and party aggrandisement is shown by the C.P.P. policy with regard to cocoa buying. Beckman observes that the farmer-traders in the cocoa areas were the 'natural heirs' to rural commercial capitalism as the European trading companies withdrew from most aspects of produce buying and retail distribution in the 1950s.[50] In 1953, the government established the Ghana Farmers' Council and this organisation eventually attained a virtual monopoly of cocoa purchasing, thereby ousting the private Ghanaian firms. The Council also used its control to reward political supporters. Meanwhile, individual officials could engage in private profiteering.

Thus the C.P.P. government and political cadres adopted what Beckman calls a 'bureaucratic monopoly solution' with regard to organising the rural cocoa economy and the wider problem of national development.[51] This statist approach received additional ideological and political support when world cocoa prices began to fall in 1960, since this appeared to legitimise the 'Left' group's claims that only a socialist solution could free Ghana from dependency and poverty.

Earlier it was suggested that in certain ways the dilemmas facing African governments in the last 30 years have not been particularly unique. This said, however, in one crucial respect at least, the recent political and government processes typical of many African countries have clearly been very different indeed from those that existed in most, perhaps all, of the countries that passed through the crisis of modernisation at an earlier date. Furthermore, the problems associated with the modernisation process may perhaps be present to a far greater extent in Africa than in many other Third World countries. We refer here to what might be called the question of ruling-class or elite accountability. How can those in control of the state apparatus be compelled to act in ways that further the long-term pursuit of national needs and aspirations, in particular the attainment of industrial development, so that some social groups besides the rulers and their immediate circle eventually obtain certain advantages. In a society committed to a basically capitalist or mixed-economy approach to economic development there is also the problem of inducing governments to set up an appropriate environment in which a productive expansionary capitalism can flourish rather than one characterised by speculation and the pursuit of 'booty'. The factors historically associated with elite or ruling-class accountability during the modernisation process elsewhere have often been conspicuous by their absence in many African countries.

1. Few African societies prior to colonial rule possessed ruling or dominant classes in the usual Marxist sense, that is, groups able to extract economic surplus on a continuous basis from the mass of the population by virtue of their capacity to monopolise ownership of, or exercise some form of permanent control over, the means of production, or both. Colonialism imposed a metropolitan ruling class but the changes that followed stopped some way short of altering the underlying configuration of social inequalities to the point where a group approximating to a 'dominant' class could emerge. Perhaps this had crucial consequences. For, given a strong economic base and/or status esteem, a socially legitimate claim to rule at the national level and a firm, experienced grasp on state power, such a dominant class, in any given country, might have felt both sufficiently secure and effective to be able to impose a radical programme of structural change as a prerequisite for genuine modernisation, whilst tolerating and facilitating the emergence of potential class rivals. As it was, for the most part the political elites who won power lacked a predictable source of wealth and status, independent of state office, were chronically insecure and inexperienced and had few claims to legitimate rule beyond the initial euphoria of Independence.

2. Although colonial governments wrought many changes they did not succeed in cementing the highly diverse and often relatively unhierarchical societies brought together within the artificial colonial boundaries into genuine nation states. The experience of externally imposed nationhood, the reality of discriminatory and authoritarian government, the delayed incorporation of Africans into the colonial bureaucracy at a reasonably high level, and yet, perhaps, the comparatively short duration of the colonial period and the slow, uneven and incomplete nature of economic change, were such that a proper basis for a widely shared sense of national and cultural identity was not attained.

3. In addition to a weakly developed nationalism, the absence of any

serious military threat to political autonomy from external sources since Independence (except perhaps in the case of Chad, Somalia and the front-line states of southern Africa) means that one of the historically most significant forces partly responsible for inducing elites or ruling classes to accept the need for radical reform and the urgency of state-led modernis-ation programmes elsewhere in the world has been relatively insignificant in the African context. The desire to demonstrate to the international community that in the aftermath of decolonisation the new nation can make its own unique contribution to the world community of nations has not so far proved sufficiently compelling as an ideology of change to provide a substitute for nationalism.

4. In a number of late-developing countries the possible or actual threat of external aggression and superior economic competition combined, sometimes, with the spectre of revolutionary change from below created a set of circumstances where in order to serve their own 'class' interests (reducing the likelihood of foreign usurpation of the reins of government, ensuring continued personal career advancement in an expanding, moder-nised bureaucracy and protecting the old order from being swept away completely) political rulers were also compelled to further their countries' political and economic development at the same time. The attainment of each goal became contingent upon the other. They could only retain some partial control by accepting the need for change; their ability to shape the direction of such change depended on maintaining some kind of grip on state power. Because of the historical legacy bequeathed both by the nature of pre-colonial African society and by colonialism, this coincidence of circumstances has not yet arisen in most African countries.

5. In pre-colonial Africa wealth usually depended on the inheritance or attainment of political office rather than the reverse.[52] In state societies private individual accumulation was often discouraged by political rulers and might be susceptible to political regulation and exploitation as well as to cultural demands that wealth be shared. For the most part colonialism did little to alter this situation. African enterprise was not given much help or protection from superior foreign competition, if any. In fact, some governments imposed severe restrictions on local business and yet openly served European interests. As we have argued, it is important not to exaggerate the extent to which indigenous business activity was inhibited during this time. Nevertheless, in general, colonialism also gave new impetus to the traditional African perception that office-holding and political power – now attainable at the personal level, mainly through education – were the main prizes to be won in the pursuit of career advancement and offered greater security and economic rewards than the risks and difficulties involved in productive economic ventures.

6. In addition, in most countries the heritage of the O.D.P.C.S. in the 1960s, and the opportunities this seemed to provide both for personal gain and national development, contrasted starkly with the limited economic hold maintained by the local capitalist bourgeoisies and their failure to capture state power or present any immediate threat to the ruling political elites. But the very weakness of local business interests, and the decision to neglect or suppress them, has removed yet another force which might otherwise have been capable of imposing a degree of political account-ability on African rulers: namely the growing power and demands of organised economic interest groups in an increasingly integrated economy.

Unfortunately, in a climate of political non-accountability there is little likelihood that those who lead economic enterprises, whether publicly or privately owned, can also be held fully responsible for their actions and so induced to contribute to national economic development in productive ways. In extreme cases statist development policies have usually meant that scarce resources have been poured disproportionately into wasteful official and unofficial public activities whilst remaining largely beyond the regulatory control either of market forces or organised political protest. At the same time, widespread government incompetence and oppression have also tended to stifle enterprise along a broad front so that the imperatives of accumulation cannot operate effectively. To the extent that statism distorts or suppresses the market and entrepreneurship whilst failing to provide a genuine and viable socialist alternative it inhibits economic development.

Of course, in the late twentieth century it is apparent that one or other form of bureaucratic socialism is available, in principle, as an alternative strategy for achieving industrialisation. Here, plan replaces market as the main mechanism for allocating resources, while direct political control over the means of production and consumption exercised by the state provides the basis for compelling citizens to accept changes in the way the labour process is organised in place of the haphazard economic pressures of private property and competition. Leaving aside all the difficult ques-tions concerning whether and when a given country truly merits the socialist label, some regimes calling themselves by this name do exist in Africa. More importantly, many observers, including some academics, have argued that some form of socialism offers a much more efficacious, equitable and appropriate path for African development than the capi-talist one. Be this as it may, it seems clear that modernising rulers in socialist countries whose actions and policies have been successful in raising the living standards of the masses to a greater or lesser extent (irrespective of their other achievements or failures) have been accountable for their actions in one or more very real ways, despite the absence of Western-style democratic politics.

The sources of this accountability have varied but include the following: the presence of a considerable and obvious external threat to regime, country or both; the existence of strong and widespread sentiments of national unity and pride, sometimes bolstered by a reservoir of public goodwill generated as a result of earlier years of severe repression and delayed modernisation by a former regime; a powerful sense of revolutionary mission to overcome backwardness and prove the socialist cause; and the regime's dependence on the highly organised revolutionary party – if to no other social group – with a tradition of discipline, dedication and unity, forged in the long struggle to win power, and without whose continuing support victory could not have been won and the eventual restructuring of society would be impossible. Moreover, so far, 'independent' socialist regimes have only come to power as a result of very special circumstances prevailing in particular countries, especially (but not only) the need to engage in protracted military as well as political struggles against exceptionally reactionary regimes or reluctant decolonising powers.

In most African countries neither the special circumstances of socialist revolutionary struggle, nor the existence of disciplined, united regimes controlled by leaders accountable both to a party and to their own view of themselves as agents of historical destiny, have so far been very much in evidence. African statism is not the same political phenomenon as bureaucratic socialism. As presently constituted, statism is also unlikely to provide an appropriate political system for setting in motion a successful form of state-induced productive capitalism.

❧ 6 ❧

AFRICAN BUSINESS AND FOREIGN CAPITAL: THE CONTEMPORARY SITUATION

The relations between Third World national bourgeoisies and metropolitan capital, and the scope for independent economic development given the latter's dominant position, have been the subject of much debate.

One version concerns the theory of the 'progressive' bourgeoisie.[1] This view originated in the various conferences and discussions that took place among Russian and Third World Marxists during the inter-war period under the auspices of the Third International. It was argued that some countries might contain emergent bourgeois elements who wished to establish an independent industrial base. This brought them into conflict both with imperialist interests and local mercantile and agrarian groups tied to Western capital and opposed to industrialisation. The possibility was envisaged that these progressive factions might form an alliance with nascent worker or peasant classes as part of the world-wide struggle against imperialism. However, the fundamentally dual character of the national bourgeoisie stood as a major impediment to such an alliance. Thus, as Woddis observes, in its attempt to expand the national economy the progressive bourgeoisie inevitably clashes with its own workers, whom it is attempting to exploit as a source of capital for development, and with Western interests whose grip on the local economy will be undermined by indigenous capitalist expansion.[2]

Several contemporary African writers have drawn attention to the essential weakness of the national bourgeoisie.[3] Osabo, for example, claims that the Nigerian bourgeoisie naturally wishes to retain most of the economic surplus generated within the country by the local labour force in order to build up a relatively autonomous capitalist economy. But such a policy requires a concerted attack on imperialist interests and several obstacles prevent the Nigerian bourgeoisie from adopting this course wholeheartedly: religious and ethnic differences at the national level; internal divisions within its own ranks; but above all the fear of revolutionary conflict with the masses whose labour it exploits. If such a conflict arose it could only be contained through continuing collaboration with Western interest and so the Nigerian bourgeoisie, like its counterparts elsewhere, draws back from confrontation with imperialism.[4]

Mahmoud offers a similar analysis of the Sudanese situation.[5] She argues that a clear division emerged as early as 1924 between a group of mainly agricultural capitalists, often descended from traditional religious leaders and landowners whose interests had been fostered by the colonial government, and the forerunner of today's educated elite, including some army officers. The second group evolved gradually into the Ashiqqa Party and was supported by urban businessmen and civil servants. It increasingly opposed British rule and had strong links with Egyptian nationalism. When it contested the first elections in 1953, now constituted as the National Unionist Party, it enjoyed widespread popular support, including from tenant-farmers, trade unionists and the Sudanese Communist Party. However, a series of complicated events and processes since that time have intervened to prevent the emergence of a genuinely anti-imperialist Sudanese state, capable of achieving independent industrialisation and propelling the country, eventually, towards socialism. In 1970 there was a right-wing reaction to the leftwards drift of the politics of the 1960s. Local capitalists took fright at the prospect of socialist policies and squashed radical groups. Moreover, since the early 1970s, Arab oil money and the transnational corporations have invested heavily in industrial development and large-scale agricultural schemes. More and more Sudanese capitalists from both parties have been drawn into these developments as direct or indirect beneficiaries of foreign investments. Kursany on the other hand argues that a genuinely progressive element can still be identified.[6] Its members are interested in productive rather than mercantile investment, they oppose foreign capital, live modestly and do not rely upon state protection.

The theory of the progressive bourgeoisie draws attention to a series of potentially crucial obstacles to Third World development and it has obviously helped to inform and invigorate some very fruitful research. Nevertheless, it does contain certain problems. For example, in this kind of analysis the bourgeoisie appears to be confronted by a stark choice; either support radical political groups and face future class suicide or fail to achieve 'proper' capitalist development because of the need to depend on imperialism. The truth, however, is surely much simpler than this. If a national bourgeoisie has so far proved unable to promote independent capitalist industrialisation this is because it has lacked the resources to do so and the necessary state support or has so far found other alternatives more amenable; it is not because its members see imperialism and socialism as stark and mutually exclusive alternatives. Neither of these are intrinsically desirable from their point of view. In any case, as we will argue later on (pp. 119–26), the belief that there is a fundamental contradiction between the continued incorporation of Third World countries into world capitalism and the possibility of industrialisation no longer seems as valid as it once did. Thus, some recent writers have argued that metropolitan interests are no longer opposed to development in the periphery and participation in the world capitalist order is not only compatible with industrial transformation but is one of its prerequisites.[7]

Another debate, of more recent origin, and more directly relevant to the question of African capitalism, stems from the writings of people like Baran, Fanon, Frank and Amin and other sympathisers with Neo-Marxist dependency theory. Here, it is argued that, like the various other elements of the national bourgeoisie, local business groups in Africa and elsewhere operate primarily in a comprador or 'service' capacity with regard to Western capital. In this scenario, comprador activity and the wider predicament of dependency and relative economic backwardness are inseparable aspects of the same general condition of satellite underdevelopment; each perpetuates the other. Because of its willingness, apparently, to play the role of intermediary between the Third World masses and metropolitan interests, the national bourgeoisie – or *petit bourgeoisie* as it is often labelled by Neo-Marxist writers – bears a large part of the responsibility for the continuing polarisation of the global capitalist economy. The West wishes to maintain the inequalities which have been built into its exchanges with the Third World for so long. Its ability to do so rests largely on continuing monopoly control over advanced technology, the enormous pull of its highly developed markets and its management of international capital flows, but Third World compradorship also plays a crucial part in continuing Western exploitation and domination.

There is, however, a certain ambiguity, even an unresolved contradiction, associated with the position assigned to the comprador bourgeoisie by underdevelopment theory. Thus, local business groups, among others, are collaborating with imperialism; they have shirked their historic task of leading the political and economic struggle for capitalist industrialisation. Yet, at the same time, comprador groups can also be seen as victims whose capacity to exercise real choice is severely circumscribed. Stunted growth in the national economy as a whole severely limits the range of profitable investment opportunities available to local business groups and state compradors. Net capital outflows, national indebtedness, fluctuating commodity prices, falling terms of trade, the very narrow and restricted interest displayed by foreign capital in the mobilisation of local resources, all these inhibit the growth of effective demand in the national economy so that there is a dearth of investment opportunities.[8] But local entrepreneurs also have to compete directly against foreign firms based within the local economy not just for markets but also for other scarce resources such as bank loans and government aid. Moreover, overseas companies normally enjoy distinct advantages in this and other respects, for example, their ability to draw on overseas contacts, skills and funding, the capacity to offer superior inducements in winning government contracts and other favours, the availability of tax and other concessions, but most of all their size, reputation and vastly superior technological, commercial and advertising expertise.[9]

Ousted from the most profitable fields of business endeavour by superior foreign competition and constrained by a market already limited through the effects of economic dependency, local entrepreneurs, it is said, have always been driven to adopt one or both of two extreme courses of action. They could seek the least profitable arenas of business activity – which for that very reason did not attract overseas investment – or they could establish some kind of service relationship with their foreign rivals where they might survive in a reasonably protected environment on the meagre crumbs guaranteed by the dominant partner. The classic business compradors were the small traders who participated in the import–export trade. Because their business interests depended on the local production of primary commodities for export to the advanced countries, and the importation of manufactured goods for distribution to the peasant farmers or landowners whose activities were the mainstay of the local economy, they helped to perpetuate a system of international exchange that generated severe disadvantages for their own country. In Chapter 3 we saw how creole and mulatto traders, mainly confined to the West African coast, flourished for a brief period in the mid nineteenth century in the period between the demise of the slave trade and the consolidation of European control, sharing the market with European firms, large and small. By the end of the century, and certainly by the early 1920s, most had either turned to alternative pursuits or had been relegated to a much more lowly form of compradorship as small retailers or, more usually, to the role of hinterland brokers engaged in produce buying on behalf of European firms on whom they relied for finance.

Although the European import–export companies operating in West Africa before the Second World War and colonial governments showed very little interest in the development of a local manufacturing capacity, seeing this as a threat to their immediate interests, African economies nevertheless underwent substantial economic diversification over time. As this took place, especially after 1945, so, several new forms of comprador business activity evolved.

Firstly, there were the sole representatives appointed by overseas manufacturers with no previous links to African economies. The latter were eager to gain a foothold in the expanding market for consumer goods fuelled by the post-war commodity boom and increased colonial government expenditure. Educated Africans enjoying a knowledge of local consumer preferences, a wide range of informal contacts, and preferably some kind of relevant occupational experience, were obvious candidates for such activity. Most would-be entrepreneurs lacked the capital required in order to become importers in their own right and needed help in getting started in business. Secondly, as the established European firms moved out of the import–export business and invested in manufacturing, contracting and services during the 1950s and 1960s, and were joined by newcomers to the African market as the transnational corporations set up subsidiaries, so the need rapidly grew for small ancillary firms to provide various supporting services. Leys gives the example of Kenyan lorry and garage owners who make up a large part of the petrol distribution and retail sales networks linked to the big Western oil companies.[10] The latter can reduce both their running costs and overall risks by decentralising their operations in this way whilst ostensibly encouraging 'independent' local capitalists on a franchise basis at the same time. Similar 'licensing' arrangements whereby large companies give regular contracts to Africans or hive off a small part of their commercial empire, perhaps to previous employees, exist in a number of business areas, especially repair and maintenance work on transport, plant or buildings. Many independent manufacturers also depend on large companies as their main sales outlet. In West Africa, local shoe firms, for example, may manufacture a very narrow range of products – sometimes only the soles or uppers for a particular kind of sandal – and are supplied by the 'customer' with some or all of the raw material inputs and the machinery required for production.[11]

Building contracting also offers fertile fields for these arrangements. Thus, large companies may sub-contract the least profitable and more labour-intensive aspects of their operations to jobbing builders. The latter use their social contacts with the pool of unemployed labourers found in most African cities in order to assemble a temporary work team whose members are hired on a short-term contract basis to carry out the simplest operations such as site clearance or digging foundations. Bromley and Gerry use these jobbing builders as one example of the phenomenon they have labelled as 'disguised wage labour'.[12] Here, petty producers and small capitalists appear to be self-employed, but in reality they represent a poorly paid extension of the labour force employed by foreign enterprise but without the advantages enjoyed by legally hired workers. This process enables foreign capital to minimise its permanent labour costs. 'Dependent wage work' involves a similar process except that here the small firm's financial dependence on credit or advances of raw materials enables the large company to make unfair gains by overpricing in addition, perhaps, to providing the main sales outlet for the former's products.

The implementation of indigenisation policies by African governments over the last 20 years, albeit with different degrees of seriousness and competence, has opened up yet new avenues for comprador activity. Thus, thirdly, the legal closure of certain business sectors to foreign ownership has sometimes generated evasive tactics, particularly on the part of Asian or Levantine firms whose concentration in the spheres of trade and light industry and small family-firm pattern of management has made them highly susceptible to the demand for transfer to African ownership. Evasion may take several forms including regrouping enterprises in conjunction with other non-nationals to create a larger enterprise with assets in excess of the legal minimum permitted to foreigners, marriage with local people or 'buying' the favours of well-placed government officials or politicians, with the latter assuming the role of comprador 'protector'.[13] Then there is the strategy whereby ownership is apparently transferred to indigenous proprietors but, in reality, the latter merely take on a 'fronting' role, providing illegal immunity from the indigenisation law in addition to other activities, such as championing the company's interests in dealing with government officials. Just how long such arrangements can survive, if the political climate in favour of indigenisation is strongly organised, as it appears to have been in the case of Nigeria during the 1970s, for example, and if the transfer to local ownership is firmly implemented by local officials, is not altogether clear.[14] In addition, much may depend on the skill and financial resources available to the Africans who perform the fronting operation. Able people with business interests of their own may become highly dissatisfied with a more or less passive role while the inexperienced and incompetent spokesperson is unlikely to appear very convincing to most outsiders for any length of time.

Fourthly, this kind of activity shades imperceptibly into another, fairly recent, legal form of business compradorship associated with the shift towards local ownership through the purchase of equity capital by African shareholders. Again, in Nigeria, the 1977 decree permitted minority local participation in the case of firms operating in the high-technology industries as mentioned before, but, insisted on majority (60%) or full Nigerian ownership in most other areas of business.[15] On the basis of her research into industrial firms based in Kano, Hoogvelt has indicated some of the relationships that can arise between foreign firms and Nigerians.[16] Existing local entrepreneurs may secure loan capital through government-sponsored banking schemes, family networks or accumulated business profits and then purchase a large proportion of an overseas company's available shares. Such a buyer might be a business rival or a trader heavily dependent on receiving supplies from the foreign firm in question. In Kano, Hoogvelt found that 70% of the equity sold to Nigerians by the 54 overseas companies she investigated were bought by 24 people. Many of these were substantial Muslim traders in their own right whose families enjoyed well-established business interests going back two or three generations. Six of these men bought 50% of all the divested shares.[17] Another possibility is that the foreign owners handpick the prospective shareholders, either because they wish to ensure that despite future majority indigenous ownership the company will remain under their control – for example, by distributing shares so widely that it is difficult for any one person to exercise real influence – or in order to secure shareholders and directors who seem content to remain in the background but who possess useful attributes. The first and second options are not incompatible as Hoogvelt observes.[18] Even very large shareholders, preoccupied with their own business affairs, may prefer to leave the firm's operations in the hands of the previous owner-managers, although some of the Kano traders she studied did take a very considerable interest in their new business interests. Yet another kind of relationship may involve the practice of 'arranging' for African managers or their high-up employees to become prominent shareholders or directors, thereby increasing their loyalty to the company whilst avoiding too much outside involvement.

Then there is the situation where a high proportion of those who purchase equity, especially in the case of larger, public companies, are well-placed government officials, politicians or military officers. By exploiting their official positions, influential connections or privileged access to information such people can, perhaps, ensure that an unfair proportion of government funds or private bank loans set aside for funding flow in their direction. Several researchers have argued that in the mid 1970s some of the Nigerian government's oil revenue ended up financing the emergence of a new private shareholding class.[19] It is important, however, not to confuse this particular abuse of public position with the process described by Schatz as 'pirate capitalism' – also in connection with Nigeria in the 1970s – where entrepreneurs become dependent primarily on massive government expenditure in the economy as their main source of business opportunity, though these may be closely related.[20] Also, to the extent that a very large proportion of profitable activity relies on the growing share of government expenditure in gross national production and, given that much of this is spent on imported goods and services, pirate capitalism could be said to constitute yet another form of business compradorship. Certainly, there seems to be a widespread belief that Nigeria's oil boom spawned a proliferation of commercially and service-orientated business activities that did little to increase the country's self-reliance or real productive capacity but helped to deepen Western penetration.

Another possible form of comprador activity, generated by the special circumstances prevailing during Nigeria's oil economy, is discussed by Turner.[21] She argues that as a result of the huge increase in government spending on imported manufactured goods a 'commercial triangle' emerged. This consisted of the representatives of the transnational corporations, seeking to persuade state and federal governments of the superiority of their products, the state comprador officials, who determined spending policy and allocated contracts, and private commercial middlemen. Normally Nigerian, these intermediaries cultivated special relationships with government officials and then offered their services to foreign sellers as go-betweens in exchange for fees when and if deals were negotiated between the other two parties. Because their profit depends on their ability to facilitate increased foreign penetration into the economy these private middlemen obviously deserve the comprador label. So, too, do the state officials, some of whom, according to Turner, managed to exclude the commercial entrepreneurs from these arrangements altogether.

Now it seems fairly clear from their comments that many observers of the Nigerian indigenisation programme do not believe that a genuine shift in control towards local people has taken place.[22] Even where experienced entrepreneurs become majority shareholders or directors their managerial involvement will probably be confined largely to marketing, public relations and personnel matters. Much more important, however, is Hoogvelt's point that the indigenisation measures may have substantially widened Nigerian ownership in many previously foreign-owned companies, but the latter's overseas connections and the continuing external monopoly control over the technological processes installed in the Nigerian subsidiaries means that 'real' control still eludes local people.[23] The aims behind indigenisation policy may also be in conflict. Should governments encourage widespread ownership, as happened in Nigeria where the 1977 decree limited individual share purchases to 5% of any one foreign company's stock, thereby making the exercise of local control very difficult, or should they foster concentrated ownership and therefore the possibility of much great influence by indigenous shareholders?[24] Several of the authors whose work we have discussed seem uncertain as to which alternative constitutes the greater evil.

Two main conclusions seem to follow from this discussion. One is that the recent indigenisation measures in Nigeria and elsewhere represent little more than a further twist in the long history of African economic dependency on metropolitan capitalism. The recent changes simply amount to a reconstruction of this relationship but at a higher level, with Africans being offered a further slice of the national cake in return for assuming roles that offer little real power as sleeping partners, quiescent directors or compliant shareholders. Secondly, business compradorship has changed in style over time, but not in form.

BUSINESS COMPRADORSHIP AND UNDERDEVELOPMENT: AN ALTERNATIVE VIEW

The comprador view of African capitalism would seem to be inadequate and misleading in a number of ways. Since it is an essential part of the wider Neo-Marxist theory of underdevelopment, the very considerable criticisms which have been levelled against the latter during the last 10 years or so necessarily undermine the basically collaborationist analysis of indigenous business, too. Later in this section we will examine some of the weaknesses associated with the underdevelopment perspective. Another major difficulty concerns the tensions and conflicts inherent in the relationship that supposedly exists between local and foreign capital, in particular, those that arise because African proprietors are victims of foreign domination as well as collaborators. Closely linked to this is the problem of motivation and the ways in which psychological and political as well as fundamental profit considerations shape the outlook and aspirations of indigenous entrepreneurs in ways that cannot always find proper expression solely through the acceptance of subordinate business roles. These problems will be taken up later in the chapter. Then there is the question of how prevalent comprador forms of business activity really are and why so little interest has been shown in other forms of entrepreneurship that cannot easily be accommodated by this model. We will now consider these alternative forms of African business activity with some care.

Non-comprador business activity

Most analyses of the comprador nature of African capitalism have little or nothing to say about other forms of entrepreneurship. By definition, their existence is peripheral to the main argument concerning the continuing dominance of Western interests. It is possible to stretch the notion of compradorship so as to include virtually all forms of indigenous activity on the grounds that so long as national economic dependency on foreign capital, technology and markets remains a reality, and given that powerful Western firms continue to operate in certain sectors then virtually all local proprietors are likely to have some sort of dealings with overseas companies, whether as suppliers or buyers, and all will be affected by their country's peripheral economic position. At the same time, if local firms are mostly small, compared to foreign companies, they will necessarily experience certain disadvantages. Here, merely to operate in the same universe of capitalist enterprises as metropolitan interest engenders the condition of compradorship. Pushed this far, the definition obviously becomes devoid of explanatory usefulness. Dealings between small and large firms occur everywhere in the world. In the advanced economies, to take but one example, numerous small- and medium-sized manufacturing enterprises in engineering and metal production rely on supplying various components to one or two huge corporations in the motor industry for their main sources of markets. The small–large relationship and the market-dependence factor are unavoidable and inextricable aspects of capitalist activity everywhere. No one seriously contends that in and of themselves they constitute a form of compradorship when they occur in Western economies. Nor, presumably, is the existence of different nationalities of ownership between negotiating firms to be regarded as a special feature of compradorship; certainly not in the age of the internationalisation of ownership and production characteristic of the late twentieth century. If Neo-Marxists do not intend the term to be used in this broad and indiscriminate manner, as they surely do not, it must be applicable, instead, to a rather narrower range of special activities. But *ipso facto*, it follows that other forms of non-comprador African business activity must also exist. The omission of these alternative kinds of entrepreneurship from most Neo-Marxist analyses is never really explained. What are these largely non-comprador forms of African business and what is the nature of their relationship with foreign capital?

The most obvious alternative to compradorship arises where straightforward competition takes place between local firms completely under indigenous control and foreign companies, both operating in the modern sector of the economy. In many countries, especially in West Africa but also in Kenya and Uganda, market rivalry has been a growing fact of economic life since the Second World War. For a long time, competition was mainly confined to the sphere of produce buying, retail trade, small contracting, transport and some services. But in Ghana, Nigeria and probably elsewhere too, local people were beginning to become established in a growing range of additional business activities from the 1950s onwards, some years before indigenisation policies of any substance had been introduced anywhere in Africa, and at roughly the same period that foreign firms were also attempting to diversify their economic base.[25] These included the following: wholesale trade, import–export activities, professional consultancy services, road haulage, vehicle repairs, timber and sawmilling, motorised fishing, hotels and restaurants, commercial farming involving crops other than the usual export commodities (for example, oil palm and vegetables linked to cosmetic manufacturing and food canneries) and, in addition, a wide range of light industrial activity, including furniture, garments, printing, rubber, leather and plastic products, stationery supplies, bakeries and other food processing such as vegetable oils and fruit juices, the manufacture of cement blocks and other building supplies and household metal products. By the late 1960s, some of these local entrepreneurs had built up quite large firms, employing 50 or even 100 people, and a few operated on a par with foreign subsidiaries in terms of technology, their ability to export and their relatively sophisticated management.[26]

It is true, however, that the majority of African businesses in countries like Nigeria, Ghana and Kenya, during the 1950s and 1960s, were small in size and not as yet strikingly different in organisation and technology from the vast number of one-person artisan enterprises and small workshops. Moreover, their foreign business rivals were not the subsidiaries of transnationals but Asians, Levantines and European expatriates who had lived in Africa for many years and owned medium-sized firms based on relatively labour-intensive production systems. Conflict between these struggling entrepreneurs not only for a share of the local market but also for equal access to public-sector contracts, foreign exchange, government loans and impartial bureaucratic treatment was often intense and many Africans complained bitterly that they did not enjoy the same degree of access to government resources as their overseas rivals. Partly because of the political pressure exercised by emergent local business groups, governments have introduced indigenisation measures during the last 20 years or so, though this process has been pushed much further in some countries like Kenya and Nigeria than in others. As we saw earlier, indigenisation policies would appear to have generated new forms of compradorship. On the other hand, where change has meant that large, sophisticated local firms owned almost entirely by African partners/shareholders have taken over previously foreign-owned companies operating with more advanced levels of technology and organisation, business rivalry at higher economic levels has also intensified.

A second, very large group of local proprietors whose activities cannot be subsumed under the comprador label consists of all those who compete not with foreign companies – since the latter are not especially interested in the business areas in question – but with numerous other local business rivals. Such firms are mostly small in scale, fairly simple in organisation, based on limited capital investment and cater mainly, though not entirely, for the lower end of the market. They have become differentiated from petty production in the following ways: they are enumerated in government statistics; employ at least a few permanent paid workers in addition to kinsmen and apprentices; the enterprise is conducted in a legally recognised building-cum-workshop and involves some plant and equipment, however meagre; there exists an elementary form of full-time organisation (the proprietor is not normally directly involved in production); the business is no longer dependent solely on individual clients, but a proportion of output is sold to other properly constituted enterprises; and the proprietor strives, not always very successfully, to reinvest some of the firm's profits in the pursuit of business expansion. Entrepreneurs of this kind operate in a wide range of business sectors: vehicle repairs; small-scale building contracting (usually involving private house owners or voluntary associations like churches rather than local or central government); bars, dance halls, disco parlours, hotels and restaurants in mainly poor areas; scrap-metal and spare-parts dealers; the manufacture of garments, bags, footwear, furniture and other goods mainly in small bulk orders of say 30 or 50 items for department stores, wholesale merchants–distributors (travelling to hinterland villages), schools, hospitals, and local army or police barracks; road haulage; professional services; retail distribution and many others.

Small firms like these constitute the everyday lifeblood of all modern or modernising capitalist economies. Social scientists and politicians in the advanced countries and the Third World have often been so preoccupied with the might of the transnational corporations, and the latters' enormous contributions to national employment, government revenue, exports and Gross National Product that there has been a tendency to overlook the degree to which everywhere small- and medium-sized firms constitute the numerical majority. Together their economic and political weight is also very formidable. Recent research in the advanced economies has shown, for example, that in Japan, Italy and America during the 1970s some 68%, 65% and 39% respectively of the total labour force employed in manufacturing were working in 'small' establishments of less than 200 people.[27] Even in Britain where the proportion has been quite low by international standards (estimated at 35% in 1982), census data reveals that the number of small manufacturing firms has increased rapidly in the last 20 years, so that by 1980 there were probably about 85,000 firms employing less than 100 people.

In most countries small firms of this kind are invariably owned by nationals or by immigrants who have recently secured citizenship rights. Being relatively simple in organisation and requiring resources which though not available to the majority are accessible to substantial minorities, they tend to provide the main starting point for the accumulation of capital and experience. For these reasons they also represent the obvious target for early indigenisation programmes in Third World countries. There seems no reason to believe that in those African countries where this strata of firm has yet to be completely colonised by local people this process will not continue rapidly in the near future.

In Africa, firms like these are often partly dependent on foreign companies for supplies and sales outlets, but this should not be exaggerated or misconstrued. In countries where an industrial base has been growing for some time, small companies increasingly procure a wide and growing range of services – vehicles and equipment repairs, transport facilities, and so on – as well as basic inputs of raw materials, parts and equipment, directly from other local firms, very similar in size and organisation to themselves; small workshops and factories, African merchant importers in their own right and small traders who have connections with larger import–export companies. In some business fields, like metal products and furniture manufacturing or vehicle repairs, it is often possible for inventive proprietors to improvise certain needed inputs by utilising second-hand machinery and spare parts and by recycling some used materials – though some writers regard these exercises in 'cannibalisation' not as evidence of enterprise in the true sense, but as yet another expression of dependency since it is foreign exchange shortages that normally prompt such measures.[28] In fact, obtaining supplies from large foreign or state organisations is often quite difficult because these tend to be unwilling to deal in the modest and irregular quantities required by small enterprises. On the market side, too, the needs of other local firms often provide a major source of sales outlets, especially urban market traders, up-country distributors and retailers. But job sharing between small specialist producers and sub-contracting are also commonplace. In these and other ways, an important nexus of interdependent and interlinked business relationships tends to grow up between the numerous enterprises operating at this level. Moreover, where large orders from powerful buyers are concerned, the state, and its numerous agencies at central and local level – schools, municipal offices, hospitals, state corporations and public utilities, army barracks and so on – are often much more important than foreign companies.[29]

So far we have discussed two groups of local entrepreneurs; those whose firms are too small, though thoroughly capitalist in orientation, to be of much concern to Western companies and those who run mostly medium-sized companies engaged in direct competition with foreign interests. Undoubtedly, however, there are many local proprietors who are involved in partnership arrangements with overseas firms. But there are several reasons why it may be possible to argue that these businessmen do not fit easily into the kinds of 'true' comprador situation described earlier on.

One such arrangement may arise when ambitious would-be entrepreneurs who currently lack sufficient capital and experience to launch their own business ventures form an alliance with one or more foreign residents who already possess considerable commercial expertise. Partnerships along these lines were not uncommon in Ghana, and possibly elsewhere in West Africa, too, between the 1940s and 1960s. Starting off as an employee, the African partner may eventually earn promotion to some kind of managerial position and be invited to sink a small amount of capital in the enterprise. The potential gains for the foreign owner are obvious. The African manager may be able to 'deal' more effectively with government officials, politicians, other local entrepreneurs and employees because of his greater familiarity with language, local culture and systems of patronage. In addition, the local partner's position may protect the firm from accusations that government indigenisation policies are being evaded, at least for a time.

A variation on this practice may occur where a greater or lesser proportion of the starting capital or necessary plant and equipment (perhaps second-hand, and no longer required by the European partner) used to set up an ostensibly local firm actually comes from a company operating abroad. The latter may wish to gain a foothold in the local market but lacks long-standing connections or may be too undercapitalised to establish a firm sufficiently large to exceed the minimum-size criteria dictated by government indigenisation measures. Although much more research needs to be carried out in this area, it seems highly likely that an increasing number of newly formed and 'locally' owned companies in the more developed African countries in recent years have followed this pattern, though the format has been established for several decades in countries like Ghana and Nigeria. What is happening in these cases is that one or more well-trained Africans, perhaps with specialist professional or technical qualifications and experience relevant to the business in question, provide some or most of the finance and local managerial organisation but rely on a well-established company based in Europe to provide equipment, back-up technical support and advice (including, possibly, an expatriate technician or production manager on 'loan' for a limited period), information on changing fashions and production techniques and probably the promise of later access to European markets, and so on. The African partner may be a former employee of the overseas company who once worked abroad for several years after completing an apprenticeship or technical course. As we have seen, indigenisation measures in countries like Nigeria have also obliged foreign subsidiaries already operating in Africa to invite local part-ownership and sometimes management. It is possible that technical exchanges with foreign companies based in Africa of the kind we have discussed, may figure largely in these arrangements, too, in the future.

Several important points need to be made concerning these examples of actual partnership. Firstly, many Neo-Marxist writers would view these relationships with great suspicion. Thus, collaboration becomes one of the most important prerequisites for indigenous capitalism but at the cost of strengthening economic dependency. In fact, the need for Kenyan businessmen to establish a widening range of social networks, including with foreign companies whether based in Africa or overseas, as a precondition for African business success was emphasised by Marris some years ago.[30] Moreover, some studies have shown that highly successful African entrepreneurs have often lived abroad for long periods of time and acquired European contacts.[31] It seems unreasonable to condemn those very experiences and arrangements which may help African entrepreneurs to build up a strong industrial base capable of competing in world markets.

Secondly, it is shortsighted not to realise that most Africans who enter partnership arrangements do so for sound, practical reasons. For example, they may have no alternative, given their lack of access to all kinds of resources. They may also believe that an alliance with a foreign company offers the prospect of real benefits which they can turn to their own long-term advantage. Among these might be the following: a sheltered environment in which to learn the skills of management under the tutelage of more experienced people; the opportunity to acquire a wide range of social and business contacts at home and abroad; access to technology and technical knowhow that is not so readily available to other local entrepreneurs; time in which to build upon their existing familiarity with the marketing and other problems associated with their chosen line of business; and partial immunity from the vicissitudes of the market, since their own capital and entrepreneurial inexperience are protected by the presence or assistance of foreign managers for a considerable period of time.

In short, the advantages of partnership arrangements may flow both ways. Just like his or her counterpart everywhere else, the shrewd, able and ambitious African will find ways to exploit the relationship. What seems surprising is that anyone should doubt this. Moreover, entrepreneurial skill and knowhow normally have to be acquired through concrete experience. Genetic inheritance, cultural orientations and class situation are insufficient in themselves to equip business leaders to perform competently the instant market opportunities are propitious. Becoming a successful entrepreneur is a learning experience in an environment where few things remain static for long. Initially the African partner's horizons may be fairly limited; retaining a newly acquired senior position or minority shareholding. But, given a reasonable amount of ambition, a growing awareness of the market potential and the gradual acquisition of resources and skills, many managers or directors may eventually seek either a more dominant position within the existing company or branch out on their own, perhaps in conjunction with other local people.

Research carried out in Ghana in the late 1960s revealed that some of the most successful indigenous proprietors had indeed passed through an earlier experience of this kind.[32] Their partnership arrangements, usually with foreign businessmen who had lived in Ghana for some years rather than with large companies, had been fairly short-lived. Most ended with the Ghanaian buying out the foreign partner or assuming total control. The arrangement provided one or more crucial advantages; access to bank loans or technical expertise, a series of useful contacts or a sound business reputation, assets which local partners could not initially supply for themselves. It was the Europeans who appear to have given most and gained least. If Ghanaians, and possibly their counterparts in other countries, too, were able to extract maximum advantages from relationships with Europeans in the 1950s and 1960s, when the political climate in favour of African capitalism was much less supportive than it has since become, it is difficult to see why a much greater number of equally determined individuals will not try to follow similar paths now that indigenisation measures have exposed a far higher proportion of overseas companies to the demands and ambitions of African people.

A general critique of underdevelopment theory

The strengths and weaknesses of the Neo-Marxist model have been competently and exhaustively assessed by a number of influential writers in recent years.[33] Accordingly, the discussion that follows makes no claims to present a thorough analysis of this debate and is confined to a few critical comments of special relevance to the subject of African business compradorship.

Writing mainly about Kenya and Nigeria, Beckman has argued that it is misleading to suggest Western capital still needs to hold back Third World development.[34] Profits may once have depended on the ability to squeeze surpluses out of inefficient, mainly household-based producers, primarily by manipulating prices or by preserving pre- and petty capitalist social forms as a reserve from which lowly-paid migrant wage workers could seek temporary employment in a few Western enclaves. But this has long ceased to be the only or even the main source of profit. The more advanced forms of appropriation now being established in Africa are based on the direct subordination of employees to the capitalist labour process and the attempt to extract relative rather than absolute surplus value through investment in high productivity. This means that metropolitan capital requires strong, competent domestic bourgeoisies capable of exercising state power in order to extend and consolidate the conditions for both foreign and local capitalist accumulation.

In denying that world capitalist development can be seen as a 'zero-sum' game, in which one group of countries can only grow if another group experiences permanent stagnation, Beckman's position is very much in line with Brenner's influential restatement of the theoretical Marxian position on world capitalist development, published in the *New Left Review* in 1977.[35] In any case, it is simplistic to suppose that Western interests are homogeneous, united and therefore capable of wielding concerted long-term strategies calculated to misdevelop entire regions of the global economy. Individual firms are interested in maximising gain in the pursuit of capital accumulation; they invest in the periphery as and when circumstances are propitious. It is true that the anarchy of the market – now on a global basis – makes it difficult for individual capitalists to create conditions favourable for development at the national level. Only local classes, elites and states wield the level of overall power required to ensure this kind of change. But this has always been the case. Because individual capitalist interests are inept in this respect does not mean that they are also opposed to wider development.

Then there is the question of Western technological supremacy. Underdevelopment theorists claim that any attempt by Third World countries to establish a local industrial capacity will simply increase their dependency. Industrial self-reliance and therefore freedom from indebtedness, external interference and unequal exchange require some kind of socialist path. But there are a number of difficulties with this position. Firstly, as Emmanuel has argued, the idea that Third World countries will overcome their backwardness by avoiding the use of advanced Western technology except, perhaps, in a few 'essential' sectors, and by relying, instead mainly on simpler, labour-intensive production systems, is not easy to accept since such a strategy will actually widen the technological gap between North and South.[36] It will often be very difficult for such countries to compete effectively in world markets except in manufactured exports of mediocre quality. Further, many industrial activities do not offer a range of technological options; the only choice is between one kind of advanced production system or another. None of this need matter if a given country is prepared to forgo the advantages of high technology. But it is by no means clear that most socialist Third World countries today are strongly committed to a development strategy based largely on intermediate technology as a necessary expedient for ensuring a high degree of industrial autonomy so it is not easy to see why non-socialist countries should be any different.

Secondly, technological self-reliance should not be confused with economic autarky. Even the most populous, economically advanced countries, plentifully endowed with a range of natural resources, do not necessarily wish to pursue complete economic independence. Moreover, technological advance is increasingly costly and few, if any, countries can hope to remain in the forefront of every kind of development. Indeed, the much envied post-war Japanese economic successes in world markets appear to have been partly based on a state-led strategy designed to predict future economic 'winners' and then concentrate private and public resources in the selected areas. In the highly integrated world economy of the late twentieth century most, if not all, countries exist in a state of relative economic and technological dependency, though it would be foolish to deny that some countries are much more dependent than others and that this crucially affects their economic fortunes.

Lastly, the belief that unequal control over and access to technological pre-eminence is a permanent condition seems to be based on the argument that technology is never really transferable between the more and less developed countries. Partly this is because the condition of relative backwardness is assumed to be fixed (true, by definition), and partly it arises because the transnational corporations are supposedly able to monopolise their control over technology through a blend of secrecy, collusion, corruption, threats, the manipulation of international laws pertaining to patent rights and sheer exploitation. But what really lies behind the physical and technical capacities inherent in each 'package' of equipment is a set of interlocking skills, derived in turn from the attainment of various kinds of knowledge. Now, the latter manifestly are transferable, particularly when determined governments pursue policies designed to establish extensive and advanced educational systems in their countries as well as the facilities required for scientific research.[37] This is precisely what the most rapidly industrialising countries, such as Brazil and South Korea, have been doing for a number of years. Fransman, among others, has argued that the newly industrialising countries have in fact pursued a wide range of strategies in order to build up a local technological capability and reduce their dependence on foreign companies.[38] These include the following: supervising agreements with foreign companies so as to minimise the restrictions imposed by the latter on the wider application of imported technology; insisting on considerable degrees of private, local or state participation; forbidding foreign companies to acquire local firms; encouraging the development of local heavy industry through government preferment policies, protection and subsidies; giving priority to imported technology regarded as most relevant to national development at a given time; and providing finance to enable local firms to adapt and improve imported machinery whilst utilising the results of government-sponsored research and development programmes.

In any case, it is worth mentioning that late development is not a new phenomenon. Every industrial country except Britain has faced the problem of 'catching up'. Tariff protection, subsidies, inducements to attract certain kinds of foreign investors, encouraging skilled personnel from overseas to train local technicians, sending students and entrepreneurs abroad for long periods of time, imitating, adapting and modifying imported technology in addition to building up a national scientific and educational capacity – all of these strategies and many more worked effectively for the United States, Germany, Japan and other countries in the nineteenth century. Moreover, Japan continued to copy, borrow and adopt Western technology right up to the Second World War and after.[39] Without minimising the doubtless much greater problems faced by Third World countries today, compared with previous late developers, it nevertheless seems valid to suggest that the extreme difficulties associated with the successful transplantation and absorption of foreign technology have almost certainly been exaggerated and misunderstood.

A final criticism of the dependency position concerns the question of import-substitution industry. It could be argued that one major reason why many African countries have experienced the problems that Neo-Marxists identify with the condition of economic dependency – indebtedness, limited job creation, capital outflow and so on – has more to do with the choice of development strategy than anything else. The attempt to establish a domestic industrial capacity mainly by concentrating on import-replacing industries, especially in the consumer-goods sector, has often proved to be self-terminating beyond a certain point.[40] Thus, insufficient attention may be given to the need to establish backward linkages with other sectors. Imports of equipment and loans are made easier to bear by permitting currency overevaluation, but this in turn makes the exporting of primary commodities and manufactured goods very difficult. Moreover, the income generated by such industry is often too small and inequitably distributed – given its low employment-creating capacity – to generate a home market large enough to sustain expansion. If import-substitution industry is coupled with agricultural neglect and an over-administered economy offering ample scope for bureaucratic corruption, it is not difficult to see why so many of the symptoms associated with economic dependency are all too evident in many countries.[41] However, most of this is avoidable as the case of South Korea (and some of the other South-East Asian countries) clearly demonstrates.[42] Here, from the late 1950s, governments gave priority to the creation of an export-oriented economy specialising, initially, in the kinds of manufactured goods that a labour-surplus country with a hitherto low technological capacity could manage. Gradually, through experience and with appropriate government support, a highly competitive industrial base was built up relying mainly on local capital and expertise. In the 1970s, more advanced industries were established without over-reliance on foreign capital. The foreign exchange required to finance capital imports in the early and later stages of industrialisation were obtained through utilising short-term government-guaranteed suppliers' credits, encouraging local savings, devaluations and confining foreign exchange expenditure to essential imports only. Thus, industrial expansion was financed largely by using the earnings from one phase of export growth to pay for the next. Of course, the favourable external environment provided by a period of world economic expansion during the 1960s and early 70s was very important to this process as most observers readily acknowledge. Nevertheless, the presence of a highly competent state (albeit an extremely repressive and authoritarian one) able to wield an enormous range of powers and a political and ideological system willing to foster and tolerate the emergence of potentially powerful private and public entrepreneurial groups, were also crucial. Unfortunately neither of these have been very much in evidence over the last 25 years in most African countries, as we argued in Chapter 4.

FROM DEPENDENCY TO 'PARTNERSHIP' AND RELATIVE SELF-RELIANCE?

Once the 'pure' dependency scenario is rejected and it is conceded that metropolitan capital now desires a rapid advance in the development of the productive forces in Africa, it is possible to envisage a number of changes taking place; indeed these may already be happening. Thus, the relationship between local and Western interests undergoes a fundamental shift from one of satellisation to 'partnership' on terms which if not yet equal are considerably less unequal than previously. The transition exists on several levels and involves a number of dimensions.

Firstly, if Western capital seeks a more broadly based economic development process in Africa, with all the profitable opportunities this may bring through expanding markets, a more productive labour force and greater accessibility to physical resources, then as Beckman argues, Western interests must also wish to see the emergence of competent states controlled by dynamic domestic bourgeoisies whose members can generate the conditions for capitalist advance – property rights, political stability, law and order, appropriate labour relations, agricultural development, sound administration, and so on.[43] But, secondly, the advent of a new, more intensive stage of Western involvement in Africa, while hastening the development of the productive forces, is also likely to improve the prospects for some countries to attain a much greater degree of economic autonomy. Writing about Nigeria and Kenya respectively, Beckman and Swainson argue that these changes have been associated with an increasing tendency towards the domestication of ownership and production as a growing indigenous capitalist class has moved into more and more economic sectors.[44] Nigeria and Kenya have also become increasingly internationalised and these changes seem likely to occur elsewhere in Africa, too. To this extent, therefore, dependency theorists point to certain real constraints. Developing countries that pursue a basically capitalist path cannot entirely avoid exposure to the pressures of the world economy, though their governments may try to minimise some of the more destructive consequences arising from this. The price of continued access to metropolitan technology, finance, and expertise and, above all, markets, is twofold: a corresponding insistence on the part of Western interests that they continue to be allowed access, whether directly or indirectly, to the national economy and the latter's increasing incorporation into a highly interdependent global economy. Each of these two processes – domestication and internationalisation – is a condition for the other.[45] Without growing involvement in the world economy and access to its markets and resources, a domestic bourgeoisie cannot grow stronger and contribute to national economic development. Unless domestic classes and the state are encouraged and perhaps helped to deepen and extend the process of local economic development, then metropolitan capital cannot realistically hope to see continued expansion take place in the international economy or the majority of Third World countries remain within the capitalist orbit.

Thirdly, it is probably true that in the late twentieth century both the sheer technical and financial superiority of metropolitan capital and the extent to which the world economy has become internationalised continue to make it much more difficult for any would-be industrialising country to attain not so much the status of an advanced economy but the kind of allround, self-reliant development, where most resources remain firmly under domestic ownership, characteristic of say the United States, Japan or Germany in the nineteenth and early twentieth centuries. However, as several writers have pointed out, there is no ideal, unalterable and necessary pattern of capitalist development.[46] Circumstances change as do the forms of capitalist expansion and the predominant ways in which the law of value finds expression through the activities of states, classes and individuals. Today, it is simply a fact of world economic life that, to a greater or lesser degree, all countries – including the most and the least advanced as well as those claiming to be socialist – experience a situation where their systems of production and distribution are partly owned, managed and certainly influenced by the representatives of overseas interests even as their own nationals seek similar involvements in other countries. It is the terms on which these exchanges take place and the extent to which they are, or might in future become, subject to greater mutuality that is really important, not the basic reality of extensive foreign ownership within national boundaries, *per se*.

What implications do these broader national changes have for African governments and local capitalist classes? As the capitalist relations of production penetrate further into the fabric of African economic life and foreign companies intensify their involvement, so too the role of local capital will expand both as an increasingly important element in the national bourgeoisie and as an essential agent servicing the needs of Western expansion. But as the African capitalist class grows in numbers, wealth and organisation, albeit initially and primarily in a comprador capacity, the ability of its members to wield greater influence over government policy and to express discontent concerning their unequal relationship with Western companies, as economic growth proceeds, may both become increasingly evident. In any case, as we have seen, some local business groups already operate in direct competition with overseas companies and feel deep grievances because they lack the same advantages. Moreover, in some African countries indigenous entrepreneurs have already secured certain concessions through indigenisation policies and it is difficult to see why they should not demand more. At the same time, as state officials gain experience and competence and also, perhaps, become increasingly exposed to the demands of the urban and rural masses, on whom the changes associated with more rapid and intensive capitalist development directly impinge, they may impose greater demands and restrictions on foreign capital.

As all these relationships unfold the state may also be called upon to adjudicate between the conflicting interests represented by local and foreign firms or may perceive that national development requires such intervention. In doing so, officials and politicians will not necessarily follow a consistent course of siding more with one interest rather than another. Thus, in the Kenyan case Langdon has demonstrated that during the 1970s the government sometimes acted to assist foreign subsidiaries.[47] For example, on one occasion it refused to alter the way in which excise taxes were levied, although this effectively discriminated against local competition. On another occasion, public officials worked to establish a partnership between local owners, the government and a foreign subsidiary. But there were also situations where different kinds of state aid, such as the allocation of public loans or the exercise of discretion in the interpretation of government legislation, were used so as to favour Kenyan entrepreneurs.

In short, the move to a partnership basis in the relationship between foreign capital and the different factions of the national bourgeoisie and the state means that these relations become much more complex, volatile and uncertain. They are more susceptible to changing conflicts, alliances and tensions whose resolution, one way or the other, cannot easily be predicted. Much will depend on the historical circumstances and configuration of class forces prevailing in each particular country.

In addition, there are certain tensions and conflicts inherent in the partnership relationship between the domestic bourgeoisie and foreign capital and these are likely to become highly unstable over time. It is probable, therefore, that local capitalists will increasingly strive not merely to improve their bargaining position *vis-à-vis* foreign capital but to move into some kind of hegemonic position. In doing so they will inevitably have to turn to government and politicians for assistance. Moreover, some governments, at least, may be increasingly prepared to provide such help in the years ahead, partly because of pressures emanating from within the spheres of government bureaucracy and politics itself and partly because of wider tensions operating in the economy and society. We will now consider what forces may be at work impelling both local capitalist groups and African governments to seek a greater degree of economic autonomy in their relations with metropolitan interests.

Tensions inherent in the business comprador relationship

Earlier in this chapter it was suggested that there are certain difficulties involved in regarding comprador business groups as both victims and willing collaborators. In order to explore this question we will assume for the purposes of analysis that there are, perhaps, three 'ideal-type' situations involving business collaboration and that the majority of actual arrangements approximate to one or other of these. One situation involves the frontman who is either not very competent and experienced or who lacks ambition and drive or both. This dearth of qualities means that more promising and lucrative avenues for personal advance elsewhere are closed to him. For this reason he is grateful for the rewards he receives as a frontman, providing legal or political legitimacy for a foreign company, even though these are meagre compared to the profits that accrue to the latter. Then there is the case of the hired African manager-cum-director, possibly enjoying some shareholding rights as well, who is reasonably experienced and well trained, increasingly competent at his job and ambitious to better his long-term prospects for self-improvement. Because he is both aspiring and able, he is impatient to establish his own business as soon as possible, or seek even better employment prospects. Accordingly, he is likely to feel aggrieved because other firms or managers/directors – and non-nationals at that – are in a position to pre-empt the most favourable opportunities which, had his own personal circumstances been somewhat different, he might have been able to pursue instead. Thus, ambition and ability on the one hand and lack of resources on the other mean that such a person is indeed an unwilling victim who seeks escape from his predicament. Thirdly, there is the African entrepreneur established in his own right. He forms an arrangement with a foreign firm based either on the purchase of shares – as may happen following certain kinds of indigenisation programme – or on some kind of business exchange involving a buyer–supplier relationship, except that the foreign firm in question may be the main or even sole source of market demand or inputs.

Several observations can now be made. It seems unlikely that someone occupying one of these comprador positions can be both unwilling victim, only forced by circumstances to assume a subordinate and not very profitable role, and grateful, compliant collaborator at one and the same time. This being so, it follows that in the case of our second and third ideal-type situations, those involved are likely to be less than content, given their subordinate and unequal position and current lack of opportunity to improve their situation. Conflicts and tensions in the partnership, therefore, seem very likely. Those concerned are likely to seek more promising avenues, to desire a more dominant position, to bide their time until their personal circumstances permit the formation of a breakaway or independent company or to quarrel over their share of the rewards. If these alternatives fail to produce results they may become resentful and uncooperative and this cannot fail to harm the dominant partner, too. However they are viewed, such comprador situations are inherently unstable. A changing political climate that eventually leads to state support for various indigenisation measures may be eagerly exploited by the victim-partners in the attempt to improve their own personal positions and acquire greater relative independence.

Even in the case of the frontman collaborator who is not, apparently, an unwilling victim at all, certain tensions may arise. For example, there is the possibility that he will be humiliated by other African employees or the European managers because his lack of competence is all too obvious to everyone. Alternatively, he may feel threatened, since there will be no shortage of poorly trained, impecunious local substitutes who could replace him at any time. Then there is the likelihood that in a changing political climate, where hostility to such relationships is increasing, the arrangement will be exposed by outsiders or perhaps the African partner will threaten to do so in the attempt to negotiate higher returns. The entire situation, therefore, is likely to become highly unsatisfactory to both sides. If this kind of comprador arrangement is to remain viable, the compliant frontman needs to be thoroughly indolent, unambitious and insensitive to the way others view him, as well as incompetent and lacking in opportunity. Whilst there are doubtless innumerable citizens who are highly eligible to fulfil these conditions, exactly the same is true in every other country. The existence of incompetent, untrained, unambitious people cannot, therefore, provide a satisfactory explanation for African underdevelopment. Even those whose only resort is the frontman role, may over time, gradually acquire confidence, skill, knowledge and wider personal horizons, so that they come to resemble more closely the aspiring victim, anxious to secure greater personal scope. As educational standards rise and the range of available occupational experiences widen, those Africans who are attracted by partnership arrangements with foreign firms may find that their bargaining power improves. It is difficult to believe that they will not use this to maximum personal advantage.

There is also the question of what kinds of bargain can be struck in the case of much more genuine partnerships between Africans and foreign companies of the kind described by Hoogvelt in the case of Kano in Nigeria. Here, entrepreneurs who had already built up substantial businesses of their own, normally in trade, were able to purchase considerable quantities of equity stock in overseas companies. Some assumed directorship positions but were usually sleeping partners. Alternatively, their managerial contribution was mainly confined to marketing matters. Since these entrepreneurs possess a good deal of business experience and have considerable accumulations of hard-won capital tied up in various ventures it is impossible to doubt their shrewdness and ability to look after their own interests. Presumably they can be trusted to obtain the best possible deal from their European partners and to keep a watchful eye over their new investments. It is possible to imagine that at some future time they may wish to play a much more active role if they feel that their interests are being neglected, or the European management is failing to exploit all the available opportunities. To label these arrangements as 'comprador' seems neither necessary nor helpful. In any case, relationships like these between different companies, along with interlocking directorships, sleeping partnerships, market pooling arrangements, and so on, abound all over the Western world. They are hardly unique to Nigeria.

This brings us to the underlying question of motivation. For collaboration to become a permanent obstacle to economic development it has to be assumed that, unlike aspiring capitalists elsewhere, African partners somehow operate in a kind of economic vacuum where they are relatively immune from all the incentives and pressures that provide a large part of the engine power driving the capitalist mode of production forwards: the need to seek even higher rates of return, to achieve capital accumulation and to protect the capital stock already built up, within the constraints set by a competitive market economy.[48] Now there may be situations where a capitalist rationality does not fully operate. Government officials and politicians, for example, may invest funds in a foreign company that they have obtained illegally through exploiting their position. As such they may regard their 'savings' as a gratuitous bonus with which it is possible to gamble. Even here, however, it seems much more likely that the partner or manager will not only wish to avoid losses but will also anticipate gains and be prepared to act so as to enhance these whether they are measured in terms of profits, improved career prospects due to business expansion or both.

This concern with gain must be even more pronounced, in fact unavoidable, where indigenous partners or proprietors of auxiliary firms, dependent on the fortunes of larger foreign companies, have placed some of their own capital at risk. At the very least, ownership must create a fear of loss and a determination to avoid this. However, when possession involves not just wealth like houses, consumer durables, liquid assets, but investment in capital-creating assets – the means of production and distribution – and these are inevitably exposed to the force of competition, then the possibility of failure on the part of senior partners or oneself breeds a level of concern and involvement of a much higher order. Of course, entrepreneurs can decide to convert their productive assets into government securities, real estate or land. But first they have to build up such a stock of capital and in most African countries few people have been able to live comfortably on inherited wealth alone, at least up till now.[49] In the meantime they may become 'hooked' by the compulsion to accumulate, partly because it is rewarding and partly because market pressures and the need to protect existing assets drives them to make further capital investments, and so on. Thus it would seem that African business collaborators, especially those who have invested some of their own resources, cannot evade the same remorseless logic – or wish to, in view of the potential gains from expansion – confronting other kinds of capitalists. In the long run, this same compulsion may drive them not only to seek expansion in their own service company and/or the parent firm, but also to find ways of attaining greater autonomy, since the rewards from this promise to be even greater.

Capitalist orientations towards business activity may be reinforced by certain non-economic motivations as well. One such motivation might be patriotism; a desire to see one's country take its proper place in the world of nations free from the humiliation of being constantly associated in the eyes of the international community with dependency, poverty, corruption and ineptitude. Strong sentiments of this kind may induce African entrepreneurs to demand government policies designed to foster a greater degree of national economic autonomy even if, on another level, their own immediate economic interests are tied up in some kind of collaborative arrangement and might even be threatened by such measures. Certainly, local entrepreneurs who are in direct competition with foreign firms and wish the government to curb the latters' market power for straightforward economic reasons, may find nationalist sentiments particularly useful in helping them to legitimise their grievances.

Many writers on contemporary African social and political life have commented on the widespread desire for self-employment: the yearning to be one's own master, beholden to no one.[50] In part this is associated with the problems of job insecurity and low wages in the formal sector alongside the continuing opportunities provided by petty production. For many women, the goal of self-employment normally has rather more to do with the desire to reduce economic dependence on husbands and kin, the need to be self-supporting because of marital instability or the difficulties involved in receiving regular economic support from husbands.[51] However, in addition to this blend of economic necessity and personal ambition, there seems to be a general cultural emphasis, too, on the value of independence and the significance of this should not be underestimated. If the desire for economic autonomy and the wish to be a source of support and livelihood for others is culturally supported and provides one of the mainsprings of the initial move to establish African businesses, it seems unlikely that such sentiments will evaporate completely, if at all, as and when entrepreneurs become involved in some kind of partnership arrangement with a foreign company. Moreover, once self-esteem has come to be based partly on the ability to exercise the role of autonomous decisionmaker, it cannot be easy for an entrepreneur to suddenly relinquish it and assume a subordinate position even if the economic rewards are considerable.

There is also the possibility that some entrepreneurs are strongly imbued with the impulse to win. This may be an established personality trait. Alternatively, as the old adage claims, nothing succeeds like success. The actual experience of struggling for survival and making headway in a competitive environment may be more than sufficient to explain why some African entrepreneurs, like their counterparts elsewhere, develop a 'winning streak'; the desire to outpace all their rivals including, eventually, foreign competitors. Schumpeter pointed to yet another source of entrepreneurial drive: 'the dream and the will to found a private kingdom'.[52]

The potential power of such non-economic motivations should not be underestimated just because it is difficult to quantify or weigh their causal significance.

Pressures within governments

In view of the arguments put forward in Chapters 4 and 5, it would appear that very substantial pressures indeed will be necessary in order to bring about a major shift in the policy orientation of some African governments so that they are increasingly prepared to pursue a much greater degree of relative national economic self-reliance in the future. But it is also important to ask what forces might induce them to foster a vigorous and expanding local capitalist class capable of assuming a much greater role in national development than hitherto alongside a strong state and foreign sector or even in preference to one or both of these? Three pressures that may propel at least some African governments in this direction seem especially significant: the political demands expressed by indigenous capitalist groups, as their grip on the local economy increases; the emergence of certain modernising and technocratic groups within the various branches of the government bureaucracy – 'progressive' elements of the state bourgeoisie – and the growing economic crises facing many countries alongside the increased political pressures and discontents emanating from the rural and urban masses. The first of these possible sources of change has already been dealt with (see pp. 125–6) so the discussion that follows concentrates on the second of these. We will take up the question of economic crisis and wider political unrest, and the changes these may help to generate, in the concluding chapter.

If various elite groups are able to identify their own personal ambitions with the goal of national development this may have important implications especially if they hold commanding positions in the state bureaucracy and politics. With regard to Nigeria and several other countries, some writers have alluded to the existence of such emergent groups whose members share a growing concern with the need to establish a self-reliant economy firmly under indigenous control. According to Turner these 'technocrats' are mostly employed in the state corporations.[53] They have received a thoroughly professional training in managerial, scientific or other specifically vocational areas and are experienced in running complex productive and administrative systems. Many have been trained or employed abroad for long periods, perhaps in large organisations. They are used to working as part of a team of specialists and they are imbued with Western-type universalistic (a term used by sociologists to denote a pattern of behaviour where everyone belonging to the same role category or social position is treated alike) cultural orientations. Turner contrasts these technocrats with the 'generalist administrators' who are skilled in handling social contacts and whose training was largely non-vocational. They manage committees concerned with overall policy direction. Their education, bureaucratic experience and personal aptitudes have equipped them admirably to play the role of negotiators and intermediaries who allocate government contracts between the representatives of transnational corporations in return for unofficial fees, thereby perpetuating the commercial capitalism supposedly characteristic of Nigeria during the oil boom. Some of these administrators were highly placed in government ministries and their compradorist inclinations tended to prevail, at least until the mid 1970s, as against the more disciplined economic motivation shared by the technocrats.

Beckman and Collins also give strong hints concerning the existence of a burgeoning stratum of technocrats-cum-administrators quite widely dispersed through the Nigerian public sector.[54] Similar emergent groups have also been identified in other countries, for example in the Ivory Coast from the late 1960s and in Ghana in the late 1970s. In Ghana, a rather effective and dedicated group of well-trained officials employed in the newly established Ghana Enterprise Development Commission successfully implemented the provisions embodied in the 1975 Investment Policy Decree – a measure concerned with the indigenisation of small-scale industrial entrepreneurs. Also in Ghana, Hansen and Collins have argued that one of the reforms pursued during the first Rawlings' government in 1979 involved empowering officials to break the connections that had been established during the previous Acheampong regime between certain army officers and foreign business groups, particularly the Lebanese.[55] Why should these progressive government groups believe that local private capital needs to be given much greater encouragement, rather than continuing to place primary emphasis on an ever-expanding state sector, and how might their will eventually prevail over the comprador political and bureaucratic insiders?

Firstly, a considerable proportion of the ruling stratum of politicians and officials are engaged in private business activity in their own right either as shareholders or sleeping partners in enterprises run by kinsmen, friends or foreign owners, or as part-time proprietors who manage their own firms. By itself this is probably insufficient to sway government policy. Thus, it is claimed that public officials often denigrate the abilities of local capitalists, whether for reasons of ideology or careerism.[56] Also, bureaucrats and politicians who engage in private business activity are protected from the full impact of the market because they enjoy well-paid secure jobs and they may be able to use their insider positions to obtain guaranteed government contracts or a disproportionate share of the public funding provided, ostensibly, to assist private entrepreneurs, as for example when indigenisation measures are being implemented.[57] Consequently, the private interests of many public officials may lean either towards relatively non-productive activities in real estate, commerce, financial services, importing, and so on, as several observers contend, or may involve comprador activities of one kind or another.

Nevertheless, and secondly, even where public officials are involved in private business activity of a mainly auxiliary nature, the same long-term tendencies that seem likely to induce full-time entrepreneurs to increasingly assert their independence from foreign firms while seeking to dominate the more profitable business sectors, are likely to prevail in the case of salaried people as well. To the extent that this occurs, their ability to influence government policy from within could prove immensely important in strengthening the provision of institutional support for local capital. Writers like Leys and Swainson believe that just such a process of step-by-step government support for Kenyans has been in evidence since Independence and the balance may already have tipped firmly in favour of advancing local rather than foreign interests.[58] The Kenyan situation is probably rather exceptional. According to Leys, many Kenyans who sought advancement in politics and government bureaucracy after the Second World War were already engaged in capitalist accumulation, mainly in agriculture or land ownership, so that public-sector employment was always an additional source of wealth, alongside business activity, not a substitute for it or a preferred alternative as in so many other African countries.[59] In a very short time, however, the same situation will arise elsewhere as the next generation of public officials, probably of middle-class origins, enter government service from a family background encompassing both private business and professional employment.

But, thirdly, there is a strong possibility that a high proportion of those who belong to what Turner and others have identified as the 'technocratic' stratum will also become increasingly involved in business endeavour. In fact, the flow of experienced, professional trained public-sector people into private enterprise has been well established in Nigeria, Zambia, Ghana and probably elsewhere, too, for some years.[60] If such people are as strongly imbued with the ideology of economic nationalism as has been suggested, then the combination of technical competence, discipline, the availability of wide-ranging social connections and a firm belief in the pursuit of technological independence may enable them to become highly formidable entrepreneurs. Lastly, frustration with government incompetence, in addition, perhaps, to the reality of dwindling career opportunities – if and when economic stagnation forces governments to pursue policies of retrenchment with regard to the public sector – may combine to increase the movement of technocrats and others into private activity.

Additional pressures encouraging governments to take a more positive view of local capitalism are also at work especially the following: political unrest caused by economic stagnation; the chronic shortage of foreign exchange – making it essential to encourage self-reliance, develop new sources of export earnings, perhaps including certain kinds of manufactured goods, and reduce the outflow of profits earned by foreign companies; and the dismal record exhibited by the public sector so far in most African countries. We will consider these questions in more detail in the concluding chapter.

§ 7 §

THE CULTURAL AND ECONOMIC CLIMATE

Previous chapters concentrated on the formidable difficulties faced by African entrepreneurs resulting from economic dependency and foreign competition as well as the exercise of state and political power both during the colonial period and since Independence. We have argued that in most countries these forces, particularly the latter, generated an inauspicious, even hostile climate for indigenous business activity. However, many social scientists have focussed their attention on certain additional constraints which they regard as equally or perhaps more detrimental to African capitalism than those we have so far discussed. Though not without their limitations, these views and research findings are both interesting and suggestive. To a considerable extent they complement the broad, historical macro-analyses we have already considered. Accordingly, they merit some examination.

The economists, sociologists and anthropologists whose work we will consider have explored a number of closely related themes: for example, the role of the entrepreneur in spearheading the transformation from 'traditional' to 'modern' society; the different patterns of business behaviour to be found in societies undergoing economic development; the nature of the cultural, social and economic environment for business enterprise and the various obstacles it presents, and the qualities shown by entrepreneurs themselves and the ways in which these help to determine success or failure. Although the discussion in this and the next chapter will consider these themes, it is impossible to do full justice to them all. Thus, the present chapter concentrates on what various social scientists have said concerning the effects of the cultural, social and economic climate while in the next we examine the quality of entrepreneurial endeavour and its implications for firm expansion.

TRADITIONAL CULTURE AND SOCIETY AS CONSTRAINTS ON AFRICAN BUSINESS

During the 1950s and 1960s the ideas associated with the sociology of development approach or modernisation theory interested a number of writers, including some economists.[1] In their quest for insights into the problems of economic change the modernisation theorists drew upon the discipline of sociology.[2] At that time sociology was still heavily influenced both by the theories and concepts that were deeply rooted in the West's own nineteenth-century experience of industrial transformation and by structural functionalism and the writings of its foremost exponent, Talcott Parsons. In constructing his own theoretical system, Parsons had interpreted and built on the work of earlier sociologists, particularly Spencer, Durkheim and Weber. Essentially, Parsons was interested in the question of how order is maintained in a given society through the way in which institutions complement one another and contribute to the functioning of the social whole. At the same time, he believed that the dominant value system, as embodied in culture, shapes everyday role behaviour and interactions. Socialisation ensures that individuals acquire a more or less similar 'social' personality appropriate to the kinds of role behaviour necessary for the maintenance of social structure.[3] Thus, economic and technical activities are inextricably bound up with and underpinned by the web of social relations and the cultural ethos.

Informed by these and other ideas, the modernisation theorists produced a particular set of views concerning Third World development and the factors which might either impede or hasten it. Central to their interpretation was the argument that the interdependence of structure, culture and personality meant that by their very nature most traditional societies contained built-in obstacles to change. Hagen, for example, argued that in a 'typical' pre-capitalist society the value system would characteristically emphasise the importance of respect for secular authority and religious deities and the virtues of strict loyalty to kin and community. People would reach adulthood imbued with certain deeply felt personality needs: the desire to belong and to conform to the rigidly hierarchical social order.[4] Of course, the argument that tradition and modernity are incompatible is highly suspect and has been shown to be empirically unfounded.[5] In Chapters 2 and 3 we saw how in many parts of Africa community, lineage, gender and authority relations were often adapted very successfully to the requirements and inducements of the colonial economy.

Another favourite theme found in the writings of the modernisation theorists concerns the potential advantages associated with the process of cultural diffusion between societies. This might result from travel, trade, the spread of religious ideas or colonial conquest. The evolutionary break-throughs achieved in certain societies might then become available to others. Once such cultural transplants had taken root, backward societies might be able to jump over one or more of the stages of historical evolution through which the 'donor' societies had once passed and so embark on a process of rapid change.[6] As many critics have observed, such arguments appear to equate the Third World's struggle to achieve modernisation with the process of becoming Western, ignoring the possibility that this may be neither possible nor desirable in all respects or instances.[7]

But exposure to the 'benevolent' effects of Western influence may not be the only source of change. According to writers like Hoselitz, McClelland and Hagen, some traditional societies contain special change-bearing groups whose members may be able to reverse the condition of inertia, perhaps alongside the changes brought by Western contact.[8] Because traditional interests and customs are so resistant to change, such in-novatory groups, whether they are political elites, entrepreneurs or both, will need to be equipped with very powerful ideological and psychological resources if they are to emerge at all. Rising economic opportunities alone will not usually be sufficient to generate dynamic entrepreneurs in the absence of these cultural energies. Thus, the supply of non-traditional business groups is relatively inelastic in relation to market demand at any one time. Hoselitz, for example, argued that the condition of social mar-ginality, where a given group experiences discrimination and social isola-tion by virtue of their minority ethnic, linguistic or religious status, might provide one such vital source of group innovation: the desire to seek prosperity and security through the energetic pursuit of low-status activi-ties despised by the majority.

If certain personality traits are crucial to entrepreneurial activity, par-ticularly self-reliance and a pre-occupation with individual achievement, and these are mainly acquired through childhood socialisation, then it follows that ethnicity or religious affiliation may well be closely correlated to the incidence of entrepreneurship, since these represent likely sources of the all-encompassing cultural packages which supposedly shape role orientations. LeVine, an American sociologist, explored this central theme in the context of Nigeria.[9] Using McClelland's concept of achievement motivation, LeVine tested and compared samples of secondary school children from the three largest ethnic groups: the Hausa, Yoruba and Ibo. McClelland's theory is based on the supposition that, largely through childhood experience, different 'needs' are built into the individual per-sonality, for example, the need to belong to certain groups, the need to dominate or the need to set high standards of personal achievement and gain intrinsic satisfaction from striving to attain these standards. He also assumed that it was possible to systematically measure the incidence of these psychological drives as between different individuals, groups or societies.

LeVine's attempt to measure average group scores for the level of achievement motivation resulted in the following distribution: the Ibo schoolchildren scored highest while the Hausa were ranked at the bottom. His explanation for these group differences was based on an examination of the systems of status mobility present in these societies. Among the Hausa, he argued, young men could only attain a higher social status by attaching themselves to the rich and powerful as clients and by showing respect and obedience. This route to personal success encouraged Hausa parents to foster relevant attributes in their children, particularly a marked reluctance to act independently and a desire to seek paternalistic protection. Such traits would appear to be the very opposite of those shown by people with a strong need to pursue individual acts of high self-attainment. By contrast, LeVine regarded Ibo society as much more open and relatively unhierarchical. Here, social mobility was apparently available to anyone willing to work hard through individual effort in trade or farming. Wealth from these activities, when not required for the performance of customary obligations, could be used to buy titles in prestigious societies or political support. Ibo parents, accordingly, strove to inculcate behaviour in their children commensurate with an individualistic, achievement-oriented social order. Depending on whether they were Christians or Muslims, LeVine saw Yoruba society in western Nigeria as falling somewhere in between these two extremes so that group scores reflected these eventualities.

One of the difficulties with this theory, as Cohen has pointed out, is that it seems unable to explain the real achievements of the Hausa people in West African business life over many generations and their willingness to take advantage of the new opportunities brought by capitalism.[10] There is also the problem of methodological validity. Thus, LeVine's theory is based on several assumptions: (a) people tend to project their underlying psychological predispositions into certain spheres of personal creativity and expression such as dreams (the measure used in his study), poems, essays or the graphic arts; (b) these projections can be systematically measured; and (c) concrete observable behaviour is normally shaped by and reflects the presence or absence of these underlying motivations. Many social scientists have been highly critical of these claims both in the case of McClelland's work and that carried out by others who have tried to apply his ideas.[11]

Despite these and other difficulties, a number of researchers have investigated the possible links between ethnicity, business participation and differential success rates. One such case is shown by Harris's study of entrepreneurs, again in Nigeria.[12] On the whole, he found it difficult to place much confidence in his findings; for example, census data was often incomplete and so samples were not reliable and it was difficult to establish statistically significant correlations. Moreover, the ethnic differences revealed in his data were not always consistent with the predictions suggested by various sociological theories current at the time, such as LeVine's. Thus, on one test, the Ibo emerged as lower down on the ranking distribution of entrepreneurs than the Yoruba. Harris concluded his assessment of ethnic factors by remarking that long-term economic changes will probably cancel out any cultural obstacles there may be to economic growth by drawing in increasing numbers of potential entrepreneurs and by generating major shifts in social structure. In the final analysis, therefore, the level of market opportunity is much more likely to affect the supply and behaviour of all kinds of entrepreneurs, irrespective of the prevailing socio-cultural environment, than the other way round.[13]

Even where research findings demonstrate that certain ethnic groups do appear to be preponderant in business samples, this may have little or nothing to do with cultural uniqueness. Instead, such differences may simply reflect the highly uneven regional impact of education and commerce brought about by colonial rule. For example, a study of mainly manufacturing entrepreneurs carried out in Ghana in the late 1960s found that all southern groups with a long experience of modernisation were heavily over-represented in the sample.[14] But, in addition, half of the entire sample belonged to the Akan group — made up of several sub-groups — whose members represented just 19% of the Ghanaian population in 1960. However, many of the Akan people have been heavily involved in cocoa farming for several generations with all its cumulative consequences: prosperity, early access to education and acquaintanceship with small family business activities, partly financed by cocoa incomes.

The economistic interpretation offered by writers like Harris concerning the direction in which causal influences normally operate during the process of socio-economic transformation is not only relevant and of interest, in the case of specific studies such as the one offered by LeVine, but it also has considerable bearing on the wider questions raised by modernisation theory as a whole. Thus, a major criticism that can be levelled against the writers associated with these ideas is their tendency to endow culture and entrepreneurial leadership with altogether too much explanatory weight. By the same token they underplayed the crucial significance of other forces: the national economic climate of market opportunity and investment, the configuration of local class interests and the effects of international competition and colonial policy. For Neo-

Marxists, and perhaps others as well, this fundamental misreading of the relationship between social and economic variables arose partly because the modernisation theorists allowed themselves to be unduly influenced by structural–functionalist sociology.[15] Consequently, they often failed to adopt a sufficiently historical view of the emergence of capitalism. Moreover, they apparently saw little contradiction in operating with a theoretical model of Third World development which, while stressing the benefits of increased cultural integration with the West, also assumed that it was perfectly possible for less developed countries to exist in a state of political autonomy and economic independence from the global capitalist order – as if countries, particularly poor ones, are more or less free to choose which set of world pressures to reject and which to accept without cost or constraint.

The idea that entrepreneurs operating in largely traditional situations need to be social as well as economic innovators because of the restrictive nature of the cultural climate also figures prominently in the work of certain anthropologists. Economists and sociologists tend to employ the methodology of survey research based on interviews with fairly large samples drawn from a population of mostly unrelated people. Also, when they investigate entrepreneurship they are mainly concerned with how business leaders operate in the 'macro' environment of the national economy. Anthropologists, on the other hand, tend to work with quite limited samples and their subjects are often people who operate in a relatively small-scale social environment with clear-cut boundaries, usually in rural communities or urban ethnic enclaves. Moreover, anthropological studies are often carried out over fairly long time periods and involve the exploration of community life in considerable depth. Perhaps because of the methodology they employ, the multiplex nature of the relationships they investigate and the limited scope of their enquiries, anthropological findings depicting the ways in which culture and social structure shape enterprise have often been much better received by scholars. Certainly, their studies seem more acceptable than some of the more grandiose theories and claims put forward by the modernisation theorists, despite the common thematic concerns shared by both groups of researchers.

If we now ask how anthropologists have tried to conceptualise entrepreneurship within the context of traditional societies whose members are nevertheless becoming exposed to modernising influences, we find that there is a broad measure of agreement among these writers. Thus, entrepreneurs who wish to operate within kinship or community situations, where the social pressures against individual acquisitiveness and mobility are still strong and 'big men' are expected to redistribute wealth, must find some way to resolve a central contradiction. On the one hand, business success in such situations depends on the ability of entrepreneurs to avail themselves of certain resources that only the kinship group and/or the community can provide: labour, land, capital or customers. Yet at the same time, they must find ways to reduce or partially evade their customary obligations to these same community members – and without incurring the latter's hostility – so that they can accumulate capital, instead of being compelled to redistribute it. Alternatively, or simultaneously, entrepreneurs may need to establish new relationships with individuals and groups outside the immediate community who may be able to provide certain advantages such as credit, information or market outlets.

Several anthropologists have asked how it is that certain individuals are apparently better placed to harness community resources in the pursuit of capital accumulation, whilst preventing social pressures from damaging their progress, than others. The answer seems to be that those who achieve business success in this situation tend to be people who by accident or design enjoy some kind of 'outsider' status. There are at least two ways in which this may occur.

Firstly, they may be strangers whose outsider position enables them to disregard the community's rules without fear of too much hostility. Barth's study of the various spheres of economic activity and exchange existing within the Darfur economy, in the Sudan, provides one example of this process.[16] He found that the amount of millet a farmer needed in order to brew sufficient beer to host a work party had a potential money value substantially less than the amount of cash that the same workers could earn if their labour (perhaps, through government employment) or its products (in the form of cash crops) were sold in the wider capitalist economy. But the Darfur economy was still a largely pre-capitalist one where relationships were not evaluated in terms of their potential money value. Instead, farm assistance was normally reciprocated by providing help in kind at a later date. Thus, individuals did not feel free to 'exploit' the labour provided by others by growing for the market rather than subsistence. Nor was it socially acceptable to pay out the money equivalent of the beer consumed as a kind of wage in lieu of reciprocal labour obligations, thereby saving time. Rather, it was an incoming Arab merchant who took advantage of this hitherto unexploited discrepancy in value between the traditional and cash spheres of the economy. He did this by purchasing millet which when brewed into beer was used to recruit work parties for the purpose of growing tomatoes, a crop that was later sold for a considerable profit in the market outside the village.

A second path to social innovation may be available to community insiders. Here, as members of the local community, entrepreneurs symbolically adopt a kind of 'stranger' status by virtue of their conversion to a different religion. This places them effectively under an alternative set of obligations and links them to a spiritual community whose members encourage private accumulation and economic experimentation whilst providing resources such as technical knowledge, credit or labour. Long's study of cash-crop farmers in the Serenje District of Zambia, who grew Turkish tobacco, provides one interesting example of this process.[17] Some of the entrepreneurs he studied had undergone conversion to the Jehovah's Witnesses church at some earlier point in time, often while working in one of the Copperbelt towns. Church membership provided religious justification, spiritual protection and practical assistance for the converts in their struggles to disentangle themselves from the demands of their matri-kin and concentrate instead on building up their business and nuclear family interests.

Parkin's study of the Giriama people of coastal Kenya has shown how Islamic conversion can also provide the same 'release' both from the demands of kin and community on time and capital and from the fear of group hostility towards those who are perceived to be self-seeking.[18] Parkin explains how the conversion of some young entrepreneurs to the Islamic faith might follow a long period of psychological tension and physical illness induced by the possibility of conflict with the elders whose status and power were threatened by the younger men's activities. Such 'illness' could be diagnosed as caused by powerful Islamic spirits whose appeasement required nothing less than the religious conversion of those unfortunate enough to become possessed. Once this had occurred, the Islamic ban on the consumption of alcohol and certain foods, as well as the need to follow a partly separate ritual and social life, all provided the opportunity for entrepreneurs to reduce their level of involvement in traditional society. Yet this behaviour no longer incurred community displeasure since it was now judged to be religiously determined rather than the result of selfish individualism. At the same time, the converts were still reasonably close to community affairs and so could use their social connections with the elders in order to gain access to land, reliable information, business contracts and so on.

The Fra Fra people from northern Ghana have always occupied a disadvantageous position within the emerging modern nation. Like other ethnic groups in Ghana and elsewhere in Africa, they were incorporated into the commercial economy at a relatively late point during the colonial period and therefore most members have experienced only a low level of education whilst the region they occupy, its ethnic groups and public spokesmen have enjoyed limited political influence over the distribution of national resources. Hart has argued that, largely because of these experiences of group deprivation, most Fra Fra people have continued to uphold community traditions including the emphasis on generosity and equality.[19] In fact, continuing community loyalty provides a powerful source of mutual support for migrants living in ethnic enclaves within Ghana's modern cities. This enables them to adapt successfully to the harsh demands of urban life by receiving help in obtaining accommodation, low-paid jobs and access to other kinds of income opportunities. But this emphasis on sharing and in-group support means that, should entrepreneurs manipulate community relationships rather than outside sources in order to acquire business capital and if, more seriously, they divert their business earnings mainly towards private capital accumulation and decline to share their profits generously with ethnic members, then they may be regarded as 'swindlers' whose activities threaten Fra Fra morality and security rather than public benefactors who deserve praise and recognition. Faced with this situation some entrepreneurs had tried to escape from the moral and social proscriptions against self-enrichment which threatened to impede their business activities. Some had apparently done this partly through religious conversion – either to Islam or Christianity – while others did so by moving to impersonal urban settings where individualistic behaviour was more acceptable.

The Hausa of northern Nigeria provide a very well-documented case of a quite different relationship between 'traditional' culture and business endeavour. Here, far from obstructing entrepreneurship, membership of a close-knit community with a strong emphasis on mutual support seems to have provided resources which have enabled many Hausa businessmen to pursue certain kinds of economic activity with considerable success. Consequently, individuals have not usually faced the same kinds of social constraints as entrepreneurs who operate within similar close-knit community situations elsewhere, although, as we shall see, Hausa proprietors do have to respond to some social and religious demands as one of the conditions for their continuing success.

In the pre-colonial era highly organised, professional Hausa merchants were engaged in long-distance trade linking together the various economies straddling the forest, savannah and Sahel regions. Their ability to do this was largely based on the mutual trust and active cooperation operating within the trading community. These, in turn, were sustained by a shared faith in Islam, reliance on kinship networks and the social organisation of Hausa society whereby migrants, scattered throughout West Africa, and living in ethnic enclaves within or near the various host trading societies, provided the expertise and protection required to sustain commercial activity.[20] Later on, during the colonial period, the Hausa adapted their geographically dispersed trading system in pursuit of new opportunities. One of their most notable achievements involved the expansion of the kola nut and cattle trades in Nigeria. Kola nuts are mainly consumed by people living in the savannah areas – northern Nigeria being the largest market – but as a forest product they must be purchased from southern growers. Cattle production, on the other hand, is primarily an occupation of the savannah farmers who then export live animals to the markets of the south. In the nineteenth century the forest farmers of Ashanti (in what is now Ghana) were one of the main sources of kola nuts, although the warrior aristocracy played a key role in managing the actual commercial exchanges with the Hausa traders.[21] The latter operated mainly from the transit towns situated along the northern borders of the Ashanti empire.

The first successful Hausa adaptation to changing circumstances began in the 1880s when some merchants decided to hire steamship services in order to transport kola from southern Ghana to Lagos instead of using the old overland routes. Later, they made increasing use of the railway between Lagos and Kano which was completed in 1911.[22] The second Hausa success came when the incomes of ordinary Nigerian consumers gradually rose in the early decades of the twentieth century and the Hausa played a key role in organising the complementary inter-regional trade in northern cattle and southern kola. Cohen has explained the organisation of these trades in considerable detail: the ways in which traders utilise the network of fellow migrants resident in southern towns as commission agents, informants and sources of accommodation, the social basis for credit arrangements, and much else besides.[23] He also describes the various religious and political struggles in which the traders have been embroiled at different times in the attempt to maintain some kind of ethnic autonomy within the Yoruba towns and to retain monopoly control over the cattle trade, lorry transport and other business activities.[24]

Writing about the kola trade based in Kano, Lovejoy has pointed to two further aspects of Hausa adaptability.[25] In the 1960s more than half of a sample of Kano wholesale merchants had fathers and grandfathers who were once involved in the same trade. Indeed, many came from families whose forebears had participated in the original caravan trade to northern Ashanti. Even relative newcomers normally came from families with at least 60 years' experience in some kind of trading activity. Secondly, Lovejoy observes that during the 1930s depression, with falling prices, the kola trade could only remain profitable if ways were found to deal in bulk supplies thereby lowering the costs of marketing and distribution.[26] The Hausa responded to this crisis by evolving a more specialised trading system. Big merchant wholesalers emerged who increasingly dealt in large quantities of kola while smaller middlemen and retailers, linked to the wholesalers by social ties and credit, engaged in the actual buying and selling process at each end of the commercial chain. The wholesalers financed their operations in various ways: profit reinvestment, borrowing and the increased use of weigh bills as a form of security, or a combination of these. In the 1950s, the Kano traders were also successful in persuading the local authority to build a new market with improved storage facilities.

By the mid 1970s, and no doubt largely in response to Nigeria's oil boom, the Kano traders were in the process of diversifying their business activities. In addition to long-distance trading, speculating in crop futures and hoarding, many moved into retail trading, the purchase of urban property and house building for rent and some owned shares in various banks. Moreover, the indigenisation measures at this time prompted some Kano businessmen to seek directorships in Western companies.[27] Lubeck's study of worker responses to the rash of new locally owned manufacturing firms emerging in Kano in the late 1960s and early 1970s has also shown that a good many traders were following the 'classic' path outlined by Marx and were investing their accumulated trading profits, and other financial resources, in light industries such as groundnut processing and textiles.[28] Yusaf, another observer of contemporary Hausa business practice, argues that although capital-pooling remains rare, there 'has been a noticeable growth of some family-based enterprises (reminiscent of some Chinese, Indian and Lebanese enterprises in Nigeria and other parts of the world) as practicable means of raising sufficient funds to acquire a large and costly capital asset'.[29] In Chapter 8 we will see that there are instances in other countries, too, of entrepreneurs using kinship and nuclear family networks in order to help overcome some of the limitations to one-person management.

Despite these various moves towards more modern forms of business activity, Yusaf observes that religious belief and customary ties continue to sustain a great deal of Hausa business activity. Banks increasingly serve as an important source of working capital, especially for established traders. Yet credit relations based on trust, and made possible by underlying socio-economic relationships rooted in kinship and religious affiliation, continue to oil the wheels of commerce. Relative newcomers to trade or young men from established families still obtain the capital needed for branching out by themselves by falling back on kinship aid or by contracting to serve as a client-cum-apprentice for a period of time with a wealthy entrepreneur in exchange for eventual business assistance. Furthermore, providing reciprocal business favours, giving financial aid to clients, dependants and officials, offering donations for religious purposes and generally being seen to respond to the traditional norm of generosity, all of these remain crucial requirements for business success as well as the attainment of social status. Thus, creditworthiness, access to business deals and the availability of assistance at times of need depend on the entrepreneur's ability to rely on social support from the immediate socio-economic network. The selfish trader who disregards moral values and operates his business solely on the basis of an individualistic economic calculus, may go under, especially at times of adversity.

Of course, it is possible that these very systems of customary support which have underpinned contractual relations so successfully may increasingly inhibit the emergence of more advanced types of business behaviour in the future. Yusaf hints at this in his concluding remarks when he notes the lack of proper accountancy procedures and business records in many Hausa enterprises and the unwillingness to establish legally recognised corporate forms of business organisation.[30] Clearly, much more careful research is needed in order to establish the extent to which tradition has ceased to be a vehicle for successful endeavour in recent years. In the meantime it would seem valid to make two qualifications. One is that some Hausa businessmen have already established a degree of independence from community involvement by making substantial investments in foreign companies where they may become exposed to the techniques of Western business management. Secondly, the need for capitalist entrepreneurs to try to persuade the wider public that profit-making accords with national values and generates a manifest pay-off for the community is not confined to northern Nigeria. Enterprises large and small spend considerable sums trying to achieve this goal everywhere in the capitalist and perhaps non-capitalist world. Subscriptions to educational and arts foundations or taking an active role in funding charitable activities are some of the ways in which companies attempt to woo citizens in the advanced economies.

The insights offered by these anthropological studies are fascinating and instructive. They reveal a central dilemma which takes a particularly extreme form in the case of those entrepreneurs who operate within small-scale, closed community situations. In most cases, entrepreneurial attempts to evade or reduce obligations were rather limited, despite various creative responses. Beyond a certain point the costs incurred by further efforts to manipulate social pressures seriously outweighed any likely benefits – or threatened to do so. But this is really only another way of saying that unless and until the wider society undergoes substantial socio-economic differentiation – so that each emergent class, or incipient class, possesses its own sub-culture and the means of providing viable intra-class support for fellow members – then the possibilities for corporate business endeavour and intensive capital accumulation over many areas of economic life will be held severely in check. Indeed, the ability of capitalist entrepreneurs to distance themselves socially from the pressures of community life is simply an aspect of a far wider, more complex process whereby much larger, impersonal, national markets gradually evolve along with a system for mobilising loanable funds and a supply of free wage labourers who (temporarily at least) are also separated from their community of origin.

Clearly, the historical and partly political analyses required if these processes are to be properly explored fall outside the scope of the anthropological approach, concerned as it is with highly structured, small-scale social situations. Here, as so often in the social sciences, methodology, subject matter and focal interest largely predetermine the nature of the possible discoveries and the parameters within which they fall.

Of course, African entrepreneurs who own much larger firms and who operate in a modern, urban setting are not immune to the demands of kinsmen, friends and neighbours. In Chapter 8 we will look more closely at how they respond to these eventualities. However, for these proprietors, such pressures represent only one among many problems, rather than the primary constraint on business success. In addition, most modern-sector proprietors have either already outgrown an earlier situation of symbiotic dependence upon community or, what is more likely, their emergence and expansion was never conditional upon the immediate support of neighbours and kin in the first place.

Most economists and sociologists have focussed their attention on these mainly urban entrepreneurs who operate in impersonal, highly competitive market situations.[31] Their investigations have normally involved the use of survey research techniques based on sampling frames of greater or lesser degrees of accuracy. Although most writers have been primarily concerned with the question of entrepreneurial performance they have also considered the economic constraints and opportunities prevalent both in the immediate and the national environment for African enterprise. It is to this topic that we now turn.

ECONOMIC CONSTRAINTS

The economic climate presents African proprietors with a number of problems (and possibilities). Chief among these are the following: obtaining funds for initial investment, day-to-day working capital and later expansion; the supply of skilled manual labour as well as technical and managerial personnel; the availability of viable investment opportunities; and the quality of the immediate operating environment in which firms are located, as this is affected, for example, by national infrastructure and government administration.

The supply of loanable funds

Not surprisingly, most researchers have looked at the question of capital supply in some considerable detail. On the face of it, the availability of funds would seem to be one of the most crucial factors likely to influence entrepreneurial prospects. In fact, as we shall see, most studies have not really found this to be the case, at least with respect to initial finance. Moreover, there is considerable agreement concerning other aspects of capital supply as well.

The amounts of capital invested by African entrepreneurs when they first ventured into business were usually quite small: between a few hundred and one or two thousand pounds with the distribution skewed towards the lower figure. One example will serve to illustrate this point. Harris found that the median value of the initial assets invested by a sample of Nigerian manufacturers in the mid 1960s was less than £1,000. [32] Most writers agree, however, that though the starting capital available to most Africans was normally relatively meagre, even in the case of the largest firms, the amounts involved were nevertheless beyond the means of most citizens, given the average income levels prevailing among the poor majority at the time when most of these businesses were established in the 1950s, 60s and early 70s.[33] Thus, the majority of successful proprietors did not come from the most disadvantaged social strata. Most had parents, siblings and kinsmen who enjoyed a modest degree of prosperity and considerable experience of the money economy.

Some entrepreneurs established their first 'proper' firm following a fairly long spell when they had operated in petty production, perhaps as market traders or artisans. For example, Garlick's study of Ghanaian traders carried out in the early 1960s revealed that Kwahu people from the Eastern Region tended to hold a predominant position in retail trade in Accra.[34] For many, tailoring, petty commerce and small-scale cash-crop farming had provided the most common points of entry into retail trade. More typically, however, the entrepreneurs investigated in these studies founded their first and main businesses after spending a period of time in employment during which they gained commercial or technical experience and managed to save. In fact personal savings – usually derived from earnings in employment – were by far the most important source of starting capital.[35] About three-fifths of the respondents included in the various studies began in this way. Family loans or gifts or a loan/advance from a commercial bank, government institution or hire purchase credit were of roughly equal importance as sources of starting capital after personal earnings. A small number of proprietors obtained their starting capital after receiving advances from customers, help from friends, gifts from a previous employer, gratuities at the termination of employment or by utilising an income from some kind of inherited asset such as a farm.

In the case of finance for business expansion most studies again paint a rather similar picture. Thus, reinvested profits were by far the most important source of capital for purchasing new equipment, extending plant, increasing the firm's distribution system, or whatever. This was so among Nigerian bakers, Ghanaian manufacturers and leading firms in Zambia where four-fifths of business expansion was financed in this way.[36] Even the sample of government-assisted proprietors in Kenya, studied by Marris and Somerset, who had received substantial loans accounting for the greater part of their capital from external sources through the I.C.D.C., had still relied on reinvested profits to finance more than half their firms' expansion.[37]

Profit reinvestment as the main source of finance offers several advantages. One is that entrepreneurs can approach business growth, and the numerous organisational problems this creates, on a step-by-step basis. They can consolidate their achievements as they go along, gradually acquiring the skills needed without overtaxing their capacity to cope at any one time. Secondly, since it is their own hard-won capital they place at risk they are presumably more likely to tread carefully and provide the increased input of effort, time and skill commensurate with the firm's growing organisational needs than might be the case if, for example, capital had been obtained primarily through bureaucratic corruption.

Nevertheless, self-financing was not the only source of funds for expansion. Also, there are often times when entrepreneurs need quick injections of funds in order to take advantage of new market opportunities. Akeredolu-Ale, for example, has argued on the basis of his study of entrepreneurs in Lagos State in Nigeria, that obtaining funds for expansion created far more problems for his sample than obtaining starting capital.[38] In Kenya and Zambia, too, local proprietors have often found that commercial banks are reluctant to provide credit facilities, let alone long-term loans.[39] Although 78% of the most successful Zambian entrepreneurs studied by Beveridge and Oberschall did receive bank loans at some time, many were refused loans for long periods and encountered prejudice from European officials. In some African countries businessmen have also obtained funds for expansion through hire purchase arrangements, advances from important customers, receiving credit from firms supplying materials or equipment, family loans or injections of capital from partners. For the most part, however, these capital sources have been marginal up till now compared to self-financing or bank/government loans.

Many small African firms also face very real cash-flow problems related to the financing of day-to-day operations. The difficulty of securing regular bank overdraft facilities is one aspect of this. But there are others too; for example, the need to provide extended credit to clients in order to secure their custom or tying up large sums of money in stocks of raw materials in case of future delays in delivery.

Sooner or later most African firms will require some form of external finance, just like their counterparts in other countries, and banks will need to play a major role in this. Although distrust, especially during the colonial period and just afterwards, largely explains why European commercial bank officials have often been reluctant to cater for the needs of African entrepreneurs this is not the only reason for the latters' frequent failure to benefit from bank facilities. Also in recent years new circumstances have intervened to improve prospects for local borrowers.

Firstly, studies have suggested that part of the problem in securing loan assistance stems from the reluctance shown by would-be borrowers themselves in approaching bank officials in the first place. There may be many reasons for this, such as the fear of being rejected, an unwillingness to open up the firm's operations to outside inspection or the inability to prepare a feasibility study. In addition, as Marris and Somerset have observed in the case of Kenya, many Africans simply lack experience in dealing with officialdom and believe they cannot cope with the formalities demanded by this new type of relationship.[40] They may move in a quite different social world from that inhabited by the more educated people who work in large institutions. Whatever the reason, smaller entrepreneurs, especially, often seem unwilling to even apply for loan facilities. In Ghana during the late 1960s, for example, one researcher found that 54% of the entrepreneurs included in the survey, with firms of below average size, had never tried to obtain any kind of commercial loan, while another 19% had only submitted one application. Most of the smaller proprietors who did apply for loans had received some kind of assistance sooner or later (67%), and their success rate was not significantly lower than in the case of the more successful entrepreneurs with firms of above average size (81%).[41]

Secondly, the need for collateral security and/or the ability to show some evidence of reasonably efficient business operations, including up-to-date and properly kept accounts, are not unreasonable demands on the part of bank officials, especially in the case of requests for sizeable long-term loans. These stipulations are standard practice world-wide; their application to African entrepreneurs does not necessarily imply unfairness or discrimination. The businessman whose operations can only be accounted for in terms of scraps of paper stuffed into a pocket or a series of verbal agreements with clients may be quite correct to assume that any requests for a loan will not be well received, but this is hardly a criticism of normal bank practice. In fact, official insistence that accounts are regularly examined and advice is accepted as part of a loan agreement may help to generate more effective management and increase profitability. Bank preferences for customers who own houses or land is one reason why so many African entrepreneurs tend to plough a considerable proportion of their profits into various forms of property acquisition.

Thirdly, in many countries it has become much easier for indigenous entrepreneurs to gain access to loans in recent years. Schatz, for example, quotes figures given in the *Lagos Daily Times* of 29 June 1974 where it was pointed out that approximately half of the credit provided by the large foreign banks at that time was being granted to Nigerians.[42] Not only have some governments insisted that Western banks set aside a much higher proportion of their loanable funds specifically for African borrowers, but state funding agencies and national banks have also been established. State or central banks can influence private foreign agencies by threatening to block foreign exchange flows and profit repatriation, withholding licences, insisting on local or government shareholding arrangements, and so on. In some countries, state banks have offered guarantees in the event of default by African borrowers and this has helped to increase the availability of funds. Lastly, although a scarcity of institutional finance must obviously constitute a serious, potential impediment to business expansion, historically it has also been the case that joint business endeavours – involving greater or lesser degrees of public participation through share flotations, company mergers, partnership agreements, and so on – have always provided very significant avenues for capitalist expansion. On this point, the evidence offered by most studies on African enterprise reveals a rather depressing picture of marked reluctance, to date, to embark on such ventures or to carry them through successfully.[43]

This leads onto another important debate. Thus, despite the frequently heard complaint by local entrepreneurs that capital shortage has been a major barrier to business advance, some researchers have been rather sceptical regarding these claims. There are several reasons for this: the widespread unwillingness to invite outside participation, the evidence that in many firms machinery is often substantially under-utilised, and the fact that self-financing has apparently served the majority of indigenous proprietors quite well. Also, most of the studies carried out in the 1960s and early 1970s failed to establish a very convincing correlation between profitability and firm expansion on the one hand, and the amount of starting capital available to entrepreneurs on the other.[44]

Further evidence pointing in the same direction can be gleaned from the records of various local and central government agencies that have tried to assist local enterprise. Both Kilby and Schatz have attempted such an assessment in the context of Nigeria for the years between the mid 1940s and the late 1960s.[45] During this period there were a number of government programmes designed to help local businesses. The Federal Loans Board, which began operations during the mid 1950s, was particularly important. The Board applied very rigorous standards to loan applicants. It insisted on evidence of managerial competence and project feasibility and normally lent only to industrial entrepreneurs whose firms were already well established, albeit in sectors that were relatively new to Nigeria. Reviewing the evidence concerning the Board's operations be- tween 1956 and 1962 Schatz discovered that most loan applications (82%) were turned down on one or more of the following grounds: an obvious lack of business skill, the inability to produce proper records of past activity, a lack of relevant experience, projects unsupported by proper investigation, and a tendency to request finance for projects falling outside the Board's declared ambit.[46] Of the 44 loans that were actually made during the first five years of operations only 38% of the relevant firms were later judged to be operating successfully. On the basis of these and other findings Schatz concluded that a shortage of capital was actually an 'illusion'. The real problem facing Nigerian businessmen was the dearth of viable projects for investment. The supposedly unsatisfied demand for capital was largely false in the sense that most loan claimants were unable to offer workable schemes capable of absorbing loan capital effectively. After examining similar evidence from other countries, for example Sierra Leone, Ethiopia and the Sudan, Schatz argued that these findings had widespread validity.

Before leaving this discussion it is important to sound a note of caution. Most of the evidence used to substantiate the argument that capital availability is perhaps less of a problem than most businessmen have proclaimed is based on studies carried out some years ago. At that time – in the 1950s and 1960s – the development of manufacturing industry was still in its infancy in most African countries. This being so it was inevitable, as one writer has argued, that the majority of enterprises established by Africans at that time were 'characterized by simple technologies and low investment thresholds'.[47] Depending on the economic sector, it was per- fectly possible for many indigenous entrepreneurs to carve out niches for themselves at this level and yet flourish. Some members of this first generation of African industrialists have probably built up much larger enterprises by now; many were already in the process of doing so when these studies were being conducted. Their very success, along with other important changes – increased involvement by foreign companies in some African economies, the expansion of the state sector, partnerships between local and overseas capital and attempts to provide state support and some public funding for indigenisation measures (albeit in a half-hearted and biased fashion in many cases) – have combined to create a rather different investment climate today. Consequently, and depending on the economic sector in question, business opportunities today probably presuppose a higher level of managerial and technical resources if African entrepreneurs are to compete successfully with large foreign firms. But this may mean that in many fields of enterprise the question of capital supply is now much more crucial than it once was. However, only careful research can tell us whether capital availability has now become the major problem which African entrepreneurs themselves have always claimed.

The availability of suitable labour

During the colonial period European employers and officials tended to regard migrant labourers as 'target workers' primarily interested in short-term employment.[48] It was widely believed that African workers preferred leisure (or traditional occupations) to further increases in wages, once their initial economic 'needs' had been satisfied – the famous 'backward sloping supply curve' for labour. This generated an indisciplined, unskilled and uncommitted workforce. Considerable doubt had already been thrown on this image of the African worker by the late colonial period. Moreover, by the 1950s and 1960s most rural migrants moved to urban centres in search of employment with the intention of remaining for a large part, perhaps most, of their adult lives. But in addition, the work carried out by researchers such as Kilby and Wells and Warmington, in mainly foreign-owned manufacturing establishments in Nigeria, revealed that low productivity, high absenteeism, and so on, mainly occurred in firms that lacked suitable training schemes, where production systems were uncoordinated, the quality of supervision was poor and incentive systems were inadequate.[49] In short, labour problems were generally no worse than in European factories and had similar causes.

On the whole, these findings are probably equally applicable to the larger African companies which operate with much the same kind of technology and organisational structures as their foreign counterparts. However, a rather different situation may prevail in the smaller, more labour-intensive firms of the kind that most indigenous proprietors have so far tended to run. Here, any difficulties in labour relations are generally caused either by the rather authoritarian style of personal management which some African entrepreneurs seem to prefer (as, for example, in the case of the Hausa traders-turned-industrialists Lubeck studied in Kano) or they flow from the very smallness of the firm, its lack of resources and the extreme pressures under which such enterprises are compelled to operate, or both of these.[50]

For example, in many small manufacturing and perhaps building firms, where machinery is limited to one or two items, the production system may be highly dependent on the contribution made by a nucleus of skilled workers. Particularly at times of relative economic buoyancy, some skilled workers may be able to find more attractive work in large companies or they may be able to make a reasonable living through self-employment.

These alternative income opportunities may increase their bargaining power *vis-à-vis* small local employers. They may be able to demand contract or part-time work so that their contribution to the labour process is irregular and unpredictable. Alternatively, they may be in a position to negotiate high wages, bonus payments or a quasi-partnership, profit-sharing status within the enterprise. There is also the real possibility that they will set up in direct competition with the original firm at some future time. It is the unsatisfactory nature of these arrangements that provides many entrepreneurs with one of the chief motivations for seeking to change over to a rather more capital-intensive production system based mainly on semi-skilled operators whose lack of skill means they occupy a more vulnerable position in the labour market.[51]

Some proprietors who own very small firms may find it necessary to employ immediate family members or more distant kinsmen. Such employees can often be paid very low wages and expected to forgo the demand for the proper terms of service normally anticipated – though not necessarily received – by non-family workers. Apprentices, too, and perhaps journeymen, who have not yet graduated to proper employee status, may offer similar advantages. Yet, whether they are the result of necessity, or a personal preference for a paternalistic labour system, these kinds of employee relationships often bring disadvantages: an unwillingness to cooperate, the risk of pilfering, the 'withdrawal' of labour as soon as the owner is absent from the premises, low productivity and probably a general lack of discipline, especially on the part of kinsmen.[52]

More recently, the interest in labour problems has shifted to the question of the availability and aptitudes of supervisory, technical and managerial personnel. Several writers claim that the supply of such high-level skills now constitutes a major impediment to firm expansion and the ability to compete successfully. One observer of the Nigerian scene, Akeredolu-Ale, has argued that high-level personnel of competence and integrity will normally prefer to seek employment in the public sector or in overseas firms.[53] This applies to highly qualified Nigerians as well as expatriates. Consequently, African employers often have to make-do with 'residual staff': the technically less skilled, relatively inexperienced, not very committed managers and technicians, perhaps of dubious character. He also points out that though overseas companies have been regarded as favourable environments for the acquisition of managerial and technical skills this is often not the case.[54] African 'managers' employed in foreign firms normally do so at lower, non-executive levels or they occupy posts as personnel officers or in public relations rather than in the sphere of production. Other writers, by contrast, disagree and argue that employment in expatriate companies in Africa or overseas can be highly beneficial for future entrepreneurial attainment.[55] In addition, as Marris has argued, the ability to move comfortably in Western business circles, whether in Africa or abroad, and to establish wide-ranging contacts, is absolutely essential if indigenous entrepreneurs are to have any chance of taking their place as equal partners with foreign firms in due course.[56]

It is not easy to resolve these differences of interpretation. However, it may be that though Akeredolu-Ale's observations were probably quite valid for the Nigerian situation at the time of his research (in the late 1960s), circumstances may have changed since then. In Nigeria, and elsewhere, indigenisation measures and increased government pressure on big foreign firms to train and employ local people at the highest levels may well have helped to raise the general level of managerial skills among African managers and business leaders since that time. Again, more research is urgently needed in this as well as other areas.

Investment opportunities and the economic environment

Earlier on we considered the ideas put forward by Schatz, an economist who has written extensively about Nigeria. In various writings, he suggested that the main problem faced by Nigerian entrepreneurs was the lack of viable investment opportunities.[57] More recently, Schatz has applied a similar argument as part of his attempt to explain what he calls the 'inelasticity of domestic supply' in the Nigerian economy despite the oil boom of the 1970s and early 1980s, that is, Nigeria's relatively poor growth performance in response to an enormous increase in domestic demand.[58] Basically, he regards the scarcity of viable investment opportunities as due to two main factors.

Firstly, there is the problem of entrepreneurial deficiency. Many Nigerian proprietors do not possess the organisational and technical skills needed to ensure the success of their investments and which the economy needs. Consequently, many projects are either badly conceived or inaccessible to most entrepreneurs. Unlike many other commentators of the Nigerian business situation, however, Schatz believes that the shortcomings of Nigerian entrepreneurs, though real enough, have almost certainly been exaggerated.[59] Thus, the second and most important factor which underlies the dearth of viable investment opportunities for indigenous enterprise is the generally unfavourable economic environment.[60] This creates a wide range of special difficulties not usually encountered in more developed economies. The unpredictable nature of the economic environment generates a host of immediate problems which affect all enterprises, foreign as well as indigenous, but these impinge much more dramatically on the latter than the former because local entrepreneurs have fewer resources, are relatively inexperienced and usually operate on a smaller scale. This makes their businesses much more vulnerable to uncertainty. Among the environmental constraints discussed by Schatz are the following. The picture he paints is widely applicable outside Nigeria.

Poor infrastructure, for example, the erratic telephone system, inadequate port facilities and badly surfaced roads all result in delays. They also push up the cost of handling inputs and outputs and absorb scarce capital because of the need to hold large stocks of goods as a reserve against likely shortages. Haphazard supplies of water and electricity may disrupt production runs. Many entrepreneurs are forced to locate their firms on low-cost sites lacking in all kinds of facilities and perhaps remote from main roads. Because they lack useful overseas and local contacts, so that their sources of information are sparse and unreliable, it is not easy for them to obtain discounts from suppliers. Their small-scale operations further reduce this possibility. Materials and spare parts often arrive not only late, so that orders cannot be met on time, but goods may also suffer damage during transit.

Schatz refers to a number of additional problems. The delays, shortages, disruptions, high cost of materials and other difficulties mean that entrepreneurs require proportionately more capital than would normally be the case if the same business was located in an advanced economy. In common with other writers, Schatz also lists some of the obstructive tendencies associated with corrupt, incompetent government bureaucracy at several levels. Regulations are often unnecessary, needlessly complicated and are frequently changed without warning. Applications for official licences, loans, tax exemptions, customs clearance, or whatever are subject to delays more often than not. In general, officials often show a marked reluctance to assist local entrepreneurs at all, unless requests for help are accompanied by 'gifts'.

Then there are the difficulties involved in competing with overseas companies.[61] In part, these are due to the latters' superior resources. But, at least until quite recently, foreign companies operating in Nigeria, and elsewhere, were also eligible to receive much more government aid in the form of tax inducements, customs exemptions, substantial site aid and other benefits. In those business fields characterised by relatively low capital-entry requirements and simple technology, where most local businesses tend to congregate, competition is often excessive and this reduces growth opportunities, even for the more efficient firms. In addition, local firms often cannot afford to engage in costly advertising campaigns or build up extensive marketing and distribution networks. This further reduces their ability to compete in national markets and burdens them with high unit selling costs.

Finally, Schatz tries to verify his claim that the absence of viable investment opportunities for local enterprise mainly results from the particularly damaging impact of the economic environment on African firms. To do this he refers to the wide range of fiscal inducements and investment allowances provided exclusively for overseas companies by the Nigerian government in the early 1970s. He then cites evidence to suggest that without these special benefits only about 25% of the investment undertaken at the time by foreign firms would have actually taken place.[62] Thus, Western capitalists were doubly protected against the vicissitudes of an operating climate which hurt local firms badly; they possessed vastly superior resources, anyway, and they were cosseted by government aid.

❦ 8 ❧

ENTREPRENEURIAL ENDEAVOUR, BUSINESS SUCCESS AND SOCIAL ORIGINS

Previous chapters focussed mainly on the way in which African capitalism has been continuously shaped and often constrained by a whole series of interdependent factors. The present chapter, however, places the spotlight much more firmly on the actors themselves and the business organisations they have striven to create. Thus, it is important to see local entrepreneurs not simply as passive owners and managers, buffeted by external forces, but also as actual and potential agents of change whose decisions contribute to the gradual transformation of that same environment in which they struggle to survive. Once we regard them in this light it becomes relevant to ask how important is the quality of entrepreneurial endeavour in determining business success (or failure) and therefore the prospects for firm expansion since it is primarily in this way that African proprietors may affect the wider economy.

A number of economists and sociologists have explored this question in some detail. The discussion that follows draws extensively upon their research findings. Most writers have observed that the management practices and business strategies displayed by many African proprietors leave much to be desired. Indeed, some researchers claim that self-imposed limitations have often retarded African capitalism more than any other single factor, although they also acknowledge the difficulties posed by the external environment. Before we consider these findings, however, it is important to note that the data we will discuss was derived partly from questionnaire surveys based on interviews with pre-selected samples of respondents. This methodology does present its own peculiar problems of validity and interpretation.

For one thing, each respondent is treated as a discrete entity rather than as a member of an on-going community. Also, this approach tends to deal with each separate aspect of business organisation. Accordingly, it is not easy to gain a coherent overall view of the entrepreneur at work in his socio-economic milieu or of the entrepreneurial role in its totality. Similarly, it is difficult to build up a picture of how each business organisation has evolved and changed over time. Detailed case studies based on intensive observation of the kind that anthropologists pursue would not present these difficulties. But such studies are expensive as well as time-consuming and they tend to concentrate on a few key informants. Moreover, the information they generate is often qualitative and does not lend itself readily to mathematical measurement, whereas it is this kind of supposedly 'representative' and precise data that many economists and sociologists wish to collect.

Secondly, survey research is generally subject to certain limitations because of the problems involved in data collection. But the latter are probably even more formidable in Africa than in the more advanced countries. In fact the studies were normally based on rather limited samples and were derived from particular business groups. Only in one or two studies, for example, those carried out by Marris and Somerset in Kenya and Beveridge and Oberschall in Zambia, do we encounter careful attempts to incorporate and compare entrepreneurs operating in a wide range of sectors.[1] Moreover, the studies were conducted in countries with quite different socio-economic structures and historical backgrounds and the samples varied quite a lot even within the same country. Consequently, the evidence is not necessarily comparable between studies or countries and any generalisations derived from the existing research must be treated with caution.

Bearing these limitations in mind we turn now to the question of African entrepreneurial endeavour; how important is the style and quality of business leadership in determining success or failure irrespective of the pressures exercised by the external environment? The researchers in this field have paid particular attention to four main areas: the propensity to innovate; the ability to develop an effective organisational framework for dealing with production, marketing, procurement and financial management; the arrangements entrepreneurs prefer to adopt with respect to the various social relationships (with workers, customers, partners, managers, kinsmen and so on) which sustain everyday business life; and the commitment and strategies pursued with respect to long-term capital accumulation. Although these different aspects of entrepreneurial activity are obviously indistinguishable from one another in practice, their delineation provides a useful way of structuring the discussion and so we will proceed on this basis.

Innovation

It was Joseph Schumpeter who focussed attention on the central relevance of original innovation to the process of economic development. He argued that the ability to innovate – that is, to make new combinations in the sphere of business organisation, marketing, distribution or production – was the single most vital function of the business entrepreneur.[2] This special contribution was quite distinct from other aspects of business activity such as risk taking, technical invention or routine management and should be treated as such. Whilst recognising the importance of Schumpeter's insights later writers have insisted that in the 'real' world economic development depends just as much on imitative innovation (whereby later entrepreneurs transfer original discoveries to enterprises, sectors, regions and countries far and wide) as it does on the initial breakthrough, perhaps more so.[3] Furthermore, innovation at secondhand normally requires virtually the same degree of risk, prescience and problem-solving ability. Moreover, it is probably unrealistic to expect Third World entrepreneurs to forge entirely new innovations except, possibly, in those business fields dependent on intermediate technology, since it is the very scarcity of skill, capital, organisational and technological capacity that renders these countries less developed in the first place.

For these and other reasons most writers have not regarded innovation as a particularly important criterion of African business performance. Nevertheless, there is some scope for meaningful innovation on the part of indigenous proprietors. This might involve: being one of the first local entrepreneurs to implement an organisational technique or technological process previously monopolised by foreign companies; extending a market distribution system so as to tap income groups or localities not formally reached by indigenous or overseas businesses; or simply adapting an imported commodity, practice or item of equipment so as to meet local or environmental needs or cultural tastes. Any of these will demand skill and courage.

A few writers have tried to assess the incidence of innovation, in this more limited sense, among African entrepreneurs and its relevance to business success. In Nigeria, Akeredolu-Ale chose his final sample on the basis of a proven capacity for innovation along the lines just discussed.[4] He found that access to previous managerial training and experience, the willingness to delegate authority and the quality of financial control were much more crucial for business success, though in the absence of a non-innovating control group it is difficult to evaluate his findings. A study (mainly of manufacturers) carried out in Ghana identified two types: the propensity for design or craft inventiveness and a capacity for basic organisational innovation (for example, being one of the first indigenous proprietors to enter a particular industry or establish a system of production control in a new activity or region).[5] Creative craftsmanship had not been particularly relevant to business expansion. Proprietors who were highly inventive in this sense were usually reluctant to undertake any activity that might reduce their scope for personal creativity. In activities like jewellery-making or wood-carving dependence on a few highly skilled craftsmen producing for a limited, probably wealthy clientele or occasional buyers could work very well. However, this style of enterprise does not provide a basis for capturing a large share of the market for most kinds of consumer goods (garments, furniture, shoes, bags and so on), particularly the mass market where low unit costs, long production runs, a wide distribution system and the ability to respond quickly to changing tastes are absolutely essential. 'Basic innovation', on the other hand, approximating much more closely to the Schumpeterian model, had apparently contributed to business success. Of the manufacturers who owned the largest firms 42% had engaged in innovatory activity at some time compared to 11% of those with below-average-sized firms.[6] Nevertheless, it was also clear that the ability to pioneer some kind of organisational improvement was important for firm expansion only in those cases where manufacturers had also established complementary and efficient systems of marketing, training or production control. It would appear that by itself basic innovation is unlikely to be especially crucial for business success.

Production and marketing

Most studies have revealed a veritable catalogue of organisational deficiencies which, it is claimed, are commonplace in many African firms. These include the following.

Labour productivity may be low because of insufficient job training, poor selection techniques, or the absence of systematic procedures for checking the quality and quantity of work output. Employees are often poorly motivated because wages and conditions of work are inadequate and incentives such as bonus payments or increments are either non-existent or unrelated to performance. Consequently, workers are prone to absenteeism and pilfering, waste and low output are often endemic.[7] Researchers have pointed out that equipment is often substantially under-utilised in African firms.[8] Machinery may also be improperly handled by poorly trained workers and irregularly maintained. There is often little attempt to subdivide the work process in an orderly, efficient way. In many firms enormous increases in productivity could be attained without the need for additional investment if the systems for coordinating the spatial, temporal and skill relations between the different work tasks were properly thought out and firmly implemented.[9]

Several writers claim that managerial deficiencies are even more evident in the case of marketing.[10] In general, keeping abreast of market fluctuation need not require expensive or elaborate arrangements. Yet many proprietors, including some engaged in wholesale and retail trade, do not take the obvious steps to do so; for example, by keeping records of customer enquiries, making regular visits to fashionable department stores or obtaining trade journals and brochures containing up-to-date information from abroad. Some local proprietors make little effort to establish regular contacts with potential buyers such as government departments, market sellers operating in up-country towns, city trading stores and wholesalers.[11] Instead, they prefer to rely on the irregular custom provided by occasional passers-by and the goodwill of a local clientele living in the vicinity for whom they produce 'goods to order'. Many businessmen do not advertise regularly. Moreover, attempts to establish a proper distribution network (perhaps by employing a small, permanent staff of itinerant salesmen or commission agents or establishing retail outlets throughout the main urban centres) were often half-hearted, and poorly managed.

Financial control also leaves much to be desired. Without proper records of money transactions it is very difficult to monitor the flow of cash, stock and goods. This, in turn, deprives owners of a crucial instrument for maintaining control over productivity, checking on the performance and honesty of employees and keeping abreast of the flow of stocks and materials. Indeed, several researchers found that the quality of financial management was one of the most significant determinants of business performance.[12]

This discussion refers to some very general problems. However, several writers offer a more systematic analysis and have identified certain underlying dilemmas and patterns of organisational practice. One concerns the difficulties encountered by small entrepreneurs from a mainly artisan background when they try to build up a large manufacturing business.[13] A good many Africans move into manufacturing with little more than a vocational training and a previous record of employment as manual workers or supervisors in the modern sector. Entrepreneurs from this background are often reluctant to trade the workbench for the managerial office. Lacking confidence and commercial experience many cling doggedly to their original technical skills. They may also be unwilling or unable to give up their initial dependence on a local clientele of mainly individual buyers (with whom, perhaps, they share some kind of close personal bond). Similarly, many small entrepreneurs prefer to operate with a paternalistic system of labour relations built around a nucleus of skilled workers who are old workmates or members of the same ethnic community plus apprentices and journeymen. But where business organisation depends on familiar skills and relationships, expansion beyond a certain point may prove to be highly problematical. In order to achieve such a breakthrough, so that the firm can compete on equal terms with companies already occupying a strong market position and gain access to certain economies of large-scale production, the entrepreneur must be able to restructure his firm in two main ways.

Firstly, he needs to establish a wide range of contacts with potential buyers who are in a position to place bulk orders of standardised goods, preferably on a regular basis. This means setting up some kind of marketing and distribution system so that regular visits can be made to commercial organisations and public agencies. However a much more flexible, streamlined production system is required if firms are to cope efficiently with bulk orders and rapid changes in demand and so increase competitiveness and profitability. This presupposes a complementary and radical organisational shift in the deployment of labour, equipment and plant. Depending on the particular kind of manufacturing activity in question, several changes are likely to be crucial to such a successful transformation: introducing a more rational division of labour, in particular, substituting machinery for certain kinds of skilled labour and breaking down the labour process into easily supervised job lots; establishing some kind of departmentalised production system linked, ultimately, to an assembly-line flow; and 'routinising' day-to-day work operations through a system of rules and checks operated at every stage of the production cycle based on work norms, records and proper written or verbal instructions. To be effective such measures may also require further changes: better job-training schemes, higher-quality supervisors and the introduction of piece-rates and bonus payments linked closely to individual output.

Of course, these organisational procedures have long been standard practice in most Western firms of any size. Moreover, the appropriate knowledge and experience is easily accessible to those who live in the advanced economies. However, for African entrepreneurs – particularly, though not exclusively, those from an artisan background – direct exposure to modern forms of organisational experience is much more difficult to obtain. To carry through the transformation we have outlined, small African manufacturers must exercise considerable ingenuity and skill and they must be prepared to take tremendous risks and experiment a good deal. Not the least of their difficulties, almost certainly, is their inability to afford external advice or managerial assistance. Thus, until quite recently the majority of African entrepreneurs, even those who entered modern business from a background in commerce or administration, have found the task of organisation-building extremely formidable.[14] It is hardly surprising, therefore, that so many cling to the simpler forms of business organisation they already know or fail in their attempt to attain higher levels.

Some researchers have observed that among the rather more sophisticated, medium-sized African manufacturing enterprises it is often possible to identify two different styles of business management and types of firm organisation operating within the same industry or sector. Some businesses have attained their present form after going through the kinds of changes we have just described while others were established at a higher level of organisation from the beginning. On the basis of his study of the Nigerian bread industry, for example, Kilby distinguished between production and market-oriented entrepreneurs.[15] The first type usually possessed a sound technical knowledge of the equipment required in baking perhaps because of their vocational training and work experience. They supervised production very carefully, avoided problems of waste and pilfering and concentrated on quality control. But many lacked initiative where marketing was concerned so that lagging sales held back the full potential offered by an efficient production system. Consequently, most of these firms grew rather slowly and financed their expansion mostly out of profits. In general, those entrepreneurs who concentrated on maximising sales came from a background in commerce or trade. Some began by employing commission agents or street vendors who hawked bread through urban localities. This cheap but effective distribution system enabled these proprietors to expand quite rapidly. In fact most of the successful bakers in Kilby's study had concentrated on sales organisation in this way although some had 'jumped' into manufacturing from trade so that their operations were quite large from the beginning. However, this second group often displayed a crucial weakness: the inability to exercise proper managerial control over labour and machinery and to keep costs down.

Nafziger's research on the footwear industry, also in Nigeria, revealed a similar contrast in entrepreneurial styles.[16] Some of the smaller firms were run by people with a strong technical vocation but who lacked a proper understanding of the need to establish regular market outlets. In many of the larger firms, on the other hand, the proprietors' previous experience left them ill equipped to cope with the technical requirements of mass production (though some were also unaware of the special marketing needs involved in the footwear industry, namely the importance of flexibility). A similar pattern was also discovered among Ghanaian manufacturers.[17] One group moved into manufacturing from trade or following a spell of employment as administrators or salesmen in large companies while others relied mainly on a vocational background including, possibly, a period of part-time attendance at technical school. It is worth noting that this divergence in entrepreneurial origins and firm organisation is not unique to Africa. Research in a number of 'Third World' countries, including India, Pakistan, the Philippines, and Greece, carried out in the 1950s and 1960s revealed very similar tendencies.[18]

Though this distinction is quite useful, many African manufacturers do not belong completely in either category. Some artisan-entrepreneurs manage to obtain a degree of commercial or more advanced technical training at some point during their careers and this helps them to establish more impersonal forms of business organisation or they manage to make the transition through sheer determination, ability and a willingness to experiment. At the same time, providing they can bring in people with relevant technical experience to cope with the problems of control, or gain some first-hand knowledge in these areas, themselves – perhaps by working in a foreign firm for a while – the more market-oriented, administratively competent entrepreneurs can often overcome their initial technical limitations. What really counts is the ability to deploy a range of organisation-building skills. This, in turn, requires a willingness to forge links with various external agencies so that any deficiencies in the entrepreneur's own background and personal resources can be partly compensated. This brings us directly to the subject of the next section.

Social relationships in business

The ability to handle the problems of production, marketing and financial control does not rest solely on technical knowledge and administrative flair. We have already seen, for example, that entrepreneurial preferences for a particular kind of clientele or the desire to operate with a paternalistic approach to labour relations may set limits to the type of production system that can be utilised and inhibit market expansion. Ultimately these may reduce the potential for firm expansion. Thus, as many researchers have observed, the style of personal relations that provides the framework for business management has important implications. This is particularly crucial in four key areas of decision-making: the question of pooling capital and other skills through the formation of partnerships or companies; the willingness to delegate authority; dealing with the demands of family and kinsmen; and the ability to establish viable social networks with important agencies outside the firm who possess resources of potential value.[19] Again, all too often, African businessmen have been found wanting in these areas.

Partnerships or companies (other than between close kin) involving a genuine pooling of finance and perhaps managerial skills, have so far been quite rare in most African countries. In Kenya during the 1960s slightly more than half of the I.C.D.C.-supported firms studied by Marris and Somerset involved such arrangements.[20] But this was a very special group. Most small shops and market stalls (83%) – which were much more numerous – were owned and run by one or two people. In Zambia, even the largest and most successful businesses were normally run on a solo-management and ownership basis (90%), while in Ghana the comparable figure for the same type of enterprise was 75%.[21] The main reason for this marked reluctance to establish pooling arrangements seems to be the widespread fear that partners will cheat in some way or fail to pull their weight.[22] Alternatively, when asked, entrepreneurs claim that once someone has invested even a tiny amount of capital in their business that person will constantly interfere in the minutest details of day-to-day operations, so making efficient management virtually impossible, or they will regard the 'disappearance' of their money into a common fund as evidence that the main partner has squandered or stolen their assets.

In part, this atmosphere of suspicion and pessimism concerning the motivations of others may originate in pre-capitalist socio-economic practices. Thus, according to Hill, traditional forms of investment in West Africa, for example, involved land, houses or social dependants.[23] Also, few cultural precedents existed for non-kinsmen to combine resources on a long-term basis, leaving others to manage their capital or savings on their behalf. Be this as it may, it is quite likely that the chronic economic and political insecurity characteristic of many African countries in recent years also accounts for these problems in no small measure. Moreover, the very existence of a climate of distrust is often sufficient to deter capital-pooling arrangements in the first place, while the fear of accusations and recriminations may provoke the very outcome it was intended to avoid.

Clearly the widespread unwillingness to establish genuinely corporate forms of business arrangements is highly detrimental to African capitalism. In particular, it closes one of the most important potential avenues to firm expansion and reduces the likelihood that indigenous companies can become sufficiently competitive to mount an effective challenge to foreign companies. Nevertheless, there are some signs that change is underway. It seems likely that by exposing some local entrepreneurs to agreements involving co-management and/or ownership, both with foreigners and other nationals, the indigenisation measures introduced in Nigeria, and elsewhere, since the early 1970s have helped to create a 'nursery' environment in which a new and more appropriate climate of business cooperation (and an awareness of its advantages) can gradually emerge. The flow of much better educated professionals, administrators and technicians into private business, people whose cultural expectations have been shaped by their work experience in large public or private corporations, may also prove salutary in the long run. Indeed, there is evidence from countries like Ghana and Kenya that even before the first indigenisation programmes were introduced a small but steady movement towards partnership and company arrangements, sometimes led by the more educated and Westernised entrepreneurs, was already well under-way and was particularly noticeable in the more successful firms.[24]

Many African entrepreneurs are almost as unwilling to delegate authority to supervisors and managers as they are to share ownership. When questioned on this matter proprietors tend to argue that supervisors would cheat them in a variety of ways if they were permitted too much autonomy or were not subjected to frequent checks: stealing wages meant for the work-force, arranging private deals with customers, pocketing the difference between moneys apparently paid out to suppliers when sent to purchase raw materials (on the basis of an over-invoiced receipt) and the actual amount spent, and so on. Foreseeing these and other problems, many owners either fail to appoint proper supervisors in the first place or they refuse to permit them real authority in certain spheres and reward them inadequately for their services. Alternatively, as Marris and Somerset found in Kenya, those entrepreneurs who do hire supervisors tend to choose someone of low education, ability and ambition who will be too afraid to cheat their employer, but by the same token will also be unable to carry out their duties effectively.[25]

However talented or energetic an entrepreneur may be, there is a limit to the degree of supervision and coordination that one person can provide. Unless businessmen are prepared to delegate authority then eventually their firms will reach a point beyond where effective expansion is no longer possible. Nevertheless, it is important to note that not all African firms are confronted by this limitation. In Nigeria, Akeredolu-Ale discovered that the more successful entrepreneurs in his sample were willing to share some aspects of business leadership with hired staff.[26] Some also employed professional accountants. In Ghana, too, despite the widespread anxiety among the indigenous business community concerning the supposed un-trustworthiness of subordinates, one study found that more than three-fifths of those who were interviewed had, in fact, taken some steps in this direction and of these over half were willing to grant certain real dis-cretionary powers, for example the right to appoint, dismiss, promote or discipline other employees, to negotiate with suppliers or customers when the proprietor was absent, and so on.[27] In addition, certain strategies are available enabling entrepreneurs to avoid or minimise some of the risks associated with delegation. These might include the following: educating a son, nephew or brother in business management, accountancy or a relevant aspect of production technology with a view to offering him a position of responsibility at a later date; promoting an able employee with a long record of loyalty; appointing an experienced European manager, technician or adviser; or forming a company in partnership with suitable and trained friends or former workmates among whom specialised managerial tasks can be shared. One or more of these measures had already been adopted by some of the proprietors studied in Ghana during the late 1960s.

It seems likely that these and other practices will become more widespread among African entrepreneurs in the future. In the past the problem of delegation was linked not only to entrenched attitudes of mutual suspicion, but was also caused by the dearth of managerial staff with suitable qualifications and experience available for employment. In any case, until quite recently such high-quality personnel have normally preferred to seek better pay and prospects in foreign companies or the public sector. But there is reason to believe that these opportunities will decline as governments are forced to cut back on public-sector investments, as foreign firms are driven to come to terms with indigenisation measures and the rising numbers of young, educated job seekers are compelled to seek alternative employment outlets.

There is a certain paradox associated with the question of family or kinship relations and economic enterprise in much of Africa. Thus, there were few traditional precedents for genuine family businesses based on continuous, joint activity and ownership. Most day-to-day productive activities were executed very largely on an individual basis, although in farming the initial clearing of land prior to planting was often performed by communal work parties on the expectation of reciprocal activity and co-wives might share certain domestic tasks. Yet land and some other kinds of property were (and still are, to some extent) normally owned collectively and the products of labour were distributed on the basis of ascriptive rights and need. Also, individuals were usually able to make certain claims on the earnings or surpluses achieved by more successful people. The norm of generosity and the tendency, therefore, for wealth to be redistributed has always appeared – at least to Western observers – as a major, potential obstacle to capital accumulation. Believing that these obligations persist today, even in a modern, urban context, and that many African proprietors are unwilling or unable to resist kinship demands to any great extent, most researchers in this field have examined the links between the extended family and business enterprise in some detail, though they do not always agree as to the severity of the problem. The main research findings can be summarised as follows.

Firstly, except in commerce – market trade, shopkeeping, wholesale activity – few African firms can be labelled as genuine 'family businesses' of the kind found in certain parts of Asia and introduced into East and West Africa respectively by Indian and Levantine immigrants from the late nineteenth century.[28] In joint enterprises of this kind, immediate members of the nuclear family and/or adult siblings or perhaps in-laws pool capital, labour and profits, to a greater or lesser extent, over a considerable period of time. But it is not just the absence of traditional precedent that works against the establishment of African family businesses outside the sphere of trade. Most proprietors also anticipate a number of adverse consequences should kinsmen be permitted a direct involvement in business affairs. Family members, it is said, are unwilling to respond to the same discipline as other employees. They tend to demand special treatment and this provokes discontent among the work-force. Jealous of the owner's success and resentful of his authority, they are also prone to dishonest as well as unreliable behaviour. In any case, apart from trading, where the qualifications required for a relatively small work-force are few, most modern enterprises in manufacturing, services and contracting need to draw upon a wide range of skills especially when expansion takes place. It will not normally be possible for most entrepreneurs to secure all or even most of these from within their extended families even if they wished to do so.

Secondly, however, some studies have shown that a sizeable proportion of African entrepreneurs can and do draw certain advantages through family connections, certainly in the early stages of business growth: help with board and keep while getting established, inheriting revenue-earning assets such as cocoa farms or houses and receiving gifts or loans, normally in respect to initial capital.[29] Some entrepreneurs have also benefited from the skill, loyalty and dedication provided by a member of the nuclear family or a close relative, normally a wife, son or brother. Thirdly, and despite these advantages, it is also clear that kinship obligations sometimes create serious difficulties. Demands to provide jobs for a wide range of kin, irrespective of their qualifications, and requests for cash donations or gifts of varying amounts from a stream of 'visitors' are probably the most frequent claims.[30] Financial contributions to funerals constitute another source of difficulty, although the time spent away from management may be more damaging than the cash demands. Businessmen are often expected to finance the education of nephews, nieces and younger siblings or even provide more or less permanent support for widowed or deserted sisters, particularly in matrilineal societies.[31]

Some researchers have argued that given the relatively impersonal urban situation in which they operate and the absence of any pressing need to depend on kinsmen for mutual protection and support, most proprietors who own modern firms ought to be able to resist many of these demands on their capital and time, yet the majority fail to do so. Thus, as Nafziger observes, entrepreneurial activity often benefits from kinship connections in the early stages but later expansion may be impaired by extended family demands.[32] What is required is the will to establish a *modus vivendi* with kin based on the maintenance of a clearly understood separation between matters of business and those pertaining to kinship needs. Here, for example, the entrepreneur might agree to set aside some posts but only for suitably qualified relatives (when job vacancies arise) and in return for promises of loyal support. Alternatively, he might make small, regular contributions to certain needy individuals or perhaps agree to set up one or more brothers or nephews in a profession or business of their own and thereafter disclaim any further responsibility.

Such attempts to isolate extended family involvement from business activity are not easy and do not come cheap. Nor is there any guarantee that these arrangements will resolve all the dilemmas kinship can create. But until such time as the process of socio-economic differentiation taking place in African societies reaches a point where kinship relationships no longer extend so firmly across the growing cultural, income, educational and residential divides between classes, then serious attempts to at least neutralise the worst effects of kinship interference represent a considerable advance even if they do not offer a perfect solution. In fact, in some countries there is evidence to suggest that the more successful businessmen have tried to move somewhat beyond this point. Not only have they taken steps to partially insulate their firms from kinship claims with considerable success, but they have also endeavoured to place family loyalties at the service of their firms by awarding key positions of responsibility to one or two promising individuals after paying for the latter to receive special training.[33]

Strategies for capital accumulation

Most decisions in business obviously have some bearing on the question of firm growth and capital accumulation. However, there are some entrepreneurial practices where, according to many researchers, failure to act in the appropriate way is likely to be especially detrimental to business expansion. Perhaps the three most crucial areas of choice in this respect are the following: the propensity to reinvest profits in a series of small firms rather than concentrating initially on building up one major enterprise; the tendency to engage in lavish styles of personal consumption; and the failure to make adequate arrangements for the successful transfer of business interests to the next generation.

There is abundant evidence to suggest that African entrepreneurs are prone to spread their profits, time and energies too thinly over a variety of activities. On the basis of his study of Kumasi traders in Ghana, for example, Garlick concluded that many local businessmen regarded their commercial activities mainly as a source of revenue for buying cocoa farms or houses and as a permanent source of economic security to provide for old age as well as family support.[34] In Kenya, Marris and Somerset also found that the majority of traders and industrialists had made investments in commercial farms (68%) while more than one-third owned a stake in some additional business activity of a more elaborate nature.[35] Certainly, the tendency for entrepreneurs to plough business profits into house buying, whether for lucrative rentier purposes or as a means of demonstrating private wealth, is very widespread indeed.[36]

Some academics and a good many African politicians, journalists and public spokesmen have been highly critical of this propensity to engage in business diversification. These practices are regarded as reprehensible because they supposedly undermine the prospect for obtaining a highly productive national economy and rapid rates of economic growth. Their reasoning seems to be that by dispersing efforts and scarce capital through a number of small investments entrepreneurs effectively deprive their most important ventures of essential funds so that it becomes impossible to gain the economies of scale and compete on more equal terms with foreign companies. Secondly, by shutting out these opportunities for efficiency and growth through concentration, each individual proprietor may well end up with total assets of a lower net value than might otherwise have been possible despite the apparent proliferation of small investments. Although there is some reason to view the first argument with a certain amount of scepticism, as we will see below, the second does point to a very real problem. Thus, in their Kenyan study Marris and Somerset found that a willingness to focus on one central firm was more clearly related to overall, long-term business success than any other aspect of entrepreneurial endeavour and this was recognised by most of the able entrepreneurs in their sample.[37] Other studies have reached similar conclusions.

However, the relationship between business success and the pattern of profit reinvestment is probably more complex than these bald statements suggest. It seems very likely that the tendency to diversify too quickly and too widely is actually in part both a response to and a symptom of deeper underlying weaknesses in entrepreneurial behaviour that are even more significant in holding back business success. Here, diversification offers an escape-route from these other dilemmas even while it exacerbates these same problems. For example, the inability to deal effectively with the demands of kinship and the resultant haemorrhage of business funds may drive owners to 'conceal' or immobilise their financial resources by investing them in fixed assets such as houses, this being much easier to achieve than implementing long-term plans for business expansion. Widespread diversification may also occur because an entrepreneur is unwilling or unable to develop a more impersonal system of managerial control. Proprietors may feel that by setting up several small-scale, relatively uncomplicated businesses they can both expand their assets and still retain close personal control over all their activities.[38] Of course, this 'solution' may not, in fact, resolve the basic problem, since a proliferation of small enterprises may sap entrepreneurial energies and skills just as much as one large expanding firm and may end up being badly run and not very profitable. Alternatively, some owners may simply be ill equipped to cope beyond a certain point with all the organisational demands of firm expansion.

The claim that by dispersing their business investments too widely African capitalists threaten national development prospects needs to be considered with some care. Thus, some writers have argued that what may create difficulties for the economy as a whole may be perfectly rational from the perspective of individual entrepreneurs.[39] Investments in farms, houses, transport, and so on, may be much less risky and less demanding than expanding a plastics factory or a building–engineering firm, and may even yield a better return on capital. The haphazard economic environment, against which indigenous firms almost certainly enjoy less protection than foreign companies, the arbitrary nature of the political process in many countries and bureaucratic indifference, even obstructionism, may all combine to discourage local capitalists from sinking their assets into highly vulnerable long-term ventures which tie up considerable quantities of funds in a concentrated form.[40] Some entrepreneurs may possess certain patriotic sentiments and may, at times, seek to demonstrate these through their business activities. But neither in Africa nor elsewhere can they expect to flourish in business for long if they give greater priority to national development needs than their own immediate profit considerations, given the realities of competition and the anarchy of the market. Depending on the observer's viewpoint, it is only the market, the policies pursued by governments, or both, that can bring these different kinds of interests into some kind of harmony. It is unrealistic to expect individual capitalists to do so alone and unaided. African governments whose leaders genuinely wish to encourage a productive local capitalism must adopt national development strategies that will generate an investment climate more conducive to long-term, concentrated business activity.

Another point that needs to be made is that some degree of business diversification may actually benefit capital accumulation rather than the reverse. Thus, houses or farms not only offer a source of economic security in the event of a collapse in mainstream business ventures, but such investments also provide an excellent source of collateral. This may increase the prospects for obtaining bank or other loans thereby enhancing business growth (providing, of course, such borrowing is used wisely). In any case, whatever the motivation, from the time of the first textile magnates in early nineteenth-century Britain, capitalist entrepreneurs have always been prone to invest part of their profits in house purchases.[41] In this respect, as in so much else, African proprietors are probably very little different from their counterparts elsewhere. Furthermore, an additional business venture, established after a period of time sufficient to permit the first to undergo considerable expansion and which complements the original business, may be highly beneficial. The soap manufacturer who invests in an oil-palm plantation, the established trader who eventually sets up a factory to manufacture the type of garments she has always sold in her shops, the contractor who enters a partnership with a sawmilling firm, in cases such as these the entrepreneur is establishing vertical linkages between the different sectors of the economy, a process that is fundamental to development by any criteria.

In short, African entrepreneurs diversify for a variety of reasons and in many instances their motivations have been misunderstood and their actions have been undeservedly maligned. Much depends on the specific circumstances prevailing in each case: for example, how soon did diversification occur after the initial firm was founded; what amount of capital was involved compared to existing assets; and what connections, if any, did the later investments have to the earlier ones? Only careful research can reveal the interplay between these factors and therefore the true costs and benefits involved.

It is widely believed that most indigenous capitalists waste a considerable proportion of their profits on various displays of conspicuous consumption; house purchases, luxury imports, and building up a network of personal dependants including 'investment' in children through contracting several marriages. Again, if true, none of this is unique to entrepreneurs who may, in fact, be rather less indulgent in these respects than many political leaders and wealthy professionals. It is difficult to add anything useful to this argument because few attempts have been made to estimate the true extent of consumer extravagance and therefore its likely effects on business growth. At least one researcher, however, has tried to make some headway on this question. In his study of Lagos entrepreneurs, Akeredolu-Ale distinguished between what he called the 'profit-for-self-and-family' and the 'profit-for-business-growth' approaches.[42] The first involved a basically 'consumption–subsistence' orientation while the second was based on the desire for expansion and meant a willingness to save and to live abstemiously. He argues, no doubt correctly, that entrepreneurs entertain certain images of themselves and their activities. These inevitably affect their willingness either to succumb to the temptations of excessive consumption or to resist and engage instead in productive investment. But the ways in which entrepreneurs approach a wide range of additional matters – technical organisation, long-range planning, financial management, delegation, and so on – are also shaped by these self-images. In other words, it is not possible to consider personal consumption and its particular effects on business separately from other questions. Like excessive diversification, when carried to extreme it tends to be a symptom of a much more fundamental malorientation to entrepreneurial activity.

Since neither the Western pattern of corporate ownership nor the Asian tradition of joint-family activity have so far been widely adopted in most African countries, the dilemma of business succession has often seemed very formidable. Again, African entrepreneurs have been criticised for failing to seek 'viable' solutions. Research indicates that those proprietors who have considered this problem normally anticipate handing over their business to a son.[43] However, the common complaint is that sons or other relatives may lack the training, experience or personal attributes required for such a responsibility. In any case, young educated family members may prefer the prestige and security offered by bureaucratic or professional positions. According to some writers many local owners fail to make any proper arrangements for handing over business management at all. Such uncertainties may mean that sudden illness or death results in the virtual break up of the firm; its assets liquidised and distributed widely among many competing family claimants or an unsuitable successor soon leads the firm towards bankruptcy.[44]

In practice, the dilemmas posed by business succession are probably rather more complicated than most observers allow. For one thing, the question of business continuity within families is only one aspect of a much wider problem: the limited extent to which the Western-type business corporation – involving the wide diffusion of ownership and the ubiquity of professional hired managers – has so far emerged in Africa. More specifically, most of the enterprises studied by the writers we have discussed were relatively new. They had been established from scratch by the present owners. The majority were still young or middle aged so that the problem of succession had not yet surfaced. Although many come from families where parents, and sometimes grandparents too, had once been engaged in some kind of commercial activity, they were normally the first generation to establish modern enterprises requiring considerable investments in fixed assets, where it made sound economic sense to preserve the firm's continuity if at all possible. Thus, the ability to plan ahead for a solution to the succession problem was certainly important, but at the time when these studies were carried out it was, perhaps, not a particularly valid test of entrepreneurial competence.

The problem of business succession is complicated by, and leads on to, further considerations. Thus, what we are really discussing here is the phenomenon of the inter-generational accumulation of wealth and privilege and therefore the question of class formation. This is sufficiently important to require a separate discussion.

PATTERNS OF WEALTH TRANSFERENCE AND CLASS FORMATION

In a capitalist economy it might be highly desirable, indeed essential, for long-term national economic development if there was a steady build-up of resources in certain families which did not come to a halt within each generation but continued into the future. At a certain point in time such concentrations of wealth could then be mobilised for large-scale investments. But this, in turn, is only another way of saying that before capitalist development can make much headway the process of socio-economic differentiation or class formation must reach a certain critical point. Here we return to one of the essential changes Marx referred to in his theory of the 'primitive accumulation of capital'.

It is important to recognise that the transfer of fully fledged businesses of a reasonable size from one generation to the next represents only one way in which the transmission of wealth and privilege can take place. In the case of most African societies so far it has probably been the least significant though, arguably, this is now changing. Bearing this in mind, what can the various studies tell us concerning the different ways in which wealth and privilege have been accumulated within certain families?

Investment in children's education has almost certainly provided the most widely used and significant avenue through which one generation has sought to bestow advantages on the next in recent times. In Chapter 3 we saw how the benefits of office enabled chiefs and sometimes other traditional rulers to finance their sons' and nephews' school fees thereby providing the latter with the means of gaining early, privileged entry to bureaucratic office and lower-professional positions (in an increasingly Westernised economy) or even, in some cases, eventual access to positions of political and military leadership. At a time – before the Second World War – when the environment for business enterprises was relatively undeveloped and when colonial restrictions and foreign competition hampered most kinds of African commercial activity, this pattern of wealth transference represented a highly rational response since employment offered much better prospects for educated young people than private enterprise. The post-war expansion of public-sector employment and the promise of Independence gave further credence to this pattern of career choice and family investment.

More recently, by providing an indirect route to family privilege and class power via political/bureaucratic office, education has tended to generate obstacles to African capitalism, because in many countries an expanding public sector, buttressed by statist ideologies, has deprived local private interests of many resources and opportunities. Hopefully, this situation will give way to a more favourable climate in the near future as those who have sought careers in public life and government increasingly perceive that private capital accumulation and public-sector employment are not competing but potentially complementary activities. In some countries, particularly Kenya, Nigeria and the Sudan, these changes are already well underway.[45]

Of course, the consequences of increasing educational provision, for some, have not always worked in such a way as to undermine African capitalism. A high proportion of the businessmen studied by the writers we have discussed came from relatively comfortable 'lower-middle-class' backgrounds. Their fathers (and sometimes grandfathers) had been employed at some time in the modern sectors of the colonial economies as artisans, policemen, local government employees, storekeepers and so on.[46] Alternatively, they were involved in commercial farming or some kind of petty business activity such as hawking or produce buying.[47] Consequently, although the entrepreneurs were not as privileged as the sons of chiefs, their families had been able to finance, or part-finance, a certain level of schooling. As most studies have shown, they were much more likely to have attended – and in many cases – completed primary school than the population as a whole of the same age group. In Kenya, for example, Marris and Somerset found that 93% of their I.C.D.C. sample had received some education whereas according to the 1962 census only 32% of the whole population at that time were in the same fortunate position.[48] In some countries a substantial minority of the entrepreneurs who were studied also spent at least a few years in secondary school, an advantage which was even more likely to have been denied to their contemporaries. The experience of full- or part-time further education in the pursuit of technical, commercial or managerial qualifications after leaving school was also beneficial in certain cases.[49]

Marris and Somerset found that in Kenya the experience of secondary education was not strongly correlated to business success. They argued that this was probably because schooling at this level tends to instil and reward attitudes of passive acceptance and a respect for routinised learning, whilst creative restlessness and a problem-solving orientation are often neglected or even denigrated.[50] Clearly, formal education, whether at this or any other level, could not be expected to equip prospective entrepreneurs with all the aptitudes required for successful business activity. What education did provide, however, was confidence, basic skills in literacy and numeracy and, perhaps most important of all, it endowed a considerable proportion of these future business leaders with the qualifications needed in order to secure valuable modern-sector job experience in public institutions or foreign companies prior to starting up on their own. The first-hand administrative, technical and commercial experience gained through such employment was usually at a fairly low level.[51] Nevertheless, as clerks, supervisors, salesmen or skilled workers, the future entrepreneurs did learn the rudiments of accountancy, marketing, record-keeping and routine organisational practice – the importance of maintenance schedules, work norms, forward planning, and so on. Previous employment in a managerial or higher professional position in a large organisation or the experience of working abroad in Europe or America for some years may have provided a small number of entrepreneurs with an even better preparation for business leadership.[52]

Inter-generational accumulation has also been proceeding in ways that involve the provision of resources much more directly related to business activity. Thus, in Chapter 7 we saw that gifts and loans between family members had often provided an important source of starting capital for quite a few entrepreneurs in several countries. Inheriting small family properties, farms or houses, had also helped some by providing a supplementary source of income or the collateral required in order to negotiate bank finance.

In a few countries the transmission not just of family wealth but of assets directly created as a result of one generation's business activities, which are then placed at the disposal of the next, has been proceeding for a considerable period of time. The case of the Hausa merchants of Northern Nigeria is possibly the most well-known.[53] Here, sons, nephews or apprentice-clients do not normally inherit complete and ready-made businesses as such at the death or retirement of the founders. But they do derive a number of concrete benefits from periods of employment in their patrons' firms: commercial experience, the opportunity to establish a wide range of business contacts and the chance to earn the trust of the local trading community. In addition, there is the possibility of receiving substantial loans or gifts to invest in their own enterprise which they can build up slowly whilst remaining partially under the protection of the original firm. In this way junior enterprises grow out of the parent companies, feeding on the latters' resources until such time as a much more substantial degree of independence seems desirable.[54]

A similar process of inter-generational business mobility has been observed in the Sudan where it has occurred at several different economic levels. Duffield's analysis of the cycle of lorry ownership is particularly instructive.[55] Before and soon after the Second World War a would-be entrepreneur could acquire a small transport business by hiring out the lorry owned by a wealthy patron and then saving part of his earnings. Eventually, he would hope to buy his own first lorry. This might involve borrowing to supplement meagre savings. In time, the debts would be paid off and he could then retain all the profits from lorry ownership and perhaps go on to acquire a second or more reliable vehicle. This process of expansion might take 20 years or more. Once a regular income from lorry ownership was assured, the proprietor usually diversified into shopkeeping, house ownership, commercial farming and so on.

Nowadays, it is much more difficult for newcomers to build up in this way and compete successfully with the first generation of lorry owners. The latters' sons, however, can bypass this process either because of their educational attainments, made possible by parental investment, or through the opportunity to manage one or more of their father's businesses. Duffield also claims that many Sudanese entrepreneurs, not just lorry-owners, increasingly run family enterprises. These are not organised in the style of Asian firms where several relatives participate directly in running the same firm together. But they are family businesses in the sense that each relative runs his own branch of the increasingly diversified and yet integrated network of enterprises, all of which were originally financed from the profits earned by the original firm.

Mahmoud's study is concerned with the history and development of the Sudanese capitalist bourgeoisie as a whole, but it includes a survey of the country's leading contemporary businessmen.[56] Of the many interesting findings three are of special relevance to the present discussion. Firstly, Mahmoud demonstrates the underlying continuity in the process of indirect capital accumulation over several generations, beginning with traditional office-holding and early access to land for commercial farming, through to educational provision for sons, diversification from agriculture into trade and culminating, in the case of some families, in the establishment of modern industries by a more recent generation of educated descendants. But, secondly, nearly one-quarter of the leading capitalists in her sample – originally of non-Sudanic but mainly Arabic origin – acquired their businesses directly from their fathers or grandfathers. The latter's forebears in turn received favoured treatment from the British in the nineteenth century.[57] Thirdly, through a multiplicity of activities, pursued over a long period of time, the Sudanese capitalist bourgeoisie has consolidated its position. These activities include intermarriages between wealthy families, business partnerships in which people of immigrant and indigenous origin pool their resources, a history of involvement in politics, including a willingness to fund parties and elites favourable to local capital and the formation of 'alliances' with leading military officers and government officials based on corruption and the forging of close personal ties.[58]

AN OVERVIEW OF ENTREPRENEURIAL ABILITY

In general, the writers we have discussed share certain overall misgivings concerning the standards of business competence displayed by African proprietors. These have been summarised in various ways. Beveridge and Oberschall, for example observed that, despite the achievements shown by their sample of leading Zambian entrepreneurs in building up modern enterprises employing fairly large numbers of employees, there remained a considerable gap in terms of organisational efficiency between these local firms and the majority of European and Asian firms.[59] Few of the former could handle any but the simplest technology, had evolved beyond a solo style of management and ownership or had introduced effective, routinised systems of production control. Schatz, too, saw the need for an entrepreneurial 'leap'.[60] Though, as we saw in Chapter 7, he regarded the shortage of viable investment projects as the chief constraint on Nigerian capitalism, nevertheless, in common with other writers, he was quite clear that managerial deficiencies do create real barriers to indigenous business success. If local firms are to have any hope of carving out a leading place in the Nigerian economy then entrepreneurs must surmount three main hurdles: the ability to utilise higher levels of technology with all that this involves in terms of quality control, training and specialisation; the attainment of much greater degrees of organisational competence, in particular the willingness to delegate authority and establish more impersonal systems of control; and the establishment of wide-ranging market outlets based on an elaborate sales network and distribution system.[61]

Nafziger's Nigerian study led him to stress the complementarity between entrepreneurship and the other factors of production: labour, plant, machinery and so on.[62] As the latter increase in quantity and complexity, with firm expansion, so too the quality of managerial leadership and competence must also rise otherwise new increments of labour or capital cannot be absorbed and operations become increasingly ineffective, leading eventually, perhaps, to collapse. Nafziger argues that until recently the most able and technically qualified Nigerians, who might otherwise have gone into private business, have been attracted by employment in the public sector or foreign firms, leaving local capitalism largely devoid of high-quality personnel.

The wide range of agreement between these writers is impressive and deserves to be taken all the more seriously since their analyses are invariably rooted in solid empirical research. Nevertheless, it could be argued that the employment of a broader, comparative and macro framework might generate the basis for a rather different interpretation concerning the quality of African enterprise and this is sometimes missing in these studies. Thus, the findings we have discussed need to be qualified in several ways.

Although those social scientists who have carried out studies of entrepreneurial performance normally discuss the importance of external constraints in some detail, the very fact that their primary interest lies in investigating individual decisions means that their studies often fail to deal adequately with the interconnections between what, for want of more appropriate terms, we might call the macro- and micro-levels of analysis. Take, for example, the crucial bottleneck to business growth caused by the failure to delegate authority. Most writers see this as a personal preference on the part of entrepreneurs arising out of widespread mutual distrust and the deep psychological desire to retain absolute personal control. But this may constitute only one factor and the least important. Thus, many businessmen may simply lack the financial resources required in order to attract really able professional candidates for such managerial positions. There may be no shortage of eager low-cost applicants but they may be people who have failed to gain reasonable employment elsewhere or who were dismissed because of their lack of training, experience, probity or competence. Alternatively, part of the problem may lie with the relatively underdeveloped nature of African economies to date, so that the supply of highly eligible employees is rather limited anyway.

Similar problems may help to explain why partnerships and shareholding arrangements have so far been relatively rare in most countries. Again, there may be any number of willing candidates ready to become co-directors but they may have little to offer in the way of capital or expertise. Genuine investors, on the other hand, may prefer to seek safer outlets for their savings, in houses and farms, or if they do intend to engage in entrepreneurial activity of a more demanding nature, they may choose to establish their own businesses. The latter alternative may appear to be both more profitable than collaborating with an existing proprietor and less risky, since it is always difficult to evaluate another's abilities from the outside. Furthermore, most countries – Nigeria, Zimbabwe, the Ivory Coast and Kenya being the exceptions – do not yet possess formal capital markets.[63]

In other words, to a considerable extent the difficulties faced by African proprietors in achieving successful firm expansion almost certainly reflect the wider problems of economic and class development in the economy as a whole and are not merely the result of personal whim or inappropriate cultural orientations. Here we return to a familiar theme: the complex interrelationship between the economic environment, the level of socio-economic differentiation and enterprise development. Enterprises respond and grow in a secure economic climate offering a variety of resources and opportunities, but their expansion in turn renders them more acceptable, secure and promising as sources of employment and outlets for personal savings. In theory, by utilising these and other inputs (if and when they are offered) in productive ways, businessmen then achieve profit levels which enable them to attract yet further inflows of resources. Their actions also help to develop the wider economy through their contributions in the form of tax revenues, wage payments, dividends, export revenues, competitively priced commodities, and so on. The difficulty, of course, is for governments to enact policies or for entrepreneurs to adopt business strategies, or both, that enable these virtuous linkages to become established in the first place. Historically, this process has always been slow, hesitant and fraught with setbacks. It would be surprising if it were otherwise in Africa.

Another difficulty with the studies we have discussed is that they either fail to utilise a comparative perspective altogether – and so do not see the similarities between African firms and business elsewhere in the world – or when they do make comparisons with, say, Western companies these tend to be inappropriate and misleading. Whether implicitly or explicitly, African enterprise is normally evaluated in terms of a particular model of contemporary Western business organisation, namely the large company run by salaried, professional managers and specialists and owned by various groups of large and small shareholders or financial institutions. In one sense it is both useful and necessary to employ such a frame of reference since in the final analysis some indigenous businesses do need to evolve in the direction of corporate organisations if they are ever to compete on near or equal terms with foreign firms in Africa and abroad. On the other hand, it is also important to bear in mind the following considerations.

Firstly, the great majority of businesses found in the advanced countries today are small, private companies owned and managed by the same person or persons, just as in the majority of African firms. In fact, the largest single category of enterprises consists of the self-employed proprietor with no hired workers. Recent studies in Britain, for example, have shown that 10% of the entire work-force now belong to this group and the numbers involved are still growing.[64] Most enterprises that do engage a work-force are quite small. Again, in Britain, only 5% of all firms larger than one-person enterprises employ more than a hundred people.[65] Secondly, it is misleading to compare African firms with the Western corporate business form because the latter was the product of a long period of business evolution. Also, it took much longer to become the most important source of employment and production in some countries than in others. In the United States, the corporation, as a device for accumulating huge amounts of capital from an often unwary public at relatively little personal risk to the directors, emerged in the decades just before the Civil War. It was especially important as a means for exploiting the opportunities provided by railway construction and as a means of mobilising the vast sums of money needed for such ventures.[66]

By contrast, the private, mainly family-owned business remained the dominant vehicle of industrialisation throughout most of the nineteenth century in the advanced European countries and certainly in France and Britain. In the case of Britain, for example, Hannah has shown that as late as 1880 the hundred largest manufacturing firms only controlled 10% of the market. Amalgamations between private companies and takeover attempts began to take place in the last years of the nineteenth century, but industrial concentration remained at a much lower level compared to the United States. Not until the 1920s did substantial movements in this direction take place.[67] Indeed, some writers have explained the onset of Britain's relative economic and technological decline at the end of the nineteenth century partly in these terms, arguing that there were too many small firms clinging fiercely to their independence, unable and unwilling to finance more advanced methods of production.[68] A similar analysis has been offered in the case of France where, it has been suggested, a conservative and basically family-oriented business culture was significant in slowing down the pace of industrialisation, including the full-scale national adoption of advanced technology.[69] Germany is normally regarded as a country where the large industrial corporation, supported by finance capital, rapidly became the motor force for industrial growth. However, according to Gerschenkron, even here the statistical record suggests that this interpretation is somewhat misleading.[70] Thus, in Germany before the First World War 94.6% of all industrial enterprises employed 10 people or less and this included mining. Moreover, most of these firms were very small indeed, 2 employees per establishment was the average.

There is another way in which some of the studies of African firms tend to create a rather misleading impression of entrepreneurial failings. No doubt unintentionally, some researchers write as if these deficiencies were more or less unique to the African situation and have few really important contemporary parallels elsewhere, especially in the advanced economies. Yet some at least of the supposedly restrictive features of African enterprise are extremely commonplace outside Africa. Again, recent research on small firms in Britain has revealed that after an initial growth-spurt the majority of proprietors tend to hold back from further expansion and concentrate instead on business survival. Beyond a certain cut-off point in terms of employment – approximately 20 workers – British entrepreneurs in the 1980s seem to lack the motivation to bring in the outside, managerial skills (or take steps to acquire these additional skills for themselves through further training) required for further expansion.[71] It has been suggested that one major reason for this reluctance is the fear that further rapid growth will threaten the owner's ability to retain full personal control. Such feelings are remarkably similar to those attributed to many African proprietors and they apparently generate the same kind of problems.

In fact, all over the capitalist world, and whatever the reasons, the vast majority of small firms never attain the size, status and power of big corporations. Some firms go bankrupt and disappear. Many remain small for long periods of time and continue to be run as sole proprietorships, small partnerships or family businesses. Others are eventually swallowed up by bigger or more ambitious companies. Only a tiny minority reveal the stamina, determination, foresight and ability required in order to grow into the monolithic companies that have become so important to Western economic life. No doubt 'luck', in entering the market at the right time or reaping the benefits of political favours (market protection, government contracts, state subsidies, legislation that discriminates against business rivals, and so on), has always been a crucial element in this process as well.

Providing the political and economic environment becomes much more favourable to indigenous enterprises, there seems no reason to doubt that a similar minority of able, determined and probably privileged business leaders will not emerge and seek to impose their will on African economic life in the future, much as their Western counterparts have been doing for the last hundred years or more. For some African entrepreneurs, at least, the huge political as well as economic gains in prospect for those willing to outgrow the limitations imposed by more traditional and familiar business styles will surely come to outweigh the personal losses involved.

§ 9 §

WHAT PROSPECTS FOR AFRICAN CAPITALISM?

The emergence of indigenous capitalist bourgeoisies has been inextricably bound up with a number of processes: the growing exposure of African societies to external influences, the slow evolution of increasingly differentiated socio-economic structures, changing ideology and the nature of state power and politics. Consequently, much of the discussion in this book has been concerned with the need to explore the implications of these wider questions for local business groups. In pursuing these themes it has been argued that state power and politics have exerted a particularly profound and often retarding effect on indigenous economic activity of all kinds, including emergent capitalist classes, though other inhibiting factors have also been extremely influential.

Nevertheless, a number of forces are at work which may not only compel African governments to become more responsive to national needs as a whole, but which may also generate an improving economic as well as political climate for African capitalism in the years ahead. Indeed, these influences have already been much in evidence in some countries during the last few years.

Statist economic policies have been largely discredited and to some extent are now in retreat.[1] In many instances the wealth extracted by states over the last 25 years or so has not been productively redeployed. Much of it has been misappropriated for private or political purposes, thereby contributing to a situation of growing inequality. Alternatively, it has been invested in different kinds of public-sector enterprise, often on a huge scale. However it is measured – the return on capital outlay, the contribution to government revenue or the ability to supply sufficient goods and services at a reasonable cost – the performance of the various parastatals has often been very poor in relation to the scarce resources they have absorbed. Even some Marxist writers now seem to doubt the wisdom of trying to expand African economies by relying primarily on public enterprise, at least for the foreseeable future. Meanwhile, government at-

184

tempts at widespread economic regulation and the imposition of various demands on private producers have stifled enterprise and investment.

The result has been economic stagnation, even collapse in the case of some countries. Moreover, this has happened following a long period of rapid economic change and gradually rising living standards from the 1940s to the 1970s which not only helped to raise material expectations among ordinary people but also exposed the rural and urban masses more intensively to the imperatives as well as the inducements of the cash-nexus. Increasing inequality, repression and frustrated aspirations have all generated political tensions. Faced with the dire consequences of statism – economic decline, the threat of increased political instability and a retreat into the 'second' economy – even the most repressive and corrupt regimes have been forced to move some way towards the introduction of an economic climate more conducive to private initiative.

There are also powerful external pressures at work propelling African governments in the same direction. Thus, over the last few years the International Monetary Fund and World Bank have increasingly insisted that the allocation of further financial assistance to African governments – in the form of debt rescheduling and the provision of 'structural adjustment loans' specifically designed to help resuscitate stagnant or crisis-ridden economies – is to be conditional upon government willingness to introduce wide-ranging reforms in economic management. Some Western governments, too, are now insisting that future aid will depend partly on the willingness to place greater reliance on the operation of market forces and the rejection of what a British minister recently referred to as 'fake-socialist solutions'.[2]

By the end of 1986 some 22 African countries had accepted reform packages that qualified them to receive special World Bank loan facilities.[3] Included in this group were countries as diverse, in terms of previous political ideology and economic policy, as Guinea, Mali, Ghana, Mozambique, Kenya, the Ivory Coast, Malawi and Senegal. The precise content of these reforms has varied but certain key measures stand out. They include the following: currency devaluation, privatisation of certain state enterprises, deregulation of some areas of economic life, serious attempts to reduce inflation, cuts in public expenditure and salaries and the payment of higher producer-prices to farmers as part of a primary emphasis on agricultural revival and expansion. In some countries signs of an economic up-turn are already apparent[4] though the extent to which this is due to the reforms rather than the provision of financial help or the slightly improved world economic climate of the last few years is not altogether clear.

But economic necessity and the dangers of political unrest are not the only factors at work. Arguably, a number of important cumulative, long-term changes taking place in the social and institutional structures of most African countries are slowly but surely bringing about a fundamental shift in the crucial relationships between the sphere of private economic activity, on the one hand, and that of state power and politics, on the other. Some of these were discussed briefly in earlier chapters:

1. The rise of technocratic/bureaucratic elites imbued with a concern for national as well as personal ambition and whose members are increasingly likely to be directly or indirectly involved in private business activity on their own account.

2. The growing numbers of educated people competing for secure, high-salaried positions in government employment, and this at a time when the public sector may be contracting, may mean that private business appears increasingly attractive as an alternative.

3. The emergence of second- or even third-generation educated middle-class professionals whose families have already established a relatively secure economic base in the ownership of various kinds of wealth, including business (alongside their greater ability to gain access to prestigious avenues of employment), as a result of the inter-generational accumulation and transfer of different kinds of resources.

4. The ability of privileged political insiders and their clients to exploit their proximity to state power and office at different times since Independence in order to amass private wealth, thereby helping to deepen the destructive tendencies towards 'parasitical'[5] or booty capitalism yet also, perhaps, rendering such political beneficiaries less hostile to future private entrepreneurial rivals now that they possess sources of personal wealth that are not dependent solely on the monopolisation of political power.

To the extent that these changes are indeed taking place they offer further prospects of an improving political climate for African capitalism. Thus, the distrust of private as against collective ownership, the feeling that economic enterprise and political or bureaucratic employment were mutually exclusive and opposed avenues for personal success, the perception that an increasingly differentiated society characterised by economic pluralism and political division along class rather than communal lines represented an alien and destructive force undermining African traditions and the unwillingness of political rulers to tolerate the emergence of potentially independent class rivals or share national resources with others outside the state apparatus – all of these polarities and divisions may steadily wane as they become irrelevant as well as counterproductive from the point of view of all emergent classes including political/bureaucratic elites. Instead, the spheres of public and private, politics and economics are increasingly characterised by complementarity and interdependence in just the same way as in other developed and developing capitalist countries.

We turn now to African entrepreneurs themselves; what motivations drive them, what resources equip them to play a much more fundamental economic role in the years ahead? In some countries established business groups already possess a strong economic base from which to expand, particularly in Kenya, Nigeria, the Sudan, Ghana and, to a lesser extent, in Zambia, the Ivory Coast, Zaire, Uganda and Botswana, and perhaps elsewhere. Considerable entrepreneurial experience, access to established commercial networks and substantial accumulations of capital derived from a period of time spent in trade – in some cases extending back over several generations – furnish a springboard for advance. It may also be possible to discern at least two other emergent processes of some importance. One involves the evolution of a distinctive type of African business venture based on a series of semi-independent branch firms yet linked to a parent enterprise. This represents a positive adaptation of traditional kinship practice and may provide the potential for some kind of corporate business form. Secondly, there is evidence of a growing consciousness of common class interest expressed through such things as the placing of educated relatives in stategic bureaucratic and professional positions or in foreign companies, intermarriage with similarly placed families, cultivating a wide range of politial contacts, investing in the security of land ownership, and so on. At the same time, the expanding provision of education and technical training, the consolidation of an increasingly complex and specialised occupational system and the deepening hold of materialist values and money relations mean that technical and managerial personnel as well as potential financial collaborators are gradually becoming more available in some countries and may provide the basis for a growing number of medium- or large-scale joint business ventures along Western lines.

Until now, and with some significant exceptions, existing business groups – whether by choice or necessity – have operated mainly in commerce and distribution. Alternatively, or in addition, they have relied for profitable business on government sponsorship (state contracts), whenever political elites have permitted outsiders to benefit from such opportunities, importing activity funded ultimately by raw material exports and/or government borrowing (sometimes on a colossal scale as in Nigeria during the oil boom) or various kinds of servicing *vis-à-vis* foreign firms. Given the difficulties inherent in the economic and political environment and the prospect of high returns in relation to the relatively low risks involved, such activities represent rational responses. As the climate for enterprise improves, however, and in the long run, African capitalists will find – as their counterparts have done elsewhere – that capital accumulation which is concentrated mainly in the sphere of circulation or exchange must reach a point of self-termination. Ultimately, profits need to be transferred so as to expand the productive base itself. Only by bringing new resources into production and directly under the control of capital or by finding cheaper more effective ways to employ them is it possible to constantly extend market opportunities and develop fresh outlets for profitable investment. Capitalism is nothing if it is not expansionary. Without productive investment wealth consists of little more than bits of paper chasing round in ever-decreasing circles capable of benefiting fewer and fewer people. Despite the potential for short-term gain, this kind of capitalism is not satisfactory even from the perspective of political elites and entrenched commercial interests.

But established business groups with a history of capital accumulation do not represent the whole story. In all economies with a market orientation numerous firms are constantly being formed, many of them by first-time entrepreneurs with access to few resources. The majority of such businesses fail to expand beyond a certain point or disappear from view. However, even in the advanced economies a few individuals eventually manage to emerge from this entrepreneurial breeding ground at the lower end of the economy and become founders of important businesses.[6] No capitalist economy can afford to neglect such entrepreneurs for long or permit existing economic interest groups or political elites to act in ways that might stifle them altogether. Indeed, the very fact of their relatively humble origins, the paucity of easy or obvious alternative paths to social mobility, means that the one significant resource available to such new entrepreneurs is their personal drive to succeed at all costs and the necessity to hang on to what they have already agained. Unlike those connected to families with established wealth and power, there may be little prospect of a second chance if business fails.

In countries like Ghana, Nigeria, Zambia and Kenya the research carried out in the 1950s, 60s and 70s revealed that a considerable proportion of Africa's emergent industrialists and other modern-sector businessmen were either first-generation entrepreneurs and/or came from lower-middle class origins providing certain advantages but not a very high level. For them, a strong dose of asceticism was a necessity as well as a virtue since luck and ability were often insufficient to guarantee success. It is precisely this kind of entrepreneur whose energies and drive need to be harnessed to the yoke of national economic development at all costs and who deserves to be supported with solid, practical schemes of government assistance. The alternative scenario – where a hostile, unpredictable political and economic climate characterised by statist policies and the rest, holds sway –

means that these very same people will almost certainly be the prime casualties.

Then there is a question of the relations between foreign and local capital. In the past, Western companies have enjoyed access to superior resources of every kind and have consequently dominated the most lucrative economic sectors. Now, however, the balance of opportunity, in some countries, may be more favourably inclined towards local capitalists, allowing them to assume a more dominant role.

Indigenisation policies represent one important advance here, though a great deal more in the way of protection and assistance needs to be extended by sympathetic governments if local firms are to consolidate and deepen their hold over key sectors and eventually outflank some foreign interests. Secondly, the years of economic stagnation along with the recent world recession, the high oil prices of the early 1980s, and so on, have led to a further deterioration in Africa's foreign exchange position. More than ever before most countries – particularly the poorest and the non-oil producers, whose governments cannot easily resort to large-scale overseas borrowing in order to fund development projects or finance trade deficits – need to find ways of encouraging national self-reliance by importing fewer non-essentials, exporting more, and preferably high-value, commodities, and reducing the outflow of foreign profits. It would be unwise to underestimate the enormous difficulties this will involve. But central to such a strategy must surely be the need for a concerted and deliberate attempt to foster local initiative and effort at all levels and in every sector of the economy including local capitalism.

The role of indigenous business groups may be particularly appropriate whenever it is intended, for example, to encourage export-led growth through building up a local manufacturing capacity since here the easiest place to begin might be with the production of certain kinds of low-cost consumer goods which require relatively labour-intensive production techniques, moderate capital and reasonably straightforward technical and managerial skills. These inputs are already accessible to many African entrepreneurs. In addition, such activities may also give them an advantage over big foreign subsidiaries, whose highly sophisticated management systems and investment interests in advanced technology predispose them to dominate other sectors. Once achievements in this area have been consolidated the experience and capital gained may enable some entrepreneurs to embark on more difficult and profitable projects.

Similarly, whenever adaptability and improvisation are at a premium along with the development of intermediate technologies based on local resources, as part of a general policy for fostering self-reliance, small, local firms are likely to hold the key. In the last few years some governments have already made certain moves to encourage such activity. In Botswana, for example, the Technology Centre has tried to encourage small entrepreneurs whose firms employ easily available, simple technologies.[7] The aim is to develop products for export as well as home markets. Recently, the Kenyan government launched a scheme designed to foster small-scale rural businesses engaged in such activities as food processing, metal fabrication and the provision of various inputs for farm production.[8] The Kenyan Commercial Bank has also devised a plan to assist very small businesses operating in the informal economy where proprietors cannot usually obtain normal bank finance and who lack accountancy and managerial skills.[9] Both of these schemes are being run with the help of funding from the U.S. Aid Agency. In Ghana, too, a strong emphasis is being placed on the revival and growth of small-scale village-based industries as part of the government's Economic Recovery Programme.[10] Here, the intention is to encourage the utilisation of local resources that depend on ingenuity and skill rather than imports and this clearly favours local entrepreneurs.

Thirdly, various international (as well as Western government) initiatives are now underway which are designed not only to extend various kinds of technical, managerial and financial assistance to African firms but also to foster direct partnerships between indigenous and foreign companies. Hopefully, if these programmes prove successful they will enable the former to gain better access to Western markets, skills and other resources while providing an important learning situation from which to expand. For example, the International Finance Corporation, linked to the World Bank, launched a new initiative in November 1986 specifically designed to help African entrepreneurs.[11] The programme – the Africa Project Development Facility – has been jointly sponsored by the United Nations Development Programme and the African Development Bank. A number of Western countries – Canada, Denmark, Japan, Sweden and The Netherlands, among others – have donated funds in conjunction with the three international organisations. Brazil and India may also participate by providing technical assistance. Among other things, the International Finance Corporation will help entrepreneurs to identify and formulate sound investment projects, it will provide finance and consultancy services and secure relevant technical and managerial assistance. In addition, the organisation hopes that it will prove possible to find private overseas firms and financial interests willing to establish various partnership arrangements with some African companies.

The Centre for the Development of Industry, an organisation funded by the European Economic Community and set up under the auspices of the Lomé Convention, also operates a scheme to link up small- and medium-

sized firms in both Europe and the Third World through various partnership arrangements. The intention is to assist those who would otherwise lack the resources to invest in external markets.[12] By the end of 1985
19 projects were receiving support in Africa. Providing there are proper
safeguards to ensure that indigenous firms gain equal benefits from access
to European markets, and other resources, there would seem to be ample
opportunity for extending these connections.

Lastly, the recent years of economic stagnation have prompted some
foreign companies to reduce their investments in Africa leaving certain
activities more available to local, private and public initiatives. Yet, at the
same time, it has become increasingly evident to Western capitalist interests that their ability to anticipate significant and expanding opportunities in African countries in the years ahead depends on the attainment
of political stability and competent government but also on the existence
of strong domestic bourgeoisies capable of consolidating the conditions
for further capitalist advance. In Chapter 6 we examined some of the
reasons why such a 'partnership' arrangement might provide considerable
scope for local capitalists to assume a more prominent and determining
role than hitherto. In any case, hopefully, African governments have now
realised that if extensive investment by foreign interests is to make a useful
and lasting contribution to national development programmes then it
must be complemented by a strong domestic involvement at the same time.
In the final analysis, only powerful and capable local interests – public as
well as private – possess a degree of permanent, all-round commitment to
national need sufficient to generate the momentum required for a successful onslaught against the condition of dependent, distorted and restricted
development.

NOTES

I THEMES AND PERSPECTIVES

1 *The Long-term Commodities Problem: Implications for Developing Countries* (World Bank, Washington, DC, 1987).

2 ECONOMIC DEVELOPMENT DURING THE COLONIAL PERIOD

1 Among the most influential and well known of the Neo-Marxist writers are the following: P. Baran, *Political Economy of Growth* (Monthly Review Press, New York, 1957); A. G. Frank, *Capitalism and Underdevelopment in Latin America* (Monthly Review Press, New York, 1969) and *Lumpenbourgeoisie and Lumpendevelopment: Dependence, Class and Politics in Latin America* (Monthly Review Press, New York, 1972); S. Amin, *Unequal Development: An Essay on the Social Formations of Peripheral Capitalism* (Harvester Press, Brighton, 1976).

   S. Amin's application of underdevelopment theory to empirical and historical data derived from the West African experience is also useful: *Neo-Colonialism in West Africa* (Penguin, Harmondsworth, 1973). Again, on Africa, see G. Arrighi and J. S. Saul (eds.), *Essays on the Political Economy of Africa* (Monthly Review Press, New York, 1973). Some of the readings in the following books are also very representative of the basic Neo-Marxist position: R. I. Rhodes (ed.), *Imperialism and Underdevelopment* (Monthly Review Press, New York, 1970); and H. Bernstein (ed.), *Underdevelopment and Development* (Penguin, Harmondsworth, 1973), especially Chapters 1, 3 and 6 by C. Furtado, T. Dos Santos and G. L. Beckford, respectively.

2 S. Amin, 'Underdevelopment and Dependence in Black Africa – Origins and Contemporary Forms', *Journal of Modern African Studies*, vol. 10, no. 4 (1972).

3 *Ibid.*

4 For example see: C. Leys, *Underdevelopment in Kenya* (Heinemann, London, 1975); E. A. Brett, *Colonialism and Underdevelopment in East Africa: The Politics of Economic Change, 1919–1939* (Heinemann, London, 1973); and G. Arrighi, 'Labour Supplies in Historical Perspective: A Study of the Proletarianization of the African Peasantry in Rhodesia' in G. Arrighi and J. S. Saul

(eds.), *Essays on the Political Economy of Africa* (Monthly Review Press, New York, 1973), pp. 180–236.

5 B. Beckman, *Organising the Farmers: Cocoa Politics and National Development in Ghana* (Scandinavian Institute of African Studies, Uppsala, 1976), p. 36.

6 Amin, 'Underdevelopment', p. 3.

7 A. McPhee, *The Economic Revolution in British West Africa* (Frank Cass, London, 1971, originally published in 1926).

8 A. G. Hopkins, *An Economic History of West Africa* (Longman, London, 1973), p. 172.

9 M. Johnson, 'Technology, Competition and African Crafts', in C. Dewey and A. G. Hopkins (eds.), *The Imperial Impact* (Athlone Press, London, 1978).

10 See G. Kitching's discussion of this process in connection with parts of Kenya: *Class and Economic Change in Kenya: the Making of an African Petit Bourgeoisie, 1905–1970* (Yale University Press, New Haven, 1980), Chapter 1.

11 A general discussion of these problems can be found in E. Boserup, *Women's Role in Economic Development* (St Martin's Press, New York, 1970). For specific case studies see: S. Jacobs 'Women and Land Resettlement in Zimbabwe', *Review of African Political Economy*, no. 27–8 (1983); W. Watson, *Tribal Cohesion in a Money Economy* (Manchester University Press, 1958) especially Chapters 4 and 7; and L. Cliffe, 'Labour Migration and Peasant Differentiation in Zambia', *Journal of Peasant Studies*, vol. 5, no. 3 (1978), pp. 326–46.

12 M. J. Hay's discussion of how the Luo women of Kenya coped with male migration and improved farming methods is particularly interesting: 'Luo Women and Economic Change During the Colonial Period', in N. J. Hafkin and E. G. Bay (eds.), *Women in Africa: Studies in Social and Economic Change* (Stanford University Press, 1976).

  In the case of cocoa farming in West Africa, several writers agree that genuine entrepreneurial skill was required on the part of early farmers. The latter had to raise capital, organise labour for forest clearance and planting, operate in terms of a five or six years investment cycle (until the first harvests) and, in some instances, engage in long-distance migrations in search of suitable land. See, for example, P. Hill's study, *The Migrant Cocoa-Farmers of Southern Ghana* (Cambridge University Press, 1963); also S. S. Berry, 'Cocoa and Economic Development in Western Nigeria', in C. K. Eicher and C. Liedholm (eds.), *Growth and Development of the Nigerian Economy* (Michigan State University Press, East Lansing, 1970).

13 Hopkins, *Economic History*, p. 235.

14 For a trenchant and highly critical analysis of this and many other aspects of 'the development of underdevelopment' in the case of the Gold Coast, see: R. Howard, *Colonialism and Underdevelopment in Ghana* (Croom Helm, London, 1978), especially Chapter 5.

15 Hopkins, *Economic History*, Chapter 7.

16 The information cited in this and the following paragraph is derived from the excellent summary of these events in *ibid.*, pp. 182–5.

17 For detailed discussions of these reactions to European commercial hegemony and price fluctuations in West Africa, see: A. B. Holmes IV, 'Economic and Political Organisation in the Gold Coast, 1920–45' (unpublished Ph.D. thesis, University of Chicago, 1972), especially pp. 80–112; and A. G. Hopkins, 'Economic Aspects of Political Movements in the Gold Coast and Nigeria 1918–39, *Journal of African History*, vol. 7, no. 1 (1965–6), pp. 135–52.

18 For the West African case, see Hopkins, *Economic History*, p. 266.

19 Marx's well-known discussion concerning the crucial importance of political intervention, often involving the use of force, can be found in *Capital vol. 1* (Penguin, Harmondsworth, 1976), part VIII, 'The So-Called Primitive Accumulation', especially Chapter 26. See also K. Marx, *Pre-Capitalist Economic Formations* (Lawrence Wishart, London, 1964), especially pp. 104–18. For an excellent contemporary analysis and summary of Marx's writings on this question, see J. G. Taylor, *From Modernization to Modes of Production*, (Macmillan, London, 1979), Chapter 7.

20 Taylor, *Modernization*, Chapter 13, especially pp. 215–35. P. P. Rey and G. Dupré argue that the circulation of European goods both before and during the colonial period played an important role in reproducing the lineage mode of production and perpetuating the power of the elders: 'Reflections on the pertinence of a theory of the History of Exchange', *Economy and Society*, vol. 2, no. 2 (1973), pp. 131–63.

21 J. Iliffe, *The Emergence of African Capitalism* (Macmillan, London, 1983), Chapter 2.

22 G. Kay, *Development and Underdevelopment: A Marxist Analysis* (Macmillan, London, 1975); and Taylor, *Modernization*, especially Chapter 10.

23 Kay, *Development*, Chapter 5, especially pp. 96–105.

24 K. W. J. Post, for example, uses the term 'peasantisation' to describe this process in '"Peasantisation" and rural political movements in Western Africa', *European Journal of Sociology*, vol. 13, no. 2 (1972) pp. 223–54. See also, H. Bernstein's theorisation of the various types of African peasantries and the different stages in their relationship to Western capital: 'Notes on Capital and Peasantry', *Review of African Political Economy*, no. 10 (1977), pp. 60–73.

25 Of course, the fact that migrant wage workers were not fully separated from their means of production did not prevent them from adopting increasingly effective forms of proletarian class action in the urban and industrial areas where they were employed. For an excellent general survey and analysis of this question see: R. Cohen 'From Peasants to Workers in Africa', in P. C. W. Gutkind and I. Wallerstein (eds.), *The Political Economy of Contemporary Africa* (Sage Publications, London, 1976); and several of the articles in R. Sandbrook and R. Cohen (eds.), *The Development of an African Working Class* (Longman, London, 1975).

26 One very important theme here, which has been explored by a number of writers, concerns the way in which the continuing sexual division of labour within the family, and women's crucial role in agriculture, underpinned the profitability of the capitalist sectors. See, for example: C. D. Deere, 'Rural Women's Subsistence Production in the Capitalist Periphery', in R. Cohen, P.

C. W. Gutkind and P. Brazier (eds.), *Peasants and Proletarians* (Hutchinson University Library, London, 1979); and the references cited in note 11 to this chapter.

27 According to L. Cliffe, there was a tendency to 'traditionalise' (p. 342) marriage in Zambia during the later colonial period. This had the effect of increasing the authority exercised by fathers and husbands over women: 'Labour Migration and Peasant Differentiation: Zambian Experiences', *Journal of Peasant Studies*, vol. 5, no. 3 (1978), especially pp. 339–42. In Tanzania, the Native Authorities tried to stabilise marriage by instituting rules against desertion and adultery. D. Bryceson argues that this occurred because it was realised that marital instability represented a threat to lineage solidarity and male control: 'The Proletarianisation of Tanzanian Women', *Review of African Political Economy*, no. 17 (1980), pp. 4–27, especially pp. 15–17.

28 Arrighi, 'Labour Supplies'.

29 H. Wolpe, 'Capitalism and Cheap Labour-power in South Africa: From Segregation to Apartheid', *Economy and Society*, vol. 1, no. 4 (1972), pp. 425–56.

30 Kay, *Development*, pp. 123–4.

31 See especially R. Brenner's very important restatement of Marx's theorising on the dynamics of the capitalist mode of production and his discussion of its implications for the analysis of capitalist formations in the periphery: 'The Origins of Capitalist Development: A Critique of Neo-Smithian Marxism', *New Left Review*, no. 104 (1977), pp. 25–93.

32 *Ibid.*

33 For a discussion of this and many other themes in the 'economics of development' see H. Myint, *The Economics of the Developing Countries* (Hutchinson University Library, London, 1964).

34 In the African context see, for example: P. Kilby, *Industrialization in an Open Economy: Nigeria, 1945–66* (Cambridge University Press, 1969); and D. Rimmer, 'The Crisis in the Ghana Economy', *Journal of Modern African Studies*, vol. 4 (1966).

35 Again, see Myint, *Economics*, for discussion of this view and the 'vent for surplus' theory with which it is associated. See also G. K. Helleiner's work on Nigeria, *Peasant Agriculture, Government and Economic Growth in Nigeria* (Richard Irwin Inc., Homewood, Ill., 1976).

For an interesting critique of this theory and its application to African agriculture see J. Tosh, 'The Cash-Crop Revolution in Tropical Africa: An Agricultural Reappraisal', *African Affairs*, vol. 79 (1980), pp. 79–94.

36 This argument is developed by Hopkins in *Economic History*, Chapter 2, but especially pp. 75–7.

37 See: A. Lewis, 'Economic Development with Unlimited Supplies of Labour', in A. N. Agarwala and S. P. Singh (eds.), *The Economics of Underdevelopment: A Series of Articles and Papers* (Oxford University Press, 1963); and B. Higgins 'The Dualistic Theory of Underdeveloped Areas', *Economic Development and Cultural Change*, vol. 4 (1956), pp. 99–115.

38 I. Roxborough's excellent book contains some critical comments on several of the themes and concepts found in conventional economics: *Theories of Under-*

development (Macmillan, London, 1979), Chapters 1, 2 and 3. See also the useful critique in K. Griffin, *Underdevelopment in Spanish America* (George Allen and Unwin, London, 1969), Introduction pp. 19–50.

39 B. Warren, *Imperialism: Pioneer of Capitalism* (Verso, London, 1980).

40 *Ibid.*, especially pp. 143–52.

41 Of course, it is well known that Britain – as the world's foremost imperialist power before the First World War – had accumulated enormous investments overseas by 1914 approximately equivalent in value to one-third of her total capital stock. But this represented the end result of a process that had been going on gradually for a century and a considerable proportion of these overseas assets consisted of reinvested profits on initial outflows. Moreover, most of this capital went to the more developed, independent (or semi-independent) nations of Europe, Latin America, the United States and the British Dominions where capitalist class relations and markets were already firmly established along with determined, modernising governments. In any case, though highly important for funding certain kinds of development, especially infrastructure, British capital did not provide the main source of funds for economic transformation in these countries. For a fascinating analysis of these and other aspects of imperialism see M. Barratt Brown, *After Imperialism* (Heinemann, London, 1963) and *The Economics of Imperialism* (Penguin, Harmondsworth, 1974).

42 N. Harris, *Of Bread and Guns: The World Economy in Crisis* (Penguin, Harmondsworth, 1983), p. 30.

43 *Ibid.*, p. 31.

44 *Ibid.*, pp. 31–2.

45 See, for example, R. Roberts' account of working-class life in Salford at the time of the First World War (150 years after the onset of the factory system): *The Classic Slum* (Manchester University Press, 1971).

46 Hopkins, *Economic History*, p. 267.

47 Kilby, *Industrialization*, pp. 9–10.

48 *Ibid.*, p. 37.

49 G. Swainson, *The Development of Corporate Capitalism in Kenya, 1918–1977* (Heinemann, London, 1980), Chapter 3.

50 *Ibid.*, pp. 123–4.

51 See the discussion in Hopkins, *Economic History*, for the case of West Africa, pp. 279–84; also G. Swainson, *Development*, especially pp. 111–13 and 118–19.

52 The Ugandan case, for example, is discussed in M. Mamdani, *Politics and Class Formation in Uganda* (Heinemann, London, 1976), pp. 252–9.

53 G. Swainson, *Development*, p. 116.

54 This process is discussed in detail by Kilby, *Industrialization*, Chapter 3, in the context of Nigeria.

55 See, for example, B. Fitch and M. Oppenheimer, 'Ghana: End of An Illusion', *Monthly Review*, vol. 8, no. 3 (1966), especially pp. 40–6, and E. O. Akeredolu-Ale, *The Underdevelopment of Indigenous Entrepreneurship in Nigeria* (Ibadan University Press, 1975), pp. 42–55.

3 COLONIAL RULE AND AFRICAN ENTERPRISE

1 Reference to, and discussion of, the tendencies towards bureaucratic regulation can be found in the following studies, among others: E. A. Brett, *Colonialism and Underdevelopment in East Africa* (Heinemann, London 1973); C. Leys, *Underdevelopment in Kenya* (Heinemann, London, 1975), especially Chapter 2; A. Coulson 'Agricultural Policies in Mainland Tanzania, 1946–1976', *Review of African Political Economy*, no. 10 (1978), pp. 74–100; M. Mamdani, *Politics and Class Formation in Uganda* (Heinemann, London, 1976) especially pp. 72–9 and pp. 164–70; and R. M. A. Zwanenberg with A. King, *An Economic History of Kenya and Uganda, 1800–1970* (Macmillan, London, 1975), Chapters 2, 3, 4 and 8.

2 See the extensive discussion on restrictive colonial policy with respect to African traders in A. A. Beveridge and A. R. Oberschall, *African Businessmen and Development in Zambia* (Princeton University Press, 1979), Chapter 1.

3 Mamdani, *Politics*, pp. 164–6.

4 *Ibid.*, pp. 74–8.

5 *Ibid.*, pp. 105–7.

6 For the case of Kenya see N. Swainson, *The Development of Corporate Capitalism in Kenya, 1918–1977* (Heinemann, London, 1980), Chapter 5, p. 176.

7 Mamdani, *Politics*, p. 105.

8 Brett, *Colonialism*, pp. 208–11. Also Zwanenberg, *Economic History*, pp. 39–43.

9 R. Howard, *Colonialism and Underdevelopment in Ghana* (Croom Helm, London, 1978), p. 68.

10 See B. Campbell's chapter on the Ivory Coast in J. Dunn (ed.), *West African States: Failure and Promise* (Cambridge University Press, 1978).

11 The discussion in this and the following paragraph is drawn from Brett's analysis in *Colonialism*, Chapter 6 and especially pp. 186–202.

12 Mamdani's discussion, in *Politics*, of the Asians in Uganda is particularly instructive; see pp. 66–72 and pp. 86–8. See also Zwanenberg, *Economic History*, pp. 159–61.

13 Mamdani, in *Politics*, argues that in Uganda the restrictions on Asian businesses were very real but that, through their kinship and caste connections with wealthy, more-established wholesalers, small traders were able to operate on credit and gained access to assured supplies of imported commodities (pp. 80–1). The really crucial restriction imposed on the Asians in Kenya and Uganda was the prohibition against land purchase in most areas. This compelled the Asians to channel their energies into trade and other non-agricultural activities. See G. Swainson, *Development*, pp. 53–4.

14 Mamdani, *Politics*, summarises the Ugandan situation in the following way: 'From the outset, the thrust of colonial policy was to keep Africans in the agricultural economy and out of the marketplace . . . while allocating the trading function, through administrative encouragement, to an alien com-

munity that could easily be segregated from the mass of the colonized and thus rendered politically safe' (pp. 70–1).

15 P. Marris and A. Somerset describe the Asians in Kenya as '(P)arochial and community minded', creating an 'impenetrable and inward-looking' culture (p. 7) and 'jealously guarding for their family and friends the opportunities they had sought out' (p. 6): *African Businessmen: A Study of Entrepreneurship and Development in Kenya* (Routledge and Kegan Paul, London, 1971).

16 See G. Kitching, *Class and Economic Change in Kenya: The Making of an African Petite Bourgeoisie, 1905–1970* (Yale University Press, New Haven, 1980), Chapter 6, especially pp. 174–80.

17 R. Cruise O'Brien (ed.), *Political Economy of Underdevelopment: Dependence in Senegal* (Sage Publications, London, 1979), Chapter 3, especially pp. 101–3 and S. Amin, 'The development of the Senegalese business community', in A. Adedeji (ed.), *Indigenization of African Economies* (Hutchinson University Library for Africa, London, 1981), pp. 314–15.

18 See, for example, A. B. Zack Williams, 'Merchant Capital and Underdevelopment in Sierra Leone', *Review of African Political Economy*, no. 25 (1982), pp. 74–82.

19 There is a good deal of excellent material available on the subject of the Gold Coast mulatto traders. See, for example: M. Priestley, *West African Trade and Coast Society* (Oxford University Press, 1969); S. B. Kaplow, 'African Merchants of the Nineteenth Century Gold Coast' (unpublished Ph.D. thesis, Columbia University, 1971); and E. Reynolds, 'Trade and Economic Change on the Gold Coast, 1807–74' (unpublished Ph.D. thesis, University of London, 1971). Reynolds shows how the rising merchant class of the mid nineteenth century (their wealth based on increased exports, mainly of oil palm, and the spread of a money economy partly made possible by the growing use of British and French currencies) assumed the role of 'social provider' in the community previously held by the Fanti chiefs but whose wealth and power was waning at this time. In fact, this was one reason why these formally independent traders gradually lost out in the competitive struggle with European importers from the 1860s onwards, as oil palm prices fell and profit margins declined. Kaplow argues that the demise of the Gold Coast merchants was also related to the financial and other advantages (better overseas contacts) enjoyed by European importers and to the latter's tendency to overcharge African traders for their supplies of trade goods.

20 C. Fyfe, *A Short History of Sierra Leone* (Longman, London, 1967), especially Chapters 11, 13, 14, 18 and 22.

21 See: P. C. Lloyd, *Africa in Social Change* (Penguin African Library, Harmondsworth, 1967), p. 55 and pp. 127–32, and S. Amin, *Neo-Colonialism in West Africa* (Penguin, Harmondsworth, 1973), especially pp. 106–9.

22 In Senegal, too, there was a long history of African involvement in produce buying and import–export activity dating back to the earliest French settlements in Saint Louis and Gorée. In the nineteenth century black Senegalese traders played a leading role in the gum export trade and in opening up the groundnut economy at the end of the century, though by this time most

Africans were middlemen-contractors rather than merchants in their own right. See Amin, 'Senegalese business' in A. Adedeji (ed.), *Indigenization*, especially pp. 309–12.

23 C. Gertzel, 'Relations Between African and European Traders in the Niger Delta, 1880–1896', *Journal of African History*, vol. 3, no. 2 (1962), pp. 361–6.

24 See A. B. Holmes IV, 'Economic and Political Organisations in the Gold Coast, 1920–45' (unpublished Ph.D. thesis, University of Chicago, 1972), p. 67.

25 *Ibid.*, p. 68.

26 R. J. Southall, 'Farmers, Traders and Brokers in the Gold Coast Economy', *Canadian Journal of African Studies*, vol. 12, no. 2 (1978), pp. 185–211.

27 *Ibid.*, p. 189.

28 Gertzel, 'Relations', pp. 362–3.

29 Southall, 'Farmers', pp. 190–4.

30 *Ibid.*, pp. 195–6.

31 *Ibid.*, p. 196 and Holmes, 'Gold Coast,' pp. 72–3.

32 P. T. Bauer, *West African Trade: A Study of Competition, Oligopoly and Monopoly in a Changing Economy* (Routledge and Kegan Paul, London, 1954), pp. 15–18.

33 *Ibid.*, Chapters 2 and 8.

34 Writing about the Gold Coast, on the other hand, Howard (*Colonialism*, pp. 59–60) disputes the argument that European investment was considerable as well as crucial for economic development. The actual sums invested by trading companies, she argues, were quite small though much greater amounts of capital were needed by mining companies.

35 *Ibid.*, pp. 60–5.

36 *Ibid.*, pp. 72–3.

37 Holmes, 'Gold Coast', pp. 74–6.

38 Bauer, *West African Trade*, pp. 109–10.

39 This view is especially pronounced in the writings of Howard, *Colonialism*, (see Chapter 4), Zack Williams, 'Merchant Capital', and Amin see n. 17. However, to a lesser extent it is also possible to discern similarities in the interpretation of the relevant 'facts' and events in the work of Bauer, *West African Trade*, and Holmes, 'Gold Coast'.

40 According to Holmes ('Gold Coast', pp. 70–2), the trend towards business concentration in the Gold Coast was much less marked in the case of cocoa buying, where the entry of new firms was unrestricted and competition was normally quite keen. Nevertheless, it was not easy for Ghanaians to succeed in this field.

41 *Ibid.*, p. 68.

42 Bauer, *West African Trade*, p. 65.

43 *Ibid.*, pp. 122–4.

44 *Ibid.*, Chapter 10.

45 References to discriminatory and unfair banking practices in West Africa are legion and can be found, for example, in the following: Amin, 'Senegalese business' in A. Adedeji (ed.), *Indigenization*, p. 313; Bauer, *West African Trade*, pp. 186–8; Howard, *Colonialism*, pp. 134–40; and E. O. Akeredolu-Ale, 'Private

Foreign Investment and the Underdevelopment of Indigenous Entrepreneurship in Nigeria', in G. Williams (ed.), *Nigeria: Economy and Society* (Rex Collins, London, 1976), p. 108.

46 This argument is suggested by Howard, *Colonialism*, pp. 138–44.

47 See Holmes, 'Gold Coast', pp. 113–14.

48 These schemes, the reasons behind them and the problems encountered by their proponents are discussed in detail in A. G. Hopkins, 'Economic Aspects of Political Movements in the Gold Coast and Nigeria, 1918–39', *Journal of African History*, vol. 7, no. 1 (1965–6), pp. 133–52 and Holmes, 'Gold Coast', pp. 95–134.

49 For example, Howard, *Colonialism*, pp. 113–16.

50 A. G. Hopkins, *An Economic History of West Africa* (Longman, London, 1973), pp. 265–6.

51 See the excellent general discussion of rural capitalism and the origins of class differentiation in J. Iliffe, *The Emergence of African Capitalism* (Macmillan, London, 1983), Chapter 2.

52 P. Hill, *The Migrant Cocoa-Farmers of Southern Ghana* (Cambridge University Press, 1963), especially Chapter 7, pp. 186–95.

53 B. Beckman, *Organising the Farmers: Cocoa Politics and National Development in Ghana* (Scandinavian Institute of African Studies, Uppsala, 1976), pp. 39–40.

54 For the case of Uganda, see Mamdani, *Politics*, especially Chapter 4 and pp. 151–6. Particularly relevant here for the Tanzanian situation is the article by P. Raikes, 'Rural Differentiation and Class Formation in Tanzania', *Journal of Peasant Studies*, vol. 5, no. 3 (1978), pp. 285–325. The Kenyan case is discussed later in this chapter in the section on 'Traditional authority' and in Chapter 5.

55 Pre-colonial long-distance trade in West Africa is discussed extensively by Hopkins in *Economic History*, Chapter 2, especially pp. 58–65.

56 Beveridge and Oberschall, *Businessmen in Zambia*, Chapter 1, observe that in Northern Rhodesia, for example, the long-distance fish trade was one of the very few business fields in which Africans were permitted to flourish during the early colonial period.

57 See, for example, A. Cohen, *Custom and Politics in Urban Africa* (Routledge and Kegan Paul, London, 1969), and the references cited in Chapter 7.

58 J. S. Hogendorn, 'The Origins of the Groundnut Trade in Northern Nigeria', in C. K. Eicher and C. Liedholm (eds.), *Growth and Development of the Nigerian Economy* (Michigan State University Press, 1970).

59 For example, see A. Nypan, *Market Trade: A Sample Survey of Market Traders in Accra* (African Business series, no. 2, Economic Research Division, University College of Ghana, 1960).

60 Beveridge and Oberschall, *Businessmen in Zambia*, Chapter 2.

61 See the discussion in Bauer, *West African Trade*, Chapter 2 and pp. 61–2.

62 See the brief but useful survey of craft activities in Hopkins, *Economic History*, pp. 250–2; also M. Peil, 'West African Urban Craftsmen', *Journal of Developing Areas*, vol. 14 (1979), pp. 2–22; P. C. Garlick's account of the changing patterns of Kwahu enterprise in Ghana and the tendency for many Kwahu to work at tailoring and shoemaking as a path to capital accumulation for eventual trading activity, is especially interesting; 'The Development of Kwahu Business Enterprise in Ghana

since 1874 – An Essay in Recent Oral Tradition', *Journal of African History*, vol. 8, no. 3 (1967), pp. 463–80.

63 Hopkins, *Economic History*, pp. 250–52.

64 Howard, *Colonialism*, pp. 72–3.

65 For example, Mamdani, *Politics*, p. 177 and the discussion in the final section of this chapter.

66 P. Kilby, *African Enterprise: The Nigerian Bread Industry* (Hoover Institution Press, Stanford, Calif., 1965).

67 Bauer, *West African Trade*, especially Chapters 1 and 2.

68 *Ibid.*, pp. 31–4.

69 Holmes, 'Gold Coast', especially pp. 72–6 and 115–34 and Hopkins, 'Economic Aspects', pp. 143–9. Hopkins's article is more concerned with the difficulties of raising finance and setting up business organisations with respect to the problem of independent export activity. Some of the difficulties encountered by the scheme organisers were outside their control but others were related to the question of trust and cooperation between the African participants.

70 See: Zwanenberg, *Economic History*, pp. 160, 168–9 and 173–4; and Mamdani, *Politics*, Chapter 3, especially pp. 65–6.

71 Mamdani, *Politics*, pp. 67–72.

72 Brett, *Colonialism*, Chapter 8, p. 242.

73 Marris and Somerset, *African Businessmen in Kenya*, pp. 143–4. See also Mamdani *Politics*, pp. 80–1.

74 N. Swainson, *Development*, p. 54, observes that another key aspect of business organisation and entrepreneurial behaviour conducive to Asian success in Kenya was the willingness to form partnerships and pool capital.

75 *Ibid.*, p. 84.

76 P. C. Garlick, *African Traders and Economic Development in Ghana* (Clarendon Press, London, 1971), especially pp. 85–6; and H. L. Van der Laan, *The Lebanese Traders of Sierra Leone* (Mouton, The Hague, 1975), especially Chapters 1, 3, 5 and 11.

77 Van der Laan, *Lebanese Traders*, Chapters 11 and 18 and especially pp. 233 and 312–13.

78 For example, Bauer, *West African Trade*, pp. 79–86.

79 Van der Laan, *Lebanese Traders*, pp. 77–8, 227–8, 232–3 and 248. See also Lloyd, *Africa*, pp. 127–30.

80 M. Kilson, *Political Change in a West African State: A Study of the Modernisation Process in Sierra Leone* (Harvard University Press, Cambridge, Mass., 1966), pp. 57–86.

81 J. Depelchin, 'The Transformations of the Petty Bourgeoisie and the State in Post-Colonial Zaire', *Review of African Political Economy*, no. 22 (1981), especially pp. 22–4.

82 M. G. Schatzberg, *Politics and Class in Zaire: Bureaucracy, Business and Beer in Lisalu* (African Publishing Company, New York, 1980).

83 M. Duffield, *Maiurno: Capitalism and Rural Life in Sudan* (Ithaca Press, London, 1981), Chapter 4, and F. B. Mahmoud, *The Sudanese Bourgeoisie: Vanguard of Development?* (Zed Books, London, 1984), Chapter 2.

84 Mahmoud, *Sudanese Bourgeoisie*, pp. 143–4.

85 G. Kitching, *Class and Economic Change in Kenya: The Making of an African Petite Bourgeoisie, 1905–1970* (Yale University Press, New Haven, 1980), pp. 254–72.

86 M. Cowen and K. Kinyanjui, 'Some Problems of Income Distribution in Kenya', Institute for Development Studies, Nairobi, Discussion Paper, 1977.

87 Kitching, *Class*, pp. 159–64.

88 *Ibid.*, Chapter 7.

89 Kilson, *Political Change*, p. 86.

90 In Uganda, for example, the government established a land bank in 1950 but it was prepared to offer loans to traders as well as farmers. A few years later in 1954, an African Loan Fund was set up to assist farmers outside Buganda who had no ownership rights to land. See Mamdani, *Politics*, pp. 200–4. Mamdani also refers to various other measures designed to help Ugandan entrepreneurs: the removal of a legal ban on mobile wholesalers; courses offered in Entebbe to teach Africans the rudiments of business financial organisation; and the provision of funds to build shops in main trading centres which indigenous traders could rent.

91 This is a point made by E. K. Hawkins in his analysis of African participation in the road transport industry: *Road Transport in Nigeria* (Oxford University Press, London, 1958), p. 46. See also the general discussion in Chapters 3 and 4 of his book.

92 P. Kilby, *Industrialization in an Open Economy: Nigeria, 1945–66* (Cambridge University Press, 1969), pp. 311–55.

93 N. Swainson, *Development*, pp. 112–13.

94 *Ibid.*, pp. 180–2.

95 For the Nigerian case, for example, see Kilby, *Industrialization*, pp. 61–2.

96 *Ibid.*, pp. 61–6.

97 See, for example, Hawkins, *Road Transport*, p. 51, and Mamdani, *Politics*, pp. 200–1. Mamdani observes that the entry of many Ugandans into transport was also helped by a government decision to open up an increasing number of lorry and bus routes to indigenous proprietors by granting them exclusive licences. Several quite sizeable African-owned bus companies rapidly emerged.

98 P. Kennedy, *Ghanaian Businessmen: From Artisan to Capitalist Entrepreneur in a Dependent Economy* (Weltforum Verlag, Munich, 1980), pp. 129–30.

4 GOVERNMENT, POLITICS AND AFRICAN CAPITALISM SINCE INDEPENDENCE

1 Writing about America in the early decades after 1776, Lipset argued that economic development, including the establishment of a manufacturing capacity, was perceived by contemporaries as a patriotic necessity. The very substantial help provided by government at both federal and state level for local business included financial assistance, granting franchises to certain companies especially those involved in construction, protective tariffs and granting charters to banks partly on the condition that they provided loans for transport companies. In addition, huge amounts of public capital were invested in various infrastructural projects by state, county and city governments. Public-sector and private economic activity were perceived as complementary to one another not as mutually exclusive activities, as has been the

case in some African countries: S. M. Lipset, *The First New Nation* (Heinemann, London, 1963), especially Chapter 1, pp. 47–56.

2 The argument that Western capitalism now wishes to encourage rapid Third World development rather than hinder it, as may once have been the case, is considered in some detail in Chapter 6.

3 On the other hand, it may be easier and more profitable for corrupt government officials to use foreign firms, operating in Africa, as a source of private funds rather than local firms. The former possess greater resources, less opportunity to mobilise popular support and as non-citizens their ability to flourish ultimately depends on state support, including the provision of numerous inducements.

4 See the article by L. L. Rood, 'Nationalization and Indigenization in Africa', *Journal of Modern African Studies*, vol. 14, no. 3 (1976), pp. 427–47, and A. Adedeji (ed.), *Indigenisation of African Economies* (Hutchinson University Library for Africa, London, 1981), Chapter 1.

5 A particularly thorough account of the events surrounding the promulgation of the Nigerian Decrees, and their contents, can be found in C. S. A. Ogbuagu, 'The Nigerian Indigenization Policy: Nationalism or Pragmatism,' *African Affairs*, vol. 82 (1983), pp. 241–66.

6 See the discussions on particular countries by individual contributors in Adedeji (ed.), *Indigenisation*.

7 These programmes are discussed in B. Dinwiddy, *Promoting African Enterprises* (Croom Helm in association with the Overseas Development Institute, London, 1974). See also the article on Malawi by W. Ettema, 'Small-scale Industry in Malawi', *Journal of Modern African Studies*, vol. 27, no. 3 (1984), pp. 487–510.

8 P. Kennedy, *Ghanaian Businessmen: From Artisan to Capitalist Entrepreneur in a Dependent Economy* (Weltforum Verlag, Munich, 1980), p. 24.

9 On Lesotho, see A. Singh's discussion concerning government attempts to encourage African enterprise in M. Fransman (ed.), *Industry and Accumulation in Africa* (Heinemann Educational Books, London, 1982), pp. 301–21. The forms of government assistance provided in Swaziland are discussed by Dinwiddy in *African Enterprises*, Chapter 9.

10 See N. Swainson, 'The Rise of a National Bourgeoisie in Kenya', *Review of African Political Economy*, no. 8 (1977), p. 42.

11 Restrictions on the borrowing activity of foreign firms in the local economy were introduced by the Kenyan Central Bank from 1974 onwards. See *ibid.*, p. 42.

12 For a discussion of the wide range of government measures employed by the governments of the N.I.C.s of South East Asia, see, for example, M. Fransman, 'Conceptualising Technical Change in the Third World in the 1980s: An Interpretative Analysis', *Journal of Development Studies*, vol. 21, no. 4 (1985), pp. 572–652.

13 This is discussed by D. Goulet, 'Development as Liberation: Policy Lessons from Case Studies', *World Development*, vol. 7, no. 6 (1979), pp. 555–66.

14 J. Iliffe, *The Emergence of African Capitalism* (Macmillan, London, 1983), Chapter 4. The term 'nurture capitalism' was originally used by S. P. Schatz in his book *Nigerian Capitalism* (University of California Press, Berkeley, 1977).

15 Iliffe, *Emergence*, p. 80.

16 Except where specific references are made to the contrary, much of the discussion that follows is not particularly applicable to Kenya and Nigeria since each government's record with regard to local capitalism has been much more positive in these countries, as Iliffe observes. Kenya's case is discussed in some detail in Chapter 5 while the Nigerian situation receives a good deal of attention in Chapter 6.

17 See B. Degefe's discussion in the chapter on Ethiopia in Adedeji (ed.), *Indigenisation*, especially p. 261.

18 The literature on Tanzanian socialism is vast, but for a general overview of some of the main debates, see for example: J. Barker, 'The Debate on Rural Socialism in Tanzania', in B. U. Mwansasu and C. Pratt (eds.), *Towards Socialism in Tanzania* (Tanzanian Publishing House, Dar es Salaam, 1979), pp. 95–126; G. Kitching's assessment of the Ujamma policies and their consequences and shortcomings in his *Development and Underdevelopment in Historical Perspective: Populism, Nationalism and Industrialisation* (Methuen, London, 1982), Chapter 5, pp. 104–24; and P. F. Nursey-Bray, 'Tanzania: The Development Debates', *African Affairs*, vol. 79, no. 314 (1980), pp. 55–78.

19 These measures are discussed in detail by A. A. Beveridge and A. R. Oberschall, *African Businessmen and Development in Zambia* (Princeton University Press, 1979), Chapter 1.

20 C. L. Bayliss, 'The State and Class Formation in Zambia' (unpublished Ph.D. thesis, University of Wisconsin, Madison, 1978). See especially her concluding chapter.

21 See Dinwiddy, *African Enterprises*, Chapter 3.

22 For a general discussion of the Ivory Coast situation see, for example: S. Amin, *Neo-Colonialism in West Africa* (Penguin African Library, Harmondsworth, 1973), pp. 48–66; and R. Sandbrook, *The Politics of Basic Needs: Urban Aspects of Assaulting Poverty in Africa* (Heinemann, London, 1982), pp. 83–90.

23 R. Sandbrook with J. Barker, *The Politics of Africa's Economic Stagnation* (Cambridge University Press, 1985), pp. 120–1.

24 See B. Campbell, 'The Ivory Coast', pp. 66–116, especially pp. 88–110, in J. Dunn (ed.), *West African States: Failure and Promise* (Cambridge University Press, 1978).

25 These policies and their consequences for Ghanaian entrepreneurs are discussed in detail by J. D. Esseks, 'Economic Independence in an African State: Ghana 1956–65' (unpublished Ph.D. thesis, Harvard University, 1967). Also, by the same author, 'Government and Indigenous Private Enterprise in Ghana', *Journal of Modern African Studies*, vol. 9, no. 1 (1971), pp. 11–29.

26 Concrete evidence concerning the link between political affiliation and receiving government favours is naturally difficult to verify, whether in Ghana or elsewhere. Nevertheless, some data is offered tentatively in Kennedy, *Ghanaian Businessmen*, pp. 132–4. A more general discussion of the relationship between government and business success in Ghana during and after the Nkrumah years can be found in P. Kennedy, 'Indigenous Capitalism in Ghana', *Review of African Political Economy*, no. 8 (1977), pp. 30–4.

27 See R. Cruise O'Brien (ed.), *Political Economy of Underdevelopment: Dependence in Senegal* (Sage, London, 1979), especially Chapter 3, pp. 108–11.

28 *Ibid.*, pp. 108–9.

29 Amin, *Neo-Colonialism*, pp. 326–7.

30 Cruise O'Brien (ed.), *Political Economy*, pp. 109–10.

31 M. Mamdani, *Politics and Class Formation in Uganda* (Heinemann, London, 1976), especially pp. 236–7 and 261.

32 *Ibid.*, pp. 261–76.

33 M. Mamdani, 'Class Struggles in Uganda', *Review of African Political Economy*, no. 4 (1975), especially pp. 50–3.

34 See C. Clapham, 'Liberia', in J. Dunn (ed.), *West African States: Failure and Promise* (Cambridge University Press, 1978), Chapter 4, especially p. 128.

35 For example, see D. G. Gould, 'The Administration of Underdevelopment', in G. Gran (ed.), *Zaire: The Political Economy of Underdevelopment* (Praeger, New York, 1979), Chapter 5; and J. Depelchin, 'The Transformations of the Petty Bourgeoisie and the State in Post-Colonial Zaire', *Review of African Political Economy*, no. 22 (1981), especially pp. 32–8.

36 For the case of Sierra Leone see C. Allen in J. Dunn (ed.), *West African States: Failure and Promise* (Cambridge University Press, 1978), Chapter 8, especially pp. 203–5. In Senegal, despite the restrictions imposed on them, the Levantines retained a dominant hold, particularly in commerce, at the end of the 1970s. See Cruise O'Brien (ed.), *Political Economy*, pp. 106–8. According to Essex, 'Economic Independence', the overall rate of Levantine immigration into Ghana actually increased between 1957 and 1962. A powerful economic nexus between the Asians/Levantines and senior military and public officials still flourished in Ghana at the end of the 1970s, although corruption during the Acheampong regime included certain elements of the indigenous capitalist class, too. See the discussion by E. Hansen and P. Collins, 'The Army, the State, and the "Rawlings Revolution" in Ghana', *African Affairs*, vol. 79 (1980), especially pp. 13–17.

37 The discussion in this and the following paragraph is drawn from M. Mamdani's detailed analysis of these events and policies, in *Politics*, pp. 260–81.

38 See especially, the references cited in notes 31–5. The manipulation of 'official' position by military officers seeking to gain special access to resources for engaging in rice farming, again during the Acheampong regime in Ghana, is discussed by A. Shepherd, 'Agrarian Change in Northern Ghana: Public Investment, Capitalist Farming and Famine', in J. Heyer, G. Williams and P. Roberts (eds.), *Rural Development in Tropical Africa* (Macmillan, London, 1981), pp. 165–92, especially pp. 173–4.

39 The Nigerian case is discussed in some detail in Chapter 6, pp. 109–11 and 131–2.

40 G. Hyden, *No Shortcuts to Progress* (Heinemann, London, 1983), p. 50.

41 See, for example: A. Coulson, 'Agricultural Policies in Mainland Tanzania', *Review of African Political Economy*, no. 10 (1977), pp. 74–100; and O. Oculi, 'Dependent Food Policy in Nigeria, 1975–1979', *Review of African Political Economy*, no. 15/16 (1979), especially pp. 64–8. A number of the contributors to the book by J. Heyer *et al.* (eds.), *Rural Development*, are also critical of colonial and more recent policies with respect to the African peasantry.

42 B. Beckman, *Organising the Farmers: Cocoa Politics and National Development in Ghana* (Scandinavian Institute of African Affairs, Uppsala, 1976), p. 183.

43 *Ibid.*, p. 22.

44 N. Chazan, *An Anatomy of Ghanaian Politics 1969–1982* (Westview Press, 1983), especially pp. 194–5.

45 Clearly, this is a huge subject in its own right. This discussion is only intended to

point out the relevance of contemporary African political tendencies to economic life and to local capital, in particular. For thorough analyses of these
questions from different points of view, see for example: R. H. Jackson and C.
G. Rosberg, *Personal Rule in Black Africa* (University of California Press,
Berkeley, 1982), and Sandbrook, *Politics*, Chapter 5.

46 Sandbrook, *Politics*, pp. 88–9.
47 See the discussion of Weber's work in R. Bendix, *Max Weber: An Intellectual
Portrait* (Methuen, London, 1966).
48 Sandbrook, *Politics*, p. 89.
49 For the case of Zaire see: J. MacGaffey, 'How to Survive and Become Rich
Amidst Devastation: The Second Economy in Zaire', *African Affairs*, vol. 82
(1983), pp. 351–66; and R. Lemarchand, 'Politics of Penury in Rural Zaire: The
View from Bandundu,' in G. Gran (ed.), *Zaire: The Political Economy of
Underdevelopment* (Praeger, New York, 1979), Chapter 12.
50 MacGaffey, 'How to Survive', pp. 355–7.
51 Chazan, *Anatomy*, pp. 191–202.
52 See the discussion of the various forms of tax evasion in Sandbrook, *Politics*,
p. 122.
53 The effects of poor economic management and, in particular, of excessive
monetary expansionism in fuelling inflation and undermining incentives is
discussed extensively by T. Killick, for the case of Ghana, *Development Economics in Action: A Study of Economic Policies in Ghana* (Heinemann, London,
1978), particularly pp. 156–60, but see also Chapters 4, 7, 8 and 9.
54 G. Williams, 'Marketing Boards in Nigeria', *Review of African Political Economy*, no. 36 (1985), pp. 5–6.
55 See, for example, Depelchin, 'Transformations'.

5 CLASS FORMATION AND STATE POWER

1 The literature on class in Africa and the methodological and definitional
problems involved in its analysis is obviously vast. See, for example, the
readings in P. C. W. Gutkind and P. Waterman (eds.), *African Social Studies: A
Radical Reader* (Heinemann, London, 1977), part V, and especially the section
by G. Williams, 'Class Relations in a Neo-colony: The Case of Nigeria', pp.
284–94. Also, R. Cohen, 'Class in Africa: Analytical Problems and Perspectives', in J. Saville and R. Miliband (eds.), *The Socialist Register* (Merlin Press,
London, 1972).
2 G. Hyden uses the term 'uncaptured' in his *Beyond Ujamma in Tanzania:
Underdevelopment and an Uncaptured Peasantry* (Heinemann, London,
1980).
3 See P. Hill's work on cocoa farming in Ghana which examines the subject of
'wage' workers in some detail: *The Migrant Cocoa-Farmers of Southern
Ghana* (Cambridge University Press, 1963). J. Iliffe's book, *The Emergence of
African Capitalism* (Macmillan, London, 1983), contains an excellent summary of the material on capitalism and peasants in Africa (Chapter 2).
4 The complex question of compradorship is considered in some depth in
Chapter 6.

5 See A. Cournanel, 'Ideology and Development in Guinea', in H. Goulbourne (ed.), *Politics and State in the Third World* (Macmillan, London, 1979), pp. 178–200, especially pp. 184–92.

6 J. K. Nyerere, *Ujamma: Essays on Socialism* (Oxford University Press, Dar es Salaam, 1968), especially Chapters 1 and 2.

7 A. Gerschenkron, *Economic Backwardness in Historical Perspective* (Harvard University Press, Cambridge, Mass., 1966), Chapter 1.

8 In Japan, for example, initial disappointment with early reliance on private enterprise led the new modernising government, after the Meiji Restoration, to act as an entrepreneur. Investments were made in a wide range of heavy and light industries, mining and railways. Most of these state enterprises, once safely established, had been sold to private Japanese entrepreneurs by the mid 1880s. Government preferential treatment towards certain politically favoured individuals was also important in fostering the emergence of a class of business leaders. See J. Hirschmeier and T. Yui, *The Development of Japanese Business, 1600–1973* (George Allen and Unwin, London, 1975), especially pp. 86–8 and 95–9. Also J. Halliday, *A Political History of Japanese Capitalism* (Monthly Review Press, New York, 1975), pp. 42–61. Interestingly, the trade treaties imposed on Japan in 1853 by the Western powers precluded the possibility of using tariff protection as a weapon for encouraging Japanese industry until the end of the century.

9 Gerschenkron, *Economic Backwardness*, especially pp. 6–11.

10 G. White, 'Developmental States and Socialist Industrialisation in the Third World', *Journal of Development Studies*, vol. 21, no. 1 (1984), pp. 97–120.

11 *Ibid.*, pp. 102–3.

12 H. Alavi, 'The State in Post-Colonial Societies: Pakistan and Bangladesh', *New Left Review*, no. 74 (1972), pp. 59–81.

13 These ideas originate in the work of N. Poulantzas, *Political Power and Social Classes* (New Left Books, London, 1973).

14 J. G. Shivji, *Class Struggles in Tanzania* (Monthly Review Press, New York, 1976). Some writers have also stressed the growing convergence of interests between the emerging 'Kulak' class of better-off peasants and the bureaucratic–political elite/ruling class: H. U. E. Thoden Van Velzen, 'Staff, Kulaks and Peasants' in L. Cliffe and J. Saul (eds.), *Socialism in Tanzania*, vol. 2 (East Africa Publishing House, Nairobi, 1973), pp. 153–79. For the case of Mali see C. Meillassoux, 'A Class Analysis of the Bureaucratic Process in Mali', *The Journal of Development Studies*, vol. 6, no. 2 (1970), pp. 91–110.

15 M. von Freyhold, 'The Post-Colonial State and it's Tanzanian Version, *Review of African Political Economy*, no. 8 (1977), pp. 75–89.

16 J. Saul, 'The State in Post-Colonial Societies – Tanzania', in J. Saville and R. Miliband (eds.), *The Socialist Register* (Merlin Press, London, 1974). See also the very influential writings of A. Cabral, especially his argument that the *petit bourgeoisie* in Guinea Bissau must repudiate the temptation to become 'bourgeois' and take over the leadership of the revolutionary movement, thereby committing class suicide: *Unity and Struggle* (Heinemann, London, 1980), pp. 134–7.

17 See references cited in notes to Chapter 2, no. 19.

18 B. Moore, *The Social Origins of Dictatorship and Democracy* (Penguin, Harmondsworth, 1967), Chapter 1.

19 *Ibid.*, p. 32. But see also F. Bedarida, *A Social History of England, 1851–1975* (Methuen, London, 1979), Chapters 2 and 5. Bedarida cites figures showing that between 1880 and 1895 members of the landed aristocracy held 47 of the positions in the various Cabinets, compared to 30 men drawn from the bourgeois class. The respective numbers changed to 13 and 23 between 1905 and 1914 (p. 130).

20 Moore, *Dictatorship and Democracy*. See Chapter 5, pp. 228–313. In Japan, for example, the merchant class who grew wealthy as a result of the changes imposed on the nobility during the Tokugawa period, were never permitted to translate this wealth into political power and remained excluded from state office.

21 T. Skocpol, *States and Social Revolutions* (Cambridge University Press, 1979), especially pp. 25–32. Another writer who has stressed both the capacity of state officials to use the 'governing apparatus' as a 'source of power independent of that held by a class because of control over the means of production' (p. 7) and the 'revolutionary potential of the state apparatus under certain specific internal and international conditions' (p. 3) is E. K. Trimberger, *Revolution From Above: Military Bureaucrats and Development in Japan, Turkey, Egypt, and Peru* (Transaction Books, New Brunswick, NJ, 1978).

22 See Trimberger's account of the emergence of an increasingly urbanised aristocracy, dependent on state support, office and favour, in the 250 years preceding the Restoration, and the factors that enabled one particular section of this nobility to gain bureaucratic ascendancy: *Revolution From Above*, Chapter 3 pp. 41–104 and especially pp. 49–55, pp. 57–61 and pp. 63–70.

23 See note 8 and references.

24 Some observers have been somewhat doubtful concerning the past achievements of, and future prognosis for, the Kenyan economy stressing, for example, the stagnation of agriculture as an impediment to further industrial expansion, the reality of continued dependency on foreign technology and markets and the politically repressive nature of the Kenyan regime. See the various contributors to the *Review of African Political Economy*, no. 17 (1980): R. Kaplinsky, 'Capital Accumulation in the Periphery – The Kenyan Case Re-examined', pp. 83–105; J. S. Henley, 'Straw Men Rule OK?', pp. 105–8; and C. Leys, 'Kenya: What Does "Dependency" Explain?', pp. 108–13.

25 C. Leys, 'Capital Accumulation, Class Formation and Dependency: The Significance of the Kenyan Case', in J. Saville and B. Miliband (eds.), *Socialist Register* (Merlin Press, London, 1978), p. 251.

26 Leys, 'Capital Accumulation', pp. 246–9.

27 P. Marris and T. Somerset, *African Businessmen* (Routledge and Kegan Paul, London, 1971), Chapter 2, especially pp. 25–9 and 37–43.

28 Leys, 'Capital Accumulation', p. 248.

29 G. Kitching, *Class and Economic Change in Kenya: The Making of an African Petit Bourgeoisie* (Yale University Press, Newhaven and London, 1980), Chap-

ters 7 and 9, especially pp. 188–9 and 239–79. See also the more detailed discussion of Kitching's work in Chapter 3 of this book.

30 N. Swainson, *The Development of Corporate Capitalism in Kenya, 1918–1977* (Heinemann, London, 1980), Chapter 5, particularly pp. 173–80.

31 *Ibid.*, pp. 180–2. See also the discussion of Swainson's work on pp. 26–7 in Chapter 2.

32 Leys, 'Capital Accumulation', pp. 248–51. See also Leys' earlier work, *Underdevelopment in Kenya: The Political Economy of Neo-Colonialism* (Heinemann, London, 1975), Chapter 2. Here Leys argued that despite Independence the Kenyan bourgeoisie remained basically subordinate to foreign capital and was little more than an 'auxiliary' class dependent on government protection (see Chapter 5), a position which he repudiated a few years later.

33 Leys, 'Capital Accumulation', p. 251–61.

34 Leys, *Underdevelopment in Kenya*, Chapter 3, especially pp. 85–102.

35 Leys, 'Capital Accumulation', pp. 257–9.

36 N. Swainson, *Corporate Capitalism*, Chapter 5, pp. 119–211.

37 See Leys' detailed analysis of this process, *Underdevelopment in Kenya*, Chapter 3.

38 See the discussion in the previous chapter, p. 67.

39 On the case of Swaziland, for example, see B. Dinwiddy, *Promoting African Enterprises* (Croom Helm in association with the O.D.I., London, 1974), Chapter 9; and I. Winter, 'The Post-Colonial State and the Forces and Relations of Production: Swaziland', *Review of African Political Economy*, no. 9 (1978), pp. 27–43, especially pp. 39–43.

40 C. L. Bayliss, 'The State and Class Formation in Zambia' (unpublished Ph.D. thesis, University of Wisconsin, Madison, 1978).

41 See the discussion in Chapter 3, pp. 50–6 and para. 3 on page 101.

42 For the most part, however, and unlike central Kenya, commercial agriculture in Ghana, as elsewhere in West Africa, was not usually based on clear individual private property rights in land at that time.

43 More than one-half the Ghanaian manufacturers – mostly based in Accra – studied by the author in the late 1960s had started their first businesses (usually in manufacturing) before 1960 and nearly one-third began before 1952; P. Kennedy, *Ghanaian Businessmen* (Weltforum Verlag, Munich, 1980) pp. 39–45.

44 See: B. Fitch and M. Oppenheimer, 'Ghana: End of an Illusion', *Monthly Review*, vol. 18, no. 3 (1966); and R. Rathbone, 'Businessmen in Politics: Party Struggle in Ghana', *Journal of Development Studies*, vol. 9, no. 3 (1972–3), pp. 391–401.

45 *Ibid.*, pp. 66–72.

46 See J. D. Esseks, 'Government and Indigenous Private Enterprise in Ghana', *Journal of Modern African Studies*, vol. 9, no. 1 (1971), pp. 11–29; and discussion in previous chapter, p. 68.

47 See Fitch and Oppenheimer, 'Ghana', Chapter 4, especially p. 55. Also, D. Austin, *Politics in Ghana, 1946–1960* (Oxford University Press, London, 1964), Chapter 6.

48 Austin, *Politics*, Chapters 1 and 2.
49 B. Beckman, *Organising the Farmers: Cocoa Politics and National Development in Ghana* (Scandinavian Institute of African Studies, Uppsala, 1976); see Chapter 1, pp. 30–1 and chapter 8, especially pp. 232–5.
50 *Ibid.*, Chapter 3, especially pp. 85–91.
51 *Ibid.*, pp. 234–8.
52 The relationship between pre-colonial state power, trade and wealth acquisition is discussed with reference to the case of the Ashanti in, for example, K. Arhin, *West African Traders in Ghana in the Nineteenth and Twentieth Century* (Longman Group, Bristol, 1979). For a more general discussion involving an interesting attempt to apply a theoretical Marxist 'mode of production' analysis to West Africa, see E. Terray, 'Long-distance Exchange and the Formation of the State; the Case of the Abron Kingdom of Gyaman', *Economy and Society*, vol. 3, no. 3 (1974).

6 AFRICAN BUSINESS AND FOREIGN CAPITAL: THE CONTEMPORARY SITUATION ●

1 The reader is referred to the article by A. Gordon, 'The Theory of the "Progressive" National Bourgeoisie', *Journal of Contemporary Asia*, vol. 3, no. 2 (1973), pp. 192–203, for a detailed historical analysis of the background to this theory in its various forms.
2 J. Woddis, 'Is there an African National Bourgeoisie?', in P. C. W. Gutkind and P. Waterman (eds.), *African Social Studies: A Radical Reader* (Heinemann, London, 1977).
3 For example, see the following writers: C. Ake, 'The Political Context of Indigenisation', in A. Adedeji (ed.), *Indigenisation of African Economies* (Hutchinson University Library for Africa, London, 1981); E. Hutchful, 'A Tale of Two Regimes: Imperialism: the Military and Class in Ghana', *Review of African Political Economy*, no. 14 (1979), pp. 36–55; and S. Osabo, 'The Deepening Crisis of the Nigerian National Bourgeoisie', *Review of African Political Economy*, no. 13 (1978), pp. 63–77.
4 Osabo, 'Deepening Crisis'.
5 F. B. Mahmoud, 'Indigenous Sudanese Capital – A National Bourgeoisie?', *Review of African Political Economy*, no. 26 (1983), pp. 103–19. Also by the same author, *The Sudanese Bourgeoisie: Vanguard of Development?* (Zed Books, London, 1984), especially Chapter 7.
6 I. Kursany, 'Role of the National Bourgeoisie in the National Democratic Revolution', *Review of African Political Economy*, no. 26 (1983), pp. 119–23, Special Issue on the Sudan.
7 See, for example, the argument developed by B. Beckman in his two articles: 'Imperialism and the National Bourgeoisie', *Review of African Political Economy*, no. 22 (1981), pp. 5–19; and 'Whose State? State and Capitalist Development in Nigeria', *Review of African Political Economy*, no. 23 (1982), pp. 37–51.
8 Of course, other factors are also at work in reducing market demand, including

poor-resource endowment and climatic uncertainty, the continuing predominance of peasant agriculture and low population in relation to land area. According to R. Sandbrook, 16 African countries have populations of less than 2 million people and another 20 countries contain between 2 and 10 millions: *The Politics of Africa's Economic Stagnation* (Cambridge University Press, 1985), pp. 15–20.

9 For a useful, basic analysis of the power of the transnational corporations and their global operations see, for example: R. J. Barnet and R. Müller, *Global Reach: Power of the Multinationals* (Simon and Schuster, New York, 1976); and H. Radice (ed.), *International Firms and Modern Imperialism: Selected Readings* (Penguin, Harmondsworth, 1975).

10 C. Leys, *Underdevelopment in Kenya* (Heinemann, London, 1975), pp. 159–63.

11 P. Kennedy, 'The Role and Position of Petty Producers in a West African City', *Journal of Modern African Studies*, vol. 19, no. 4 (1981), pp. 565–94, especially p. 573.

12 R. Bromley and C. Gerry (eds.), *Casual Work and Poverty in Third World Cities* (John Wiley, London, 1979), especially Chapter 1.

13 See P. Collins's account of evasion tactics and the problems faced by public officials charged with the implementation of indigenisation decrees, especially in Ghana and Nigeria, in 'The Management and Administration of Parastatal Organisations for the Promotion of Indigenous Enterprises: A West African Experience', *Public Administration and Development*, vol. 1 (1981), pp. 121–31.

14 See the analysis of the pressures behind the Nigerian Indigenisation Decree by C. S. A. Ogbuagu, 'The Nigerian Indigenisation Policy: Nationalism or Pragmatism?', *African Affairs*, vol. 8, no. 2 (1983), pp. 241–66.

15 T. Forrest, 'Recent Developments in Nigerian Industrialisation', in M. Fransman (ed.), *Industry and Accumulation in Africa* (Heinemann Educational Books, London, 1982), p. 337.

16 A. Hoogvelt, 'Indigenisation and Foreign Capital: Industrialisation in Nigeria', *Review of African Political Economy*, no. 14 (1979), pp. 56–68.

17 *Ibid.*, pp. 62–3.

18 *Ibid.*, pp. 63–6.

19 See, for example, P. Collins, 'Public Policy and the Development of Indigenous Capitalism: The Nigerian Experience', *Journal of Commonwealth and Comparative Politics*, vol. 15 (1977), pp. 141–3.

20 S. P. Schatz, 'Pirate Capitalism and the Inert Economy of Nigeria', *Journal of Modern African Studies*, vol. 22, no. 1 (1984), pp. 45–57.

21 T. Turner, 'Commercial Capitalism and the 1975 Coup', in K. Panter-Brick (ed.), *Soldiers and Oil: the Political Transformation of Nigeria* (Frank Cass, London, 1978), pp. 166–200, especially p. 167.

22 Doubts are expressed by E. O. Akeredolu-Ale, 'Private Investment and the Underdevelopment of Indigenous Entrepreneurship in Nigeria', in G. Williams (ed.), *Nigeria: Economy and Society* (Rex Collins, London, 1976), pp. 115–19. Also see references cited in notes 15, 16 and 21, by Forrest, Hoogvelt and Turner respectively.

23 Hoogvelt, 'Indigenisation', p. 59.

24 This, and several other issues relating to indigenisation, its implementation and the consequences for the West African case, are discussed in considerable detail by P. Collins in 'The State and Industrial Capitalism in West Africa', *Development and Change*, vol. 14 (1983), especially pp. 410–11.

25 The emergence of African entrepreneurs in certain modern business fields other than trade as early as the 1940s and early 1950s, in some countries, can be seen from the following studies, for example: P. Kilby, *African Enterprise: The Nigerian Bread Industry* (Hoover Institution Press, Stanford, Calif., (1965); Mahmoud, 'Sudanese Capital'; M. Duffield, *Maiurno: Capitalism and Rural Life in Sudan* (Ithaca Press, London, 1981); and P. Kennedy, *Ghanaian Businessmen: From Artisan to Capitalist Entrepreneur in a Dependent Economy* (Weltforum Verlag, Munich, 1980), especially Chapter 2.

26 For the case of Ghana, see Kennedy, *Ghanaian Businessmen*, p. 35 and Chapter 3.

27 J. Curran, *Bolton Fifteen Years On: A Review and Analysis of Small Business Research in Britain 1971–1986* (Small Business Research Trust, London, 1986), pp. 8–9.

28 For an opposite view which sees improvisation, recycling as well as the informal acquisition of skills as useful and necessary, see K. King, *The African Artisan* (Heinemann, London, 1977), especially Chapter 4.

29 This appeared to be the case in Accra, Ghana, in the late 1970s where small manufacturing and service firms were concerned. See Kennedy, 'Role and Position', pp. 581–3.

30 P. Marris, 'The Social Barriers to African Enterprise', *Journal of Development Studies*, vol. 5, no. 1 (1968), pp. 29–38.

31 For example, A. A. Beveridge and A. R. Oberschall, *African Businessmen and Development in Zambia* (Princeton University Press, 1979), p. 132, and Kennedy, *Ghanaian Businessmen*, p. 129.

32 P. Kennedy, 'African Businessmen and Foreign Capital: Collaboration or Conflict?' *African Affairs*, vol. 77 (1977), pp. 187–8.

33 The following list includes just a few of the, perhaps, better-known critics: R. Brenner, 'The Origins of Capitalist Development: A Critique of Neo-Smithsian Marxism', *New Left Review*, no. 104 (1977), pp. 25–93; C. Leys, 'Underdevelopment and Dependency: Critical Notes', *Journal of Contemporary Asia*, vol. 7, no. 1 (1977); A. Phillips, 'The Concept of Development', *Review of African Political Economy*, no. 8 (1977), pp. 7–20; G. Palma, 'Dependency: A Formal Theory of Underdevelopment or a Methodology – for the Analysis of Concrete Situations of Underdevelopment', *World Development*, vol. 6, no. 7/8 (1978) pp. 881–924; H. Bernstein, 'Sociology of Underdevelopment Versus Sociology of Development', in D. Lehmann (ed.), *Development Theory: Four Critical Studies* (Frank Cass, London, 1979); B. Warren, *Imperialism: Pioneer of Capitalism* (New Left Review Editions, London, 1980); and the various contributors to P. Limqueco and B. McFarlane (eds.), *Neo-Marxist Theories of Development* (Croom Helm, London, 1983).

34 B. Beckman, 'Imperialism and the National Bourgeoisie', and 'Whose State?'

35 Brenner, 'Capitalist Development'. See also the brief discussion of Brenner's work in Chapter 2.

36 A. Emmanuel, *Appropriate or Underdeveloped Technology?* (John Wiley Series on Multinational Corporations, Chichester, 1982).

37 See the excellent discussion by A. Singh on the way in which the establishment of a higher educational and scientific infrastructure can give countries access to advanced technology and the need for this in Africa: 'Industrialisation in Africa: A Structuralist View', in M. Fransman (ed.), *Industry and Accumulation in Africa* (Heinemann Educational Books, London, 1982), especially pp. 32–4.

38 M. Fransman, 'Conceptualising Technical Change in the Third World in the 1980s: An Interpretive Analysis', *Journal of Development Studies*, vol. 21, no. 4 (1985), especially pp. 628–38.

39 For a fascinating account of the slow, piecemeal, adaptive nature of Japanese technological development in the textile industry see Y. Kiyokawa, 'Entrepreneurship and Innovation in Japan: An Implication of the Experience of Technological Development in the Textile Industry', *The Developing Economies*, vol. 72, no. 3 (1984). The article makes clear that Japanese manufacturers were still largely reliant on imported machinery for many aspects of textile production until the 1920s and 1930s. Only in 1937 did Japanese manufacturers begin to export certain kinds of cotton-spinning machinery developed originally to meet the country's specific requirements (pp. 228–30).

40 See the discussion by F. Nixson, 'Import Substitution Industrialization', in M. Fransman (ed.), *Industry and Accumulation in Africa* (Heinemann Educational Books, London, 1982), pp. 38–57.

41 The concept of the 'over-administered economy' and its implications for Nigerian development during the oil boom is developed by D. Rimmer, 'The Overvalued Currency and Over-Administered Economy of Nigeria', *African Affairs*, vol. 84 (1985), pp. 435–46.

42 See, for example: C. Hamilton, 'Capitalist Industrialisation of the Four Little Tigers of East Asia', in P. Limqueco and B. McFarlane (eds.), *Neo-Marxist Theories of Development* (Croom Helm, London, 1983), pp. 137–80; and A. Michell, 'South Korea, Vision of the Future for Labour Surplus Economies', in M. Bienefeld and M. Godfrey (eds.), *The Struggle for Development* (John Wiley, Chichester, 1982), pp. 189–218.

43 Beckman, 'Imperialism'.

44 *Ibid.*, especially pp. 47–51, and N. Swainson, 'The Rise of a National Bourgeoisie in Kenya', *Review of African Political Economy*, no. 8 (1977), especially p. 55.

45 For a general analysis of the growing internationalisation of the world economy and its implications for Third World development see, for example: N. Harris, *Of Bread and Guns* (Penguin, Harmondsworth, 1983), especially Chapters 4 and 5; E. A. Brett, *International Money and Capitalist Crisis: The Anatomy of Global Disintegration* (Heinemann, London, 1983), especially Chapters 5 and 6; and M. Bienefeld and M. Godfrey (eds.), *The Struggle for Development* (John Wiley, Chichester, 1982), especially Chapter 1.

46 This is a point made by Phillips, 'Concept of Development'.
47 S. Langdon, 'The State and Capitalism in Kenya', *Review of African Political Economy*, no. 8 (1977), pp. 90–8.
48 The other driving force of capitalist expansion, of course, is the inherent conflict between labour and capital.
49 Some of the reasons for this were alluded to in Chapters 2, 3, and 5; the relatively undifferentiated nature of most African societies until quite recently and therefore the absence of a 'ruling class' in the conventional sense; the constraints on capital accumulation imposed by colonialism; the tendency for the wealth of 'big men' to be dispersed because of the cultural emphasis on redistribution, kinship obligations and the practice of polygamy and equal inheritance. Nevertheless, in Chapter 8, it will be argued that inter-generational accumulation has been occurring but has involved the ability to manipulate and transfer resources across and between several different institutional processes.
50 This has been very widely documented. See, for example: A. Peace, 'The Lagos Proletariat: Labour Aristocrats or Populist Militants?', in R. Sandbrook and R. Cohen (eds.), *The Development of an African Working Class* (University of Toronto Press, 1976); M. Peil, *The Ghanaian Factory Worker* (Cambridge University Press, 1972); M. Peil, 'Workmates, Kin and Friends: The Social Contacts of West African Urban Workers', in R. L. Simpson and I. Harper Simpson (eds.), *Research in the Sociology of Work* (Jai Press, Greenwich, Connecticut, 1981); and P. C. Lloyd, *Power and Independence* (Routledge and Kegan Paul, London, 1974).
51 Again, there is now a huge literature of women's economic position in urban Africa. For a general discussion see E. Boserup, *Women's Role in Economic Development* (St Martin's Press, New York, 1970). For particular case studies see: C. Robertson, 'Ga Women in Economic Change during the Colonial Period', in N. Hafkin and E. Bay (eds.), *Women in Africa: Studies in Change* (Stanford University Press, 1976), pp. 111–34; and N. Nelson, 'How Women and Men Get By: The Sexual Division of Labour in the Informal Sector of a Nairobi Squatter Settlement', in R. Bromley and C. Gerry (eds.), *Casual Work and Poverty in Third World Cities* (John Wiley, London, 1979), Chapter 14.
52 J. A. Schumpeter, *The Theory of Economic Development* (Harvard University Press, Cambridge, Mass., 1934), p. 93.
53 Turner, 'Commercial Capitalism and the 1975 Coup', pp. 176–9 and 190–3.
54 Beckman, 'Imperialism,' p. 13; and Collins, 'The State and Industrial Capitalism', p. 419.
55 M. A. Cohen, *Urban Policy and Political Conflict in Africa: A Study of the Ivory Coast* (University of Chicago Press, 1974), p. 140. For the case of Ghana see: Collins, 'Management and Administration'; and E. Hansen and P. Collins, 'The Army, the State and the "Rawlings Revolution" in Ghana', *African Affairs*, vol. 79 (1980), pp. 3–23, especially pp. 16–19.
56 See, for example, T. Forrest, 'Recent Developments'.
57 E. O. Akeredolu-Ale ('Private Investment', pp. 109–10) comments on the ability of top bureaucrats and politicians, generally, to exploit their position for material gain.

58 C. Leys, 'Capital Accumulation, Class Formation and Dependency: The Significance of the Kenyan Case', in J. Saville and R. Miliband (eds.), *The Socialist Register* (Merlin Press, London, 1978); and N. Swainson, *The Development of Corporate Capitalism in Kenya, 1918–77* (Heinemann, London, 1980).

59 C. Leys, 'African Economic Development in Theory and Practice', *Daedalus*, vol. 111, part 2 (1982), pp. 98–124, especially pp. 111–13.

60 See C. L. Bayliss, *The State and Class Formation in Zambia* (unpublished Ph.D. thesis, University of Wisconsin, 1978); and Kennedy, *Ghanaian Businessmen*, p. 168.

7 THE CULTURAL AND ECONOMIC CLIMATE

1 It is, perhaps, doubtful whether the people who contributed to the debates concerning the non-economic aspects of development at this time were self-consciously aware of themselves as forming an academic 'group', but the commonality of their themes has certainly led later critics to identify them as such. These writers came from a number of disciplines including economics, sociology, anthropology, psychology, political science, history and public administration. The references cited here represent only a small proportion of the writers (and their works) associated with this approach.

M. Nash, 'Some Social and Cultural Aspects of Economic Development', *Economic Development and Cultural Change*, vol. 7 (1959), pp. 137–50; B. Hoselitz, 'Economic Growth and Development: Non-economic Factors in Economic Development', *American Economic Review*, vol. 47 (1957), pp. 28–41. Also the collection of readings by B. Hoselitz, *Sociological Aspects of Economic Growth* (Free Press, New York, 1960); N. Smelser, 'Mechanisms of Change and Adjustment to Change', in B. F. Hoselitz and W. E. Moore (eds.), *Industrialization and Society* (U.N.E.S.C.O. and Mouton, The Hague, 1963). W. E. Moore, *Social Change* (Prentice Hall, Englewood Cliffs, New Jersey, 1963); W. W. Rostow, *The Stages of Economic Growth: A Non-Communist Manifesto* (Cambridge University Press, 1960); D. Lerner, *The Passing of Traditional Society: Modernising the Middle East* (Free Press, New York, 1958). There are several useful collections of readings covering many aspects of Modernisation Theory, for example: A. and E. Etzioni (eds.), *Social Change* (Basic Books, New York, 1964); and J. E. Finkle and R. W. Gable, *Political Development and Social Change* (John Wiley, New York, 1966).

2 One writer who has shown this very clearly is A. M. Hoogvelt, *The Sociology of Developing Societies* (Macmillan, London, 1976), part I, especially Chapter 3. But see also: J. R. Gusfield, 'Tradition and Modernity: Misplaced Polarities in the Study of Social Change', *American Journal of Sociology*, vol. 72 (1967), pp. 351–62; and H. Bernstein, 'Modernisation Theory and the Sociological Study of Development', *Journal of Development Studies*, vol. 7 (1971).

3 See, for example, T. Parsons, *The Social System* (The Free Press, Glencoe, Ill., 1951).

4 This theory is elaborated in considerable detail and with several case studies, including one based on the 'colonial situation', in E. Hagen, *On the Theory of*

Social Change: How Economic Growth Begins (The Dorsey Press, Homewood, Ill., 1962). Another writer who emphasised the obstructionist nature of
traditional values is G. Foster in 'Peasant Society and the Image of the Limited
Good', *American Anthropologist*, vol. 67 (1965), pp. 293–315.

5 See, for example, such studies as: T. S. Epstein, *Economic Development and
Social Change in South India* (Manchester University Press, 1962); and F. G.
Bailey, *Caste and the Economic Frontier* (Manchester University Press, 1957).

6 S. N. Eisenstadt, 'Social Differentiation, Integration and Evolution', *American
Sociological Review*, vol. 29 (1964), pp. 375–86; and T. Parsons, 'Evolutionary
Universals in Society', *American Sociological Review*, vol. 29 (1964), pp.
330–57. Parsons' ideas on this subject were later presented in a more complete
form in his *Societies: Evolutionary and Comparative Perspectives* (Prentice
Hall, Englewood Cliffs, NJ, 1966).

7 See the references cited in note 2 and especially Hoogvelt, *Developing Societies*,
part I. Many writers have presented damaging critiques of this and other
assumptions and ideas found in the writings of some modernisation theorists,
for example: A. G. Frank, *The Sociology of Development and the Underdevelopment of Sociology* (Pluto Press, London, 1970); N. Long, *An Introduction to
the Sociology of Rural Development* (Tavistock Publications, London, 1977);
and J. G. Taylor, *From Modernisation to Modes of Production* (Macmillan,
London, 1979), Chapters 1 and 2.

8 Hoselitz, 'Economic Growth'; Hagen, *Theory of Social Change*; and D.
McClelland, *The Achieving Society* (C. Van Nostrand, Princeton, NJ, 1961).

9 R. A. LeVine, *Dreams and Deeds: Achievement Motivation in Nigeria* (University of Chicago Press, 1966).

10 A. Cohen, *Custom and Politics in Urban Africa* (Routledge and Kegan Paul,
London, 1969), pp. 187–90.

11 See, for example, J. H. Kunkel, 'Values and Behaviour in Economic Development', *Economic Development and Cultural Change*, vol. 12, no. 3
(1965). Also, J. H. Kunkel, *Society and Economic Behaviour: A Behavioural
Perspective of Social Change* (Oxford University Press, 1970).

12 J. R. Harris, 'On the Concept of Entrepreneurship, with an Application to
Nigeria', in S. P. Schatz (ed.), *South of the Sahara* (Temple University Press,
Philadelphia, 1972), pp. 5–27. See also Harris's discussion of the 'supply' versus
'demand' debate in 'Some Problems in Identifying the Role of Entrepreneurship
in Economic Development: The Nigerian Case', *Explorations in Entrepreneurial History*, 2nd series, vol. 7, no. 3 (1970).

13 Kilby, another economist working in Nigeria, also considered the relationship
between traditional culture – as represented by ethnic membership – and
business performance, as one possible variable which might affect the quality of
entrepreneurship. He concluded that traditional Nigerian culture was impeding the performance of most local entrepreneurs regardless of their particular
ethnic origins. He was also less sanguine than Harris concerning the possibility
that wider experience and training would eventually eradicate these cultural
impediments to successful business practice: P. Kilby, *Industrialization in an
Open Economy, Nigeria 1945–1966* (Cambridge University Press, 1969),
Chapter 10, especially p. 341.

14 P. Kennedy, *Ghanaian Businessmen* (Weltforum Verlag, Munich, 1980), p. 148.
15 For example, Hoogvelt, *Developing Societies*; and Frank, *Sociology of Development*.
16 F. Barth, 'Economic Spheres in Darfur', in R. Firth (ed.), *Themes in Economic Anthropology* (Tavistock Publications, London, 1967).
17 N. Long, *Social Change and the Individual* (University of Manchester Press, 1968), especially Chapters 2, 3 and 8.
18 D. J. Parkin, *Palms, Wine and Witnesses* (Intertext Books, London, 1972), Chapters 2, 3, 4 and 5.
19 K. Hart, 'Entrepreneurs and Migrants: A Study of Modernisation among the Frafras of Ghana' (unpublished Ph.D. thesis, Cambridge University, 1969). Also, K. Hart, 'Swindler or Public Benefactor? The Entrepreneur in his Community', in J. Goody (ed.), *Changing Social Structure in Ghana: Essays in Comparative Sociology of a new State and an old Tradition* (International African Institute, London, 1975).
20 See the discussion in A. G. Hopkins, *An Economic History of West Africa* (Longman, London, 1973), pp. 58–65.
21 See, for example, the discussion in K. Arhin, *West African Traders in Ghana in the Nineteenth and Twentieth Centuries* (Longman, London, 1979).
22 P. E. Lovejoy, 'The Wholesale Kola Trade of Kano', *African Urban Notes*, vol. 5 (1970), pp. 129–43.
23 A. Cohen, 'The Social Organisation of Credit in a West African Cattle Market', *Africa*, vol. 35, no. 1 (1965) and 'Politics of the Kola Trade', *Africa*, vol. 36, no. 1 (1966).
24 Cohen, 'Organisation of Credit', and *Custom and Politics*, Chapter 4.
25 Lovejoy, 'Kola Trade', pp. 138–40.
26 *Ibid.*, p. 135.
27 See the discussion in Chapter 6 and the article by A. M. Hoogvelt, 'Indigenisation and Foreign Capital: Industrialisation in Nigeria', *Review of African Political Economy*, no. 14 (1979), pp. 56–68.
28 P. Lubeck, 'Unions, Workers and Consciousness in Kano, Nigeria: A View from Below', in R. Sandbrook and R. Cohen (eds.), *The Development of an African Working Class* (Longman, London, 1975), pp. 139–60, especially pp. 140–3.
29 A. B. Yusuf, 'Capital Formation and Management Among the Muslim Traders of Kano, Nigeria', *Africa*, vol. 45 (1975), pp. 167–81; quotation is from p. 181.
30 *Ibid.*, p. 181.
31 Those urban proprietors who do orientate their business activity primarily towards a local, neighbourhood clientele often do so out of choice not necessity – as we will see in Chapter 8.
32 J. R. Harris, 'Factors affecting the Supply of Industrial Entrepreneurs in Nigeria' (unpublished mimeograph, Massachusetts Institute of Technology, 1966). Similarly, in his study of small firms in Eastern Nigeria carried out in the early 1960s, Kilby found that only 7% of these enterprises had been started with more than £500; P. Kilby, 'The Development of Small Industries in Eastern Nigeria: The Kilby Report' (Enugu, Nigeria, For the Ministry of Information,

1963). For the Kenyan case, see P. Marris and A. Somerset, *African Businessmen: A Study of Entrepreneurship and Development in Kenya* (Routledge and Kegan Paul, London, 1971), Chapter 8.

33 For example, see the data provided by A. A. Beveridge and A. R. Oberschall, *African Businessmen and Development in Zambia* (Princeton University Press, 1979), pp. 120–34. Also, Kennedy, *Ghanaian Businessmen*, pp. 145–9.

34 P. C. Garlick, 'The Development of Kwahu Business Enterprise in Ghana since 1974 – An Essay in Recent Oral Tradition', *Journal of African History*, vol. 8, no. 3 (1967), pp. 463–80.

35 For example, see the following: Kilby, 'Small Industries'; J. R. Harris and M. P. Rowe, 'Entrepreneurial Patterns in the Nigerian Saw-milling Industry', *Nigerian Journal of Economic and Social Studies*, vol. 8, no. 1 (1966), pp. 69–95; Beveridge and Oberschall, *Businessmen in Zambia*, Chapter 4, pp. 122–6; and Marris and Somerset, *Businessmen in Kenya*, p. 189.

36 P. Kilby, *African Enterprise: The Nigerian Bread Industry* (Hoover Institution Press, Stanford, Calif., 1965), p. 102; Kennedy, *Ghanaian Businessmen*, pp. 48–53; Beveridge and Oberschall, *Businessmen in Zambia*, Chapter 6, pp. 126–9.

37 Marris and Somerset, *Businessmen in Kenya*, pp. 202–203.

38 E. O. Akeredolu-Ale, *The Underdevelopment of Indigenous Entrepreneurship in Nigeria* (Ibadan University Press, 1975), pp. 77–8.

39 Marris and Somerset, *Businessmen in Kenya*, pp. 189–93; and Beveridge and Oberschall, *Businessmen in Zambia*, for a discussion of this and other difficulties faced by Zambian businessmen (pp. 150–61).

40 Marris and Somerset, *Businessmen in Kenya*, pp. 189–193.

41 Kennedy, *Ghanaian Businessmen*, pp. 51–2.

42 S. P. Schatz, *Nigerian Capitalism* (University of California Press, Berkeley, 1977), p. 70.

43 This question is examined in more detail in Chapter 8.

44 For example: Harris, 'Factors'; Harris and Rowe, 'Entrepreneurial Patterns'; Kilby, *African Enterprise*; Akeredolu-Ale, *Underdevelopment*; and Kennedy, *Ghanaian Businessmen*.

45 Kilby, *Industrialization*, Chapter 10 and Schatz, *Nigerian Capitalism*, Chapter 4. See also the earlier articles by S. P. Schatz, 'The Capital Shortage Illusion: Government Lending in Nigeria', *Oxford University Papers*, vol. 17, no. 3 (1965), pp. 309–16, and 'Aiding Nigerian Business: The Yaba Industrial Estate', *Nigerian Journal of Economic and Social Studies*, vol. 6 (1964), pp. 199–217.

46 Schatz, *Nigerian Capitalism*, pp. 66–72.

47 Harris, 'Concept of Entrepreneurship', p. 11.

48 A. L. Epstein's study, for example, of labour relations and urban life in Northern Rhodesia includes a fascinating account of European stereotypes concerning the supposed motivations and needs of migrant mine workers: *Politics in an Urban African Community* (Manchester University Press, 1958), especially Chapter 2.

49 P. Kilby, 'African Labour Productivity Reconsidered', *The Economic Journal*, vol. 71 (1961), pp. 273–91; and F. A. Wells and W. A. Warmington, *Studies in*

Industrialization: Nigeria and the Cameroons (published for the Nigerian Institute of Social and Economic Research by Oxford University Press, 1962).

50 Lubeck, 'Unions'.

51 See the discussion in Kennedy, *Ghanaian Businessmen*, pp. 90 and 95.

52 A brief account of the nature of employer–employee relationships in very small firms in Accra, Ghana, can be found in P. Kennedy, 'Workers in Petty Production, Accra, Ghana: Towards Proletarianization', *Labour, Capital and Society*, vol. 16, no. 1 (1983).

53 Akeredolu-Ale, *Underdevelopment*, p. 83. See also the comments by E. Wayne Nafziger, *African Capitalism: A Case Study in Nigerian Entrepreneurship*, (Hoover Institution Press, Stanford, Calif., 1977), pp. 234–5 and 238–40.

54 Akeredolu-Ale, *Underdevelopment*, p. 76.

55 For example: Nafziger, *African Capitalism*, pp. 146–7; and Kennedy, *Ghanaian Businessmen*, pp. 129–31.

56 P. Marris, 'The Social Barriers to African Enterprise', *Journal of Development Studies*, vol. 5, no. 1 (1968), pp. 29–38.

57 See references cited in note 45 above.

58 S. P. Schatz, 'Pirate Capitalism and the Inert Economy of Nigeria', *Journal of Modern African Studies*, vol. 22, no. 1 (1984), p. 53.

59 Schatz, *Nigerian Capitalism*, Chapter 4.

60 *Ibid.*, Chapter 6.

61 *Ibid.*, pp. 122–8.

62 *Ibid.*, p. 123.

8 ENTREPRENEURIAL ENDEAVOUR, BUSINESS SUCCESS AND SOCIAL ORIGINS

1 P. Marris and A. Somerset, *African Businessmen* (Routledge and Kegan Paul, London, 1971); and A. A. Beveridge and A. R. Oberschall, *African Businessmen and Development in Zambia* (Princeton University Press, 1979).

2 J. A. Schumpeter, *The Theory of Economic Development* (Harvard University Press, Cambridge, Mass., 1934), Chapter 2, especially pp. 65–6 and 75–81.

3 F. Redlich, 'Entrepreneurship in the Early Days of Industrialisation', *Weltwirtschaftliches Archiv*, vol. 75 (1955); and A. H. Cole, *Business Enterprise in its Social Setting* (Harvard University Press, Cambridge, Mass., 1959).

4 E. O. Akeredolu-Ale, *The Underdevelopment of Indigenous Entrepreneurship in Nigeria* (Ibadan University Press, 1975), Chapter 4, pp. 84–5 and Appendix B, pp. 108–9. See also the discussion by Beveridge and Oberschall in *Business in Zambia*, Chapter 4, pp. 216–19.

5 P. Kennedy, *Ghanaian Businessmen* (Weltforum Verlag, Munich, 1980), Chapter 5, pp. 123–7.

6 *Ibid*, p. 126.

7 For example: J. R. Harris and M. P. Rowe, 'Entrepreneurial Patterns in the Nigerian Saw-milling Industry', *Nigerian Journal of Economic and Social Studies*, vol. 8, no. 1 (1966) pp. 69–95; and F. A. Wells and W. A. Warmington, *Studies in Industrialization: Nigeria and the Cameroons* (published for the

Nigerian Institute of Social and Economic Research by Oxford University Press, 1963). See also the discussion in Chapter 7 of this book.

8 The same is often true, of course, in foreign companies and state corporations as several writers acknowledge.

9 Analyses of this kind are commonplace in the literature. For example: Beveridge and Oberschall, *Businessmen in Zambia*, Chapter 4, pp. 144–61; Harris and Rowe, 'Entrepreneurial Patterns'; P. Kilby, *African Enterprise: The Nigerian Bread Industry* (Hoover Institution Press, Stanford, Calif. 1965), Chapter 5; and A. G. Akin Ogunpola, 'Patterns of Organisation in the Building Industry', *Nigerian Journal of Economic and Social Studies*, vol. 10, no. 3 (1968), pp. 339–60, especially pp. 350–54.

10 See: Kilby, *African Enterprise*, pp. 98–101; and E. Wayne Nafziger, *African Capitalism: A Case Study in Nigerian Entrepreneurship* (Hoover Institution Press, Stanford University, Calif., 1977), Chapter 6, especially pp. 141–8.

11 For example, Kennedy, *Ghanaian Businessmen*, Chapter 3, pp. 68–73.

12 For reference to poor accountancy practices, see the following: Akeredolu-Ale, *Underdevelopment*, pp. 84–5; A. B. Yusef, 'Capital Formation and Management Among the Muslim Hausa Traders of Kano, Nigeria', *Africa*, vol. 65 (1975), pp. 167–82, p. 181; and Harris and Rowe 'Entrepreneurial Patterns', pp. 40–41.

13 This discussion draws heavily upon the author's own research in Ghana: Kennedy, *Ghanaian Businessman*, Chapter 3, especially pp. 86–91.

14 The central importance of 'organisational-building' to successful business expansion has long been stressed. See, for example: F. Harbison, 'Entrepreneurial Organisation as a Factor in Economic Development', *Quarterly Journal of Economics*, vol. 70 (1956); and C. Belshaw, 'The Cultural Milieu of the Entrepreneur', in H. G. J. Aitkin (ed.), *Explorations in Enterprise* (Harvard University Press, Cambridge, Mass., 1965).

15 Kilby, *African Enterprise*, pp. 98–101.

16 Nafziger, *African Capitalism*, Chapter 6.

17 Kennedy, *Ghanaian Businessman*, pp. 106–7 and 149–53.

18 See, for example: A. P. Alexander, 'Industrial Entrepreneurship in Contemporary Greece: Origins and Growth', *Explorations in Entrepreneurial History*, 2nd series, vol. 3, no. 2 (1966); J. J. Berna, *Industrial Entrepreneurship in Madras State* (Bombay Publishing House, 1960); J. J. Carroll, *The Filipino Manufacturing Entrepreneur: Agent and Product of Change* (Cornell University Press, Ithaca, New York, 1965); and G. F. Papanek, 'The Development of Entrepreneurship', Papers and Proceedings of the 74th Annual Meeting of the American Economic Association, *American Economic Review*, vol. 52, no. 2 (1962), pp. 46–58.

19 This aspect of firm organisation is dealt with fairly extensively in Chapter 6.

20 Marris and Somerset, *African Businessmen*, p. 254.

21 Beveridge and Oberschall, *Businessmen in Zambia*, pp. 146–7; and Kennedy, *Ghanaian Businessmen*, p. 114.

22 See, for example, J. O. Odufalu, 'Indigenous Enterprise in Nigerian Manufacturing', *Journal of Modern African Studies*, vol. 9, no. 4 (1971), pp. 603–4.

23 P. Hill, 'Some Characteristics of Indigenous West African Economic Enterprise', *Economic Bulletin of Ghana*, vol. 6, no. 1 (1962).

24 Kennedy, *Ghanaian Businessmen*, pp. 116–17; and N. Swainson, *The Development of Corporate Capitalism in Kenya: 1918–1977* (Heinemann Educational Books, London, 1980), Chapter 5, especially pp. 200–8.

25 Marris and Somerset, *African Businessmen*, pp. 116 and 122–6.

26 Akeredolu-Ale, *Underdevelopment*, pp. 84–6.

27 Kennedy, *Ghanaian Businessmen*, pp. 117–18.

28 See the discussion in Marris and Somerset, *African Businessmen*, pp. 142–5; and Beveridge and Oberschall, *Businessmen in Zambia*, pp. 134–8.

29 For example: P. C. Garlick, *African Traders and Economic Development in Ghana* (Clarendon Press, Oxford, 1971), p. 36; Nafziger, *African Capitalism*, pp. 189–91 and 205; Kennedy, *Ghanaian Businessmen*, pp. 110–12; and Beveridge and Oberschall, *Businessmen in Zambia*, pp. 229–30.

30 See Marris and Somerset, *African Businessmen*, Chapter 6, especially pp. 136–9; Kilby, *African Enterprise*, pp. 101–2; and J. R. Harris, 'Industrial Entrepreneurship in Nigeria' (unpublished Ph.D. thesis, Northwestern University, 1967), p. 284.

31 These and other disadvantages are discussed in detail by Garlick, *African Traders*, Chapter 7.

32 Nafziger, *African Capitalism*, pp. 192–3.

33 See Kennedy, *Ghanaian Businessmen*, p. 113; and Beveridge and Oberschall, *Businessmen in Zambia*, p. 231 writing about Ghana and Zambia respectively.

34 Garlick, *African Traders*, pp. 110–16 and 146–8.

35 Marris and Somerset, *African Businessmen*, pp. 122–4.

36 Out of 186 Ghanaian manufacturers, traders and contractors, studied in 1968–9, two-thirds had purchased at least one property; Kennedy, *Ghanaian Businessmen*, p. 101.

37 Marris and Somerset, *African Businessmen*, p. 123.

38 *Ibid*, pp. 122–6.

39 H. G. Aubrey, 'Industrial Investment Decisions; A Comparative Analysis', *Journal of Economic History*, vol. 15, no. 1. (1955), pp. 335–51; and K. Hart, 'Small Scale Entrepreneurs in Ghana and Development Planning', *Journal of Development Studies*, vol. 6, no. 4 (1970), pp. 104–19.

40 According to F. Riggs, the combination of bureaucratic incompetence and unpredictability, along with the threat of political interference foster in local entrepreneurs a tendency to, 'concentrate on activities which bring quick profits': *Administration in Developing Societies: The Theory of Prismatic Society* (Houghton Mifflin, Boston, Mass., (1964), p. 116.

41 See, for example, the discussion in H. Perkin's book on the importance of converting industrial profits into land and grand houses in the late eighteenth and early nineteenth centuries, as a way of attaining status and security: *The Origins of Modern English Society: 1780–1880* (Routledge and Kegan Paul, London, 1969), pp. 85–9.

42 Akeredolu-Ale, *Underdevelopment*, pp. 86–7.

43 See *ibid.*, p. 87, for the Nigerian case, and Beveridge and Oberschall, *Businessmen in Zambia*, p. 131, for the Zambian situation.

44 Garlick (*African Traders*, pp. 90–3) argues that the problem of succession is likely to be particularly acute in matrilineal societies because of the conflict between sons and sisters' sons concerning the legitimacy of their respective claims to the property of a deceased father/uncle.

45 In the case of Kenya, for example, N. Swainson (*Corporate Capitalism*, p. 204) writes: 'It is clear from the "top fifty" list (of Kenyan company directors) for 1974–5 that a larger number of the Kenyan directors have developed their *own* enterprises at the same time as holding down professional or executive positions . . . It is a mistake, therefore, in the Kenyan context, to distinguish a separate bureaucratic class . . . at this stage of accumulation there is *not* a high degree of separation between the owning and managing classes who are often interlinked.' The Nigerian situation was discussed in Chapter 6. Some of the work on Sudanese capitalism is examined later in this chapter, pp. 177–79.

46 The following examples are not untypical. In Nigeria, Harris found that 56% of his sample of local industrialists (interviewed in 1965) had fathers who were traders, artisans, public-sector workers, professionals or chiefs (J. R. Harris, 'On the Concept of Entrepreneurship with an Application to Nigeria', in S. P. Schatz (ed.), *South of the Sahara: Development in African Economies* (Temple University Press, Philadelphia, 1972) pp. 5–27, especially p. 14. Also in Nigeria, Nafziger (*African Capitalism*, pp. 174–7), discovered a very similar social background profile for his sample of local manufacturers (58%) except that a higher proportion of the fathers had held positions as government employees or professional workers. Nafziger also contrasted his own figures and those supplied by Harris, relating to fathers' occupations, with those for the adult male occupation as a whole (1952–3 Census) and found that only 21% of the latter had been engaged in similar 'modern-sector' activities. Comparable figures on fathers' occupations (small businessmen, skilled workers or artisans, public-sector workers, commercial employees and chiefs) for a sample of Ghanaian entrepreneurs (P. Kennedy, 'Some Patterns of Indigenous Business Enterprise in Ghana', unpublished Ph.D. thesis, Birmingham University, 1974, p. 144) were 55% for the sample and 14% for the adult male population in the 1948 Census. If cocoa farming is included the figures are 84% and 26%. In Zambia, Beveridge and Oberschall (*Businessmen in Zambia*, pp. 129–30) found that 70% of their leading entrepreneurs had fathers who were exposed to, and involved in, the growing money economy as miners, foremen, schoolteachers, domestic servants for Europeans, local government workers or self-employed businessmen. See also the discussion on traditional authority, education privilege and commercial activity for the cases of Zaire, Kenya, Sierra Leone and the Sudan in Chapter 3.

47 The proportions engaged in small business activities (not including commercial farmers or self-employed artisans) as indicated by the studies mentioned in the previous note were as follows: 22% (Harris), 25% (Kennedy) and 20% (Beveridge and Oberschall).

48 Marris and Somerset, *African Businessmen*, p. 211.

49 Of a sample of mainly industrial entrepreneurs in Ghana (Kennedy, p. 150) 34% had undergone some kind of full- or part-time technical training at one time or other and some had also taken a course in commerce or management (12%). These figures – for the late 1960s – are almost certainly very high compared to the population as a whole.

50 Marris and Somerset, *African Businessmen*, pp. 216–18.

51 In Zambia, 72% of the entrepreneurs studied by Beveridge and Oberschall (*Businessmen in Zambia*, pp. 122–3), who owned substantial businesses, had held positions of this kind before going into business. Most of the I.C.D.C. supported businessmen in Kenya (Marris and Somerset, *African Businessmen*, pp. 61–2) were previously employed in occupations that provided experience relevant to business activity, namely as skilled manual workers (29%), white collar jobs such as clerks (32%) or as self-employed petty traders (12%). However, Marris and Somerset argue that although these positions were inaccessible to most of the less privileged Kenyans they represented a much lower level of aspiration than the type of employment available to the more educated elite. It was partly this frustration at being excluded from the more prestigious avenues to social mobility (they argue) that provided the motivation propelling these Kenyans into business as an alternative route to success (Chapter 3).

52 This is argued by Kennedy, *Ghanaian Businessmen*, pp. 129–31 and 149. Of the most successful entrepreneurs in this sample, 37% had been through one or other of these work experiences compared to 13% of the less successful respondents. Other writers have been more sceptical concerning the 'benefits' of employment in European companies; see Akeredolu-Ale, *Underdevelopment*, p. 83.

53 See the analysis in Chapter 7.

54 This process is described by Yusuf, 'Capital Formation', pp. 167–81.

55 M. Duffield, *Maiurno, Capitalism and Rural Life in Sudan* (Ithaca Press, London, 1981), especially pp. 119–24.

56 F. B. Mahmoud, *The Sudanese Bourgeoisie: Vanguard of Development?* (Zed Press, London, 1984).

57 *Ibid.*, Chapter 4, especially p. 73.

58 *Ibid.*, pp. 99–101, Chapter 5, especially pp. 105–10, and 143–5. See also F. B. Mahmoud, 'Indigenous Sudanese Capital – A National Bourgeoisie?', *Review of African Political Economy*, no. 26 (1983), pp. 103–19, especially pp. 116–17.

59 Beveridge and Oberschall, *Businessmen in Zambia*, pp. 146–7.

60 S. P. Schatz, *Nigerian Capitalism* (University of California Press, Berkeley, 1977) p. 78.

61 *Ibid.*, pp. 81–91.

62 Nafziger, *African Capitalism*, p. 169.

63 R. M. Moose, 'Alternative Sources of Capital', in C. Lancaster and J. Williamson (eds.), *African Debt and Financing* (Institute for International Economics, Washington, DC, 1986). Ghana will soon be included in this list. See *African Business*, no. 106 (June 1987), pp. 23–5.

64 J. Curran, *Bolton Fifteen Years On: A Review and Analysis of Small Business*

Research in Britain, 1971–1986 (Small Business Research Trust, London, 1986), pp. 10–11.
65 *Ibid.*, p. 27.
66 T. C. Cochran and W. Miller, *The Age of Enterprise: A Social History of Industrial America*, revised edn (Harper and Row, New York, 1961), pp. 67–76.
67 L. Hannah, *The Rise of the Corporate Economy* (Methuen, London, 1976) p. 13 and Chapter 7, especially p. 111.
68 For example, E. J. Hobsbawm, *Industry and Empire*; (Weidenfeld and Nicolson, London, 1968), see Chapter 9, especially pp. 152–3 and 157–8.
69 One of the main proponents of this view is D. S. Landes. A very brief summary of his position can be found in *The Unbound Prometheus* (Cambridge University Press, 1969) p. 528.
70 A. Gerschenkron, *Economic Backwardness in Historical Perspective* (Harvard University Press, Cambridge, Mass., 1966), p. 64 fn. 21.
71 J. R. Doyle and C. C. Gallagher, 'Size-distribution, Potential for Growth and Contribution to Job Generation of Firms in the U.K., 1982–1984', Research Report No. 7, Newcastle University, Department of Industrial Management, p. 22. Also, Curran, *Bolton*, pp. 25–7.

9 WHAT PROSPECTS FOR AFRICAN CAPITALISM?

1 The attempt to push back the frontiers of state ownership and control is, of course, a world-wide process, at the present time; witness, particularly, the privatisation of public utilities and corporations in countries as different and far apart as Chile, India, South Korea, Canada, Britain and Japan. See, for example, the report in the British newspaper, *The Independent*, 10 April 1987.
2 Mr Christopher Patten, the Minister for Overseas Development, during a speech given in the spring of 1987.
3 See the report in the British *Guardian* newspaper by Salim Lone for the 'Third World Review' feature, 20 February 1987.
4 According to Peter Blackburn in the *Financial Times*, 6 March 1987, the situation in Ghana, especially, has undergone a marked improvement since 1984.
5 The term 'parasitical' capitalism is used by J. Iliffe in *The Emergence of African Capitalism* (Macmillan, London, 1983). See the earlier discussion of this question in Chapter 4.
6 On the other hand, of course, they may also be bought out by powerful established companies whether in the advanced countries or the Third World.
7 Reported in *African Business*, no. 97 (September 1986), pp. 61–2.
8 *African Business*, no. 106 (June 1987), pp. 55–6.
9 *Ibid.*, p. 9.
10 *African Business*, no. 93 (May 1986). The same report also points out that the Ghana National Investment Bank is now geared to helping local industries rather than those relying on imports. To qualify for a loan companies need to obtain at least 40% of their raw materials from local sources. Financial support

for this scheme is also coming from the World Bank, OPEC, the African Development Bank and other sources.

11 This is discussed extensively in *African Business*, no. 101 (January 1987), pp. 20–1. The International Labour Office, based in Geneva, has also made a recent commitment to concentrate part of its future development efforts in Africa on encouraging small businesses. This is seen as a necessary and central plank in any realistic strategy to create jobs for the growing numbers of young unemployed. See *African Business*, no. 103 (March 1987), pp. 7–8.

12 Reported in *African Business*, no. 100 (December 1986), pp. 12–13.

INDEX

Accra, 36–7
Acheampong, General, 132
'Africa of the Labour Reserves', 11, 29
'Africa of the Trade Economy', 11, 29
African Project Development Facility, 195
Akan, 139
America: business, 115, 124, 182; government and local enterprise, 64, 122; markets, 14, 41
Amin, Idi, 72
apartheid, 18
Arab: merchants in the Sudan, 141, 178; oil money in the Sudan, 105; traders in East Africa, 46
artisans, 8, 53, 57, 59, 63, 148, 176; artisan–entrepreneurs and their difficulties, 162–3, 165
asceticism, 48–50, 188
Ashanti, 144
Ashiqqa Party (Sudan), 105
Asians: family businesses, 47, 70, 145, 169, 174; legislation affecting, 13, 32, 70–1, 109; move into manufacturing, 26, 70, 114; restrictions on, 32–3, 48, 70–72; skills, 47, 178; trading interests and activities, 33, 35, 41, 44, 46–8, 93–4

Banks and banking: European banks and discriminatory practices, 13, 31, 39, 40–1, 63, 107, 149–50; local banks, 63, 151, 190; loan facilities for African entrepreneurs, 41, 54, 58, 63, 68–9, 84, 94, 109, 125, 145, 148, 151–2, 190; pressures to assist local capital, 63, 73; reluctance to borrow, 150; problems of collateral security, 40, 150
'Basic Needs' approach, 67
Bata shoes, 58
Belgian Congo: see Zaire
Belgium, 33

Benin, 66
Birmingham, 35
booty or 'parasitical' capitalism, 100, 186
Botswana, 187, 190
bourgeois hegemony, 83, 85, 87–9, 91–2, 94, 126
bourgeois-led development, 2, 86–7
Brazil, 22-3, 50, 121, 190
bread industry, 44, 114, 149, 164
Britain: business, 115, 173, 181–3; development 15, 24, 50, 60, 84, 88, 182; imperialism, 2, 15, 59, 98, 105; monarchy and nobility, 88–9
British American Tobacco Company, 58
brokers, buying agents, 34, 44–5, 49, 107
bureaucratic bourgeoisie, 69, 71–2, 76, 81, 89, 90, 99, 101, 186
bureaucratic socialism, 3, 102–3

Cadbury Brothers, 36–7
Cairo, 23
Canada, 190
cannibalisation, 116
capital accumulation: African, 51, 56, 92, 96, 133, 141–3, 146, 177–9, 187–8; as a general process, 5, 7–8, 80, 93, 102, 129; see also intergenerational wealth accumulation
capital shortage, the illusion of, 63, 151–2
capitalist: labour process, 8, 15, 80, 119, 188; mode of production, 18, 19, 129; orientation, 8, 129
Centre for the Development of Industry (European Economic Community, Lomé Convention) 190–1
Chad, 52, 101
chiefs and other traditional rulers, 11, 16–7, 35, 45; involvement in business, 51, 53–5, 98; privileges and abuse of office, 51–4, 93, 105, 176